NO STARS
TO GUIDE

NO STARS
TO GUIDE

ADRIAN SELIGMAN

SUTTON PUBLISHING

First published in 1947 by
Hodder & Stoughton Limited, London

This paperback edition first published in 1997 by
Sutton Publishing Limited
Phoenix Mill · Thrupp · Stroud · Gloucestershire · GL5 2BU

British Library in Cataloguing Data
A catalogue record for this book is available from the
British Library

ISBN 0-7509-1637-0

Cover picture: the *Olinda* at sea off the Turkish Coast.

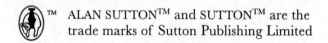 ™ ALAN SUTTON™ and SUTTON™ are the
trade marks of Sutton Publishing Limited

Printed in Great Britain by
Hartnolls, Bodmin, Cornwall.

To
D.N.A.

CONTENTS

GOD FOR ACTION . . .

THE Commander was a very odd man by normal naval standards. We always felt that his determination, when baldness crept upon him, to adorn himself with a fiery red wig, which gave him the appearance of a seaside landlady of the old school, must have had something to do with his early retirement from the Navy to a ranch in the Argentine. He had been recalled for war service with the rest of the old and bold, and he brought with him to his job a good deal of rugged individuality and such energy and drive as must frequently have given his Argentine cattle the shock of their lives. Our Senior Officer frequently gave us shocks as well; but we were secretly rather proud of his fiery presence and of his great booming voice.

It must be admitted at once that, although the organisation to which I then temporarily belonged went by the impressive title of Force "W," we were in fact "just another False Nose party" . . . one of those polyglot bands of individualists which, to the indignant paymasters and other orderly minded folk, seem to burgeon like a plague of multi-coloured fungi around the sombre fringes of the Secret Service midden. They are looked upon as the private desperadoes of the great robber barons of "I" . . . GANGS, in fact, defined by Webster's Dictionary as "Companies of persons acting together for some purpose, usually criminal, or at least not good or respectable." Their expense accounts are frequently adorned with such airy notations as "Goodwill—£10," or merely "Balance accounted for elsewhere on security grounds." They are for ever flying hither and yon upon the highest priorities; and the more important ones usually succeed in arranging for their women-folk, called P.A.'s (and referred to by some as Pleasing Appendages) to be transported to the ends of the earth and back again—also on Top Priority and "under Most Secret cover." Small wonder, then, that the expression Special Service Party is a source of considerable exasperation and mistrust to the authorities who direct the more gentlemanly activities of the armed forces of the Crown.

In April 1941, the Commander disappeared in a flurry of gin and inspiration to Greece. The great retreat from that unhappy country had begun in earnest; none the less, I distinctly remember a spirit of almost joyous exhilaration in the air of Alexandria on the day the Old Man left. We chuckled, as we always have chuckled, at what appeared to be the worst blunders on the part of those in authority. We chuckled at the antics of the wily Arab labourers and at the loiterers around the docks; but, loudest of all, we chuckled at the picture of Commander Lancelot Mathews, D.S.O., R.N. (Retired), thundering off into the forefront of the battle to "shake his gory locks" and bellow defiance at bolting allied "brass" and the ponderous Hunnish juggernaut alike.

For some time we heard no more than an occasional lurid rumour of the exploits of our Senior Officer who, with Jesse Matheson, a Canadian Lieutenant, R.C.N.V.R., had later retired (still breathing fire) to Crete. Crete fell . . . and there was no news at all for some time. Then John Hilton, a middle-aged Lieutenant-Commander R.N.R. and second-in-command of our party, received a letter from the Old Man himself. It gave us the surprising information that Jesse and he, instead of returning to allied territory, had unaccountably moved across to Turkey upon some dark errand which stank of secrecy and unaccountable, irrecoverable expenses.

After that there was silence for nearly three months until suddenly, one day towards the end of November 1941, old Mathews returned at last to Egypt. He came alone in a ship from Mersin, and his return was even more spectacular than his departure.

It was in the middle of a hot and dusty forenoon that we became all at once aware, from the boats which were berthed three deep along the quay, of a great commotion stirring up the dust round the end of No. 46 Shed. The disturbance seemed to grow and become more violent. It was like a whirl-pool, with frequent eddies of Arabs and Palestinian workmen breaking away from it, gyrating vigorously, collecting others from the outskirts and then twisting back into the central maelstrom. Now it began to move down the quay towards us. It became a great snowball, then an avalanche, thundering along the waterfront, sweeping up every living creature, (including all the dogs) and throwing them in a violently agitated cloud of dust and humanity behind it. It gained speed. Now it had a head—a spearpoint; and, as it came nearer, we recognised the fiery red wig, the bellowing voice and the powerful all-scattering advance of the Old Man.

The crowd and its leader came surging on down the jetty. The furious yapping of dogs, mingled with the screeching of Arabs, was drowned every few minutes by the mighty roars of old copper-nob from the van. We saw now that the crowd consisted of porters . . . porters carrying packing-cases, bits of machinery, crates of fruit, coils of wire and even bundles of old clothes. There must have been a hundred men staggering under all sorts of awkward and impossible loads, while the dogs and small boys darted in and out around their legs, adding their noise to the general bedlam. The Old Man, who had climbed into Greece up the precarious structure of the British Expeditionary Force, appeared to have come tumbling down again through Turkey with an avalanche of old junk and scrap iron rattling about his ears.

"Send a working party ashore to deal with all this," he bellowed as he came abreast of the boats, "and you, Hilton, come into my office a minute."

John Hilton climbed ashore and went lumbering across the jetty with the air of an amicable rhinoceros about to be involved in an embarrassing affair in the lion's den. And a little later I followed him in the hope of finding out, at first hand, what the immediate future held in store for all of us. As I neared the Commander's office, I could hear him booming away inside like a hurricane confined. When I reached the door and looked in, I realised at once that something had occurred during the last few minutes to send the Old Man into a raging fury. He had just finished reading the top letter in his "IN" basket. He snorted impatiently, then flung the letter down and proceeded to attack it so violently, with a blue pencil, that the point of the pencil broke, causing a further outburst of curses. Quietly I slipped away and took a turn up and down the quay while I waited. Half an hour later I saw the Commander burst out of the door marked S.O. "W" and go charging off down the quay again. I returned to the

office to find John sitting at old Mathews's desk with a "Most
Secret" envelope in his hand.

"Where's the Old Man rushed off to?" I asked him.

"Turkey," he replied, so gravely that anyone who had not
known John Hilton would have imagined that nothing less
than desertion or dismissal could be involved.

"Straight away? Just like that?"

"He's seeing S.O. Plans and Intelligence before he goes . . .
then he's catching the noon train."

"Just like him. What's it all about? Where's Jesse anyway?"

"Still in Turkey—at Istanbul, I think."

"And what's going to happen to you and me?"

John hesitated for a moment and looked worried. "We're
going up to Turkey, too," he said at last. "We're flying from
Cairo as soon as they can get us a passage . . . in civilian
clothes!" he added, even more gloomily.

To Turkey . . . to neutral Turkey in war-time! To a
country of gay lights, love and laughter, or so my imagination
painted it . . . to the land of the romantic Taurus express,
younger brother of the Orient express, in which lovely spies
and hired assassins jostled each other across the grim and mountainous wastes of Asia Minor, from Istanbul to far Baghdad!

"What's the job?" I inquired.

"I don't really know," answered John. "The Old Man
doesn't know himself. He's mad as a hornet about it. It's
taken him the best part of a week to get down here, with all
that gear salvaged from Crete, and all he gets is this . . . a
letter from our embassy in Ankara and a signal from C.-in-C.
telling him to get to hell back again where he came from."

He showed me the contents of the Most Secret envelope.
The signal read as follows:—

> From: C.-in-C. Med.
> To: S.O. "W" (*Senior Officer, Force "W"*).
>   You are to return forthwith to Ankara
>   reporting on your arrival to the
>   British Naval Attaché.
>   2. Letter enclosed from H.B.M.
>   Ambassador at Ankara to C.-in-C.
>   Med. refers.

The letter was wordy but informal. We could tell from its tone that it came from one of those very religious men who have frequently, and for the best of reasons, climbed to the top of our diplomatic and colonial services. There was mention in it of some unspecified commitment placed upon His Majesty's Government by a friendly power, and it ended as follows:—

> . . . involving an intimate knowledge of the Turkish coast and existing conditions upon it.
>
> I consider that Commander L. T. Mathews, R.N., would be most suitable as director of these operations, and I very much hope that he can be spared. Also at least two other officers with a sound knowledge of pilotage and, if possible, some familiarity with merchant shipping.
>
> As soon as I receive full details of the proposed plan I will communicate them to you officially through the Naval Attaché here. Meanwhile I can only repeat that the job is likely to be a most difficult one which may involve a certain amount of danger.
>
> We must leave matters in the hands of Him who watches over us and *pray constantly* that *His mercy* may be shown to us.
>
> Yours ever,
>
> .   .   .   .   .

At the bottom of the letter were five words, in heavy blue pencil, which I had seen the Old Man scrawl upon it with such violence an hour before. They were:

> GOD FOR ACTION————
>
> THEN FILE.
>
> L.T.M.
>
> 28.11.41.

I

SNOW IN THE TAURUS

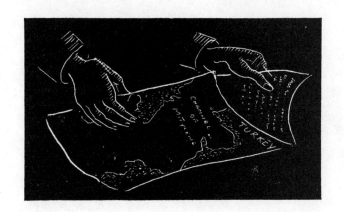

I

JOHN and I climbed into a Lockheed with a very mixed assortment of fellow-passengers—about a dozen of them in all. We were dressed in our beautiful new civilian suits of course, and everyone else in the aircraft was similarly clothed. A few of them—a stout Levantine woman and her small daughter, for instance—were obviously non-combatants; but in one or two others, an uncompromising Anglo-Saxon figure would bulge self-consciously through garments with which it had clearly long been unfamiliar. Those who had hats wore them awkwardly, having half forgotten the peace-time drill . . . the easy gestures and mannerisms with which a homburg or a trilby is donned, doffed, fiddled with, carried by the brim or hooked over the handle of an umbrella between one's knees.

John Hilton was also one of these; stolidly British in his grey flannel trousers and sports coat, rather fat, cautious to a fault and inclined always to take things too seriously. He had spent nearly thirty years in the Merchant Service, during which time he had seldom strayed more than a mile from the waterfront of any port and had obstinately refused to learn any other language than north-country English. As a result, John was for ever suspecting foreigners of trying to do him down or of laughing at him. This in turn made him try, when in a foreign land, to behave in a more proudly, even pompously British manner than was necessary; he conceived this to be his duty, though at heart (and he was a kind-hearted chap) he felt shy and uncomfortable.

John, one might have said, felt himself obliged as a Briton to accept the world as his oyster; but it was plain to see that he would have infinitely preferred "a nice pair of kippers."

As the wheels of our aircraft left the ground and we began the smooth, exhilarating upward rush into early morning sunlight, striking flat across the desert, a feeling of hilarious holiday seemed to catch me up and carry me out of myself—out of the aircraft, soaring into space—away from all anxiety, monotony and routine—out across the world to the north and east. I felt

19

in spirit like a bright new figure of Mercury from which all former worries and preoccupations had fallen away like sombre draperies—fallen back and down into the purpling smoke of Cairo and its suburbs.

I glanced across with affection at the passionless bulk of John Hilton, slumped in a seat on the other side of the cabin. The aircraft banked steeply and, pointing one wing at a group of trenches, like a cluster of maggots in the desert, seemed to heave itself round upon the end of it, while the upper wing went scything the sky above us. Away to our left now stood the Pyramids, quartered by sunlight and looking strangely neat and precise. Just ahead, a silvery strip of Nile wound its way into the smoke and disappeared among the buildings of the city. We rolled level again and steadied on a course north-east. Hilton closed his eyes and slouched down farther into his seat. His face wore an expression of anxious determination—determination not to be in any way impressed; anxiety not to show embarrassment. Through the tiny square window beside me I could see the desert stretching bare and hazy into the distance; bare and brown, brown and dusty, as it had for countless ages; as it had for the children of Israel, adventuring forth upon it to the north-eastward several thousand years ago. From two thousand feet above the sand, the horizon still looked the same for us as it had for them, and scarcely farther off. Our flight, like theirs, was an escape from Egypt; an escape to fabulous northern lands and adventures only guessed at.

Why exactly were we flying to Turkey . . . now, in this autumn of 1941, with the Mediterranean Fleet pinned down in Alexandria and Haifa, and with three great German claws striking out across Eastern Europe and over the Libyan Desert? One of these claws had already plunged deep into the Ukraine, another had gripped the Aegean, a third was tearing at the frontiers of Egypt; and, from between these exultant talons, the sorry remnants of our forces had crept and scuttled like field mice from a hawk. Turkey alone still clung to a precarious neutrality. Down her iron-bound coastline, dodging from cove to hidden cove and skittering by night around the headlands, the last allied small-craft had only recently escaped. Why, then, were an elderly Lieutenant Commander and a young Lieutenant flying back to Turkey now?

The day before we left Alexandria we had been to see the Staff Officer Intelligence; but he either would not or could not tell us much. He had looked harassed as usual when we called on him; but he had risen as we entered and shouted through the door to his assistant that he was not to be disturbed for twenty minutes. This had sounded impressive, but it could only have been done from habit or in order to give us a sense of personal importance. At any rate, the interview had lasted no more than seven minutes in all.

"You know the general picture of the Aegean?" The S.O.I. had seemed impatient or possibly worried by his lack of any real information for us. He had pulled out some chart folios and started fiddling with the tapes.

Yes, we knew the picture . . . the Germans and Italians occupied the entire sea, right up to the coasts of Turkey.

"Well, one of our Allies has got a plan for moving some ships secretly out of that area, and its going to be your job to get them out through the Aegean and down to Beirut and Syria."

He had paused there and regarded us doubtfully for a moment or two. Then he had turned back to the chart and continued:

"You see, all the waters west of the Dardanelles are C.-in-C. Med.'s responsibility, so the baby's been passed to us to look after the ships from the time they reach Istanbul till they get to Suez. . . . Of course we couldn't possibly send anything up to escort them; the Hun aircraft have got matters all their own way up there . . . it's miles out of range for our fighters, and anyway we've already lost half the ships of the Med. Fleet off Greece and Crete. . . ."

At this point he had glared at us with a sour expression, as though he half suspected that we were about to demand a cruiser each; then he had ended hastily with a frank admission:

"Look here, I simply haven't an idea how this job's going to be done. . . . All I can tell you is that since Commander Mathews went back to Turkey a week ago to see about it, I've had a letter from Ankara which told me the facts I've just given you; nothing more. You must get up to Ankara as quick as you can. . . . Matheson's up there already, of course. You'd better dash round and buy yourselves some civilian clothes, and be ready to join the aircraft for Turkey which leaves Cairo on Monday morning . . . all right?"

"So that's our great secret mission!" I remembered exclaiming. After several months spent in carrying out the monotonous and often futile tasks of a duty officer in Alexandria, this new twist to my naval life had seemed to offer the most fascinating possibilities. I could not for the life of me imagine why John and I had been chosen for the adventure, neither of us had any knowledge of the Turkish coast; but I had been quite happy to leave such matters to explain themselves later. Meanwhile, we had both gazed hopefully, though not very intelligently, at the charts; as though waiting for the S.O.I., like some modern Moses, to smite the black mountains of Turkey with his staff and create through them a convenient blue ribbon of a canal from Istanbul to Adana.

And now the desert—bare and brown beneath us on every hand . . . naked and seemingly endless. As I gazed at it, a narrow ribbon of bright green and brown with an iron grey stripe in it, loomed suddenly below us and a little to the left of our course. "Look John," I tried to shout through the heavy roar of the aircraft's engines. "That must be the sweet-water

canal to Lake Timsah—older than the Bible—old as Egypt."
But John was asleep.

My memories of that flight are very few. I do remember,
though, my first sight of the Suez Canal from the air; then
league upon league of the Sinai Desert with, far below us now,
the road and railway into Palestine, lying in disorderly curves,
like threads of grey and black cotton dropped upon the sand
from heaven. After a long time we passed over El Arish—a
quick flurry of huts and sidings; then the desert again, bare
and yellow, and we were in Palestine.

For mile after mile there was nothing to look at but this
desert. I fell to wondering about the details of our forthcoming
operation—the size of the ships involved and their nationality.
They would most likely be small Greek coasters or *caiques*, I
decided, which had succeeded in escaping from Piraeus at the
last minute. Then my thoughts turned to that violent old
mariner Commander Mathews, and to the glib young Canadian
Jesse Matheson. I wondered what they were doing in Turkey
at this moment, and whether they had already evolved some
master plan.

Jesse had come out from England with me nearly a year
before. He was something of a scallywag and apt to treat
women with contempt, whenever he could do so with impunity.
In spite of this, however, he undoubtedly had the liveliest personality of anyone in our particular crowd. I think that he
and I both saw the same colours when we looked at life, which
gave us a certain mental affinity ; but we reacted to these
colours very differently, which kept our conversation alive and
often exciting.

The aircraft droned along placidly over the flat earth. We
must have been in the air for more than an hour by now. A
little pile of black, red, brown and buff mountains appeared
for a moment in the southern distance, only to fade immediately
into the surrounding haze. I was beginning to tire of the
unending expanse of sand when suddenly, from beneath the
wing of the aircraft, swept a veritable carpet of fields, orchards
and plantations, and over to our left lay the port of Jaffa, with
the city of Tel Aviv beside it.

We landed at Lydda. The air was cold and fresh and free

from dust, so John and I climbed out of the aircraft to go for
a short stroll while waiting for the machine in which we were
to continue our journey.

I was in the mood to be excited at anything and everything.
. . . at being able, after two years in the Navy, to walk about
bareheaded in public . . . at seeing myself dressed in unconventional clothes. . . . And were they unconventional! I
glanced down at my trousers and smiled at the memory of a
forenoon spent among the shopkeepers of Alexandria. What
fun we had had in the outfitting department of a large Egyptian
store, Jane and I. The cut and the colouring of every garment
we looked at had been so startling that, in the end, we had
tried only to find something amusing. Eventually I had
walked back to tea with Jane's aunt in a confection of delicate
mauve with green stripes in it, while upon my head was a
light, biscuited-coloured felt hat. It had been surprising how
inconspicuous I had looked in the streets of Alexandria.

On the grey expanses of Lydda airfield I looked less inconspicuous. The mood of holiday, however, was still upon me;
a holiday from the irritating domestic worries and the trivial
responsibilities of naval shore base life—soon to become a holiday in a neutral country. . . .

But John Hilton was worried.

"I've been thinking about this job," he muttered, as we
reached the perimeter of the airfield. . . . "I don't know, I'm
sure," he added in a tone suggesting that nobody else could
possibly know either.

"What's actually bothering you?" John was always worrying
about something; usually about the youth and high spirits of
people like Jesse and myself, compared with his own great age
and experience.

"Well, did you measure the distance on the chart between
some of those enemy-occupied islands and the Turkish coast?"

"No."

"There's not more than two miles between them in some
places . . . less than a mile in the Samos Straits. How the hell
are we going to get through?"

"I dare say the ships they give us won't be quite as large as
that," I suggested rather weakly.

"Don't talk so bloody wet," growled John. "Half of each

of those Straits is in enemy waters. . . . Anyway, we may get
big merchant ships. Have you ever handled one?"

I could see that one of his "anxious father" moods was upon
him, so I shook my head and waited for him to go on.

"No, and nor has that young Matheson. . . . Merchant ships
aren't bloody destroyers, you know."

I smiled. Even though John was always full of grievances,
there was really no malice in him. Jesse irritated him more
than the rest of us, chiefly because the two of them were so
different in age and background; but Jesse was by no means
a fine-weather sailor, and John knew it.

"In the first place, a merchant ship has very little power for
her weight," he continued, still harping on a type of vessel
about which he alone had expert knowledge. (I felt he would
be deeply disappointed should the craft turn out to be ten-ton
caiques after all.) "It takes her a hell of a time to work up
speed, and once she gets going she takes a hell of a lot of
stopping . . . then she'll have a huge turning circle and she'll
often take a long time even to *begin* answering her helm. . . .
I tell you a merchantman's no ship to go skating around the
rocks in."

He paused to pick up a stone from the ground. He was well
into his theme now and in his element. His dire prophecies
were beginning to cheer him up rapidly.

"I had a good look on the chart at the Straits of Kos and
Khios," he went on, as we continued our stroll; and now most
of the former dullness had left his voice. . . . "Some of those
places look pretty tricky for a big merchantman, even in daytime. But as for attempting 'em by night or in bad weather, as I
suppose they'll want us to. . . . Well, in peace-time, a man might
lose his ticket for even going near 'em" (this with gloomy
relish) "and that channel inside Castelorizzo Island, on the
south coast there, east of Rhodes; why, there isn't even a
proper chart of that!"

The final statement seemed to give John so much satisfaction
that he relapsed into contented silence.

"We'd better wait and see what they've worked out for us
up in Ankara," I suggested after a pause. "The whole thing's
a bit outside the experience of any of us; but we can have a
damn good shot at it."

"You young fellas are all the same," declared John amicably
—"dashing off to sea like first-year apprentices. . . . You'll
put the ships ashore, I tell you," he pronounced with happy
conviction.

"Well, if they stay where they are, they're no use to us anyway."

John grunted but made no
reply.   I could see that his
doubts were now shelved.
Having decided that the
"young fellas" would need
careful watching, he no longer
bore them any ill will; he
was content to hug his convictions to himself—to tuck
them away in the back of his
mind, like a hidden store of
nuts, for future digestion.

From Lydda we flew on
up the coast; past the gay
white cluster of Caeserea in
the mountains, past Mount
Carmel and the busy port of
Haifa. The countryside grew
more hilly and soon a mass
of boulderous cloud covered
the sky . . . . across to Acre
and the white cliffs of Na-
koura; on past the rivers and
tree-clad gorges of Southern
Lebanon, with the snowy crest
of Hermon poking up above
the clouds behind them.

Our aircraft passed over the diminutive ports of Tyre and
Sidon, their ancient brown castles still intact, with a few
schooners lying beside them. Completely unchanged is Tyre,
on the end of its isthmus which the road neglects.

Soon afterwards, just as we were approaching the headland of
Ras Beirut, a mass of heavier cloud and rain blotted out the
view, and we stood out to sea to avoid it. For another full hour

we bumbled along—twisting this way and that to avoid the blackest squalls, till my sense of direction was gone. I grew drowsy, and dozed for a time; then, all in a moment, the sea flashed away and there beneath us lay the pale confusion of cold, grey steppes and hummocks which was Turkey.

2

THE country round the airfield at Adana was bleak and bare. It was raining. We climbed stiffly out of the aircraft and shivered. There were Turkish customs guards and sentries with ancient rifles. They looked sharp-featured little men—grey and and grim as the landscape—with fiery eyes.

There was an atmosphere of tension and distrust; it enveloped us as soon as we landed. These Turks were in a most uncomfortable corner, hanging blindly and rigidly on to their neutrality, but ready at any moment to abandon it. They hoped, of course, to be able to come in on our side; but I wondered, as I looked at these fierce little men, what they really thought of us . . . the tide of war was beginning to turn so heavily against us; not only had we been defeated by the Germans, and even the Italians, in every Middle Eastern theatre except at Malta; but now there was increasing tension in the Far East, which seemed to have been timed to support the German attack on Russia . . . to the average Turk the war must have seemed very nearly over in the early winter of 1941.

From the airfield we drove to the British Consulate. The road we took was hardly more than a track—heavily rutted and deep in mud. On the way we passed, with difficulty, a Kurdish caravan. There were no men in evidence, but the women who led the camels wore voluminous trousers in all sorts of colours, secured round their ankles in the traditional Arabian Nights style. They were heavily swathed in shawls, right up to their eyes, and some of them carried babies slung in more shawls upon their backs.

The scene was one which the dusty streets and docks of Alexandria could never have presented. It was a scene which fitted exactly that atmosphere of a thrilling and urgent secret mission which our flight from Cairo had created. I pointed it out to John, but he pretended not to be interested; he was sitting upright in one corner of the back seat, like a plump effigy of Queen Victoria, framed in the sober polished oak of his insularity.

"What a flop you'd be at a League of Nations Conference," I grinned.

"The League of Nations is dead," he observed calmly, to my mingled astonishment and delight. "It was finished the moment they let the foreigners into it."

At the Consulate they gave us the choice of remaining one night at Adana and then catching the Taurus express on to Ankara, or of continuing our journey this same afternoon in a slow train which was due to reach Ankara next day.

I plumped emphatically for going straight on. Our adventure had started so excitingly. How could we sit kicking our heels in this miserable town? It looked, in any case, no more than a jumble of mean, muddy streets without any sign of life or colour. For once John backed me up.

"All right," said Vice-Consul Ensor, "I'll get a couple of first-class seats on the slow train. No sleepers I'm afraid, but you can keep your sleeper tickets in case they tack on a wagon-lit at Kayseri; they sometimes do." So at 5 o'clock that afternoon, December 6th, 1941, we climbed into the train, which was to be our home for at least two days. John slid open the first door he came to and we stumbled through it.

It was nearly dark, and there were no lights in the compartment; but these came on shortly after we had sat down. They revealed the other two occupants—a bald-headed old Turk, with a mouth full of gold, and a small boy, possibly his son, who sniffed and sniffed and sniffed. Shortly afterwards the lights went out again. They remained out for the rest of the night.

We rumbled away across the flat, dull plain and by the time we began to climb the foothills of the Taurus it had grown quite dark; but in the star-glow it was still possible, from our darkened carriage, to see the desolate landscape growing every minute wilder. A rough but well-graded road kept us company, crossing and recrossing the tracks. Occasionally, at one of these crossings, there would be a solitary Kurd with his donkey, or a caravan collected round its fires. The train

climbed on heavily through the dusk. We could see nothing
of our companions save the occasional glow of the old man's
cigar, nor hear any sound but the tireless sniffing of the little
boy. In my imagination I began to paint a host of exciting
and improbable pictures of them against a background of fell
intrigue, through which moved the sinuous sinister figure of a
bewitching adventuress.

These pictures grew out of Vice-Consul Ensor's grave warnings to us before we left him. "Be careful who you speak to on
the train," he had said. "You never know who people are these
days." John, of course, had concurred at once; but I am afraid
that my immediate reaction was a keen desire to find out. I
do not defend it; it is a waste of time to defend the natural
impulses of one's youth. "What secrets after all could I possibly
give away?" I had asked myself. "Surely no one could imagine
that I would suddenly blurt out the reason for our presence
in Turkey!" And, apart from the bare object of our journey, I
knew nothing that was likely to be of interest to the enemy . . .
the method of operating, the detailed plan, were not only un-
known to me; I was unable even to guess at them intelligently.

The train panted on through the night. The scene grew
wilder yet. Forbidding black hills towered above us, cut up
by angry streams and rapids. Then a gibbous moon appeared.
And just as it did so, we turned away towards the mountains
and plunged into a long, steep tunnel.

When we emerged, we were high upon the side of a canyon.
Far below I could make out faintly the turbulent white course
of a torrent in spate; beyond it, the black cliffs climbed unbroken to snowy peaks, pale with moonlight. There followed
a chain of roaring tunnels, and we snarled once or twice over
hasty bridges. Then at last there came a long, long tunnel.

The little boy's sniffing was lost in tumultuous darkness.
The train lurched a ponderous rhythm in time with the old
man's cigar, which grew dimmer and smaller . . . went out.
And the night closed as black as black ink in upon us, pitch
black, noisy black—swaying blackness. The clamorous wheels
roared up louder; subsided, grew steadier, drowsier, calmer,
and finally . . .

I woke to find the train rattling over the points into Kayseri

station. Brilliant spears of sunshine darted in at the window
through the gaps in a row of stationary box cars we were
passing. Then the train halted, and we climbed out of the
carriage into deep snow.

The station was no more than a few rough huts set in the
middle of a wide plain. The plain stretched white and rolling
to the horizon in all directions save one . . . a few miles away

to the south-east stood the snow-covered pile of Mount Erdjias,
soaring in solitary magnificence out of the Anatolian plateau.
Between us and the mountain lay the small town of Kayseri—
a collection of primitive houses with the spire of a mosque
poking up from among them. There was another train in the
station besides our own, a slow train from North Turkey, which
was about to join ours; and, sure enough, amongst its coaches
there stood a wagon-lit.

We hurried across to stake our claim for sleepers; but, at
first, we could find no attendant. We did, however, meet an
English-speaking Greek, who informed us that the line was
blocked with snow for several miles west of Kayseri.

"Trains have sometimes remained at Kayseri for more than
a week," he added in a tone of melancholy relish.

We thanked him for his information and were about to climb out again into the snow, when the door of the last compartment in the wagon-lit slid violently back to reveal a little man in brown uniform trousers. His right hand was wrestling with the tabs of his braces behind, and over the other forearm were draped a towel and his uniform jacket. He gazed at us sadly for a moment but said nothing. And we, in turn, stared back in silence. He was a comic figure—about five foot four inches high, with a large, dome-shaped head that rose above a fringe of black hair, like Olympus towering above the tree line. Mournful, dark eyes peered out of a hound-like face.

John broke the spell by starting to fumble for the sleeper tickets. These he held out to the little attendant, who only diverted to them his dismal gaze, the expression on his face deepening at the same time to a look of positive horror.

"We want two sleepers," said John firmly. "*Avec bain,*" he added in a fit of misguided inspiration.

The little man (whose name turned out later to be Alphonse) merely shrugged his shoulders and withdrew into the compartment.

John took a determined stride after him. "*Nous voulez* two *dormy-vous—pronto*—get me?*"

"No speak Deutsch," replied Alphonse woodenly. This seemed fair comment upon John's atrocious mixture of languages, but was none the less a lie, as we eventually discovered.

John now placed himself squarely in the doorway, and there followed a long and tricky argument conducted in scraps of almost every European tongue except English (the only one, had John realised it, which both of them could speak perfectly). It soon became clear, however, that Alphonse himself was comfortably settled in the last available sleeper and was grimly resolved not to give it up in favour of his official bed—a tiny flap seat in the draughty corridor.

But in the end John Hilton won. "And that's that," he pronounced, heaving his bags into the compartment and shutting the door. I doubted whether it really was. Alphonse had given in too easily; there would be a snag somewhere. However, I followed John in, and offered to take the top bunk in deference to John's superior age, rank and weight and also, it must be admitted, on account of some previous experience of night trains on the Continent. "O.K. Thanks," muttered John, piling his bags upon the lower one.

As soon as my gear was stowed I tried to shut the window, which had been left open a little at the top. It would not budge an inch, no matter how hard I tugged and prised and rattled. I turned to the worthy Hilton. "See if you can fix this, John," I said. "We're going to freeze like hell to-night if you can't."

John turned from his unpacking with a scowl on his nobbly red face; but, seeing that the booby-trap to be dealt with consisted of no more than a refractory window, his expression changed to one of patient resolve. I stood aside in expectant silence as he lurched across and took hold of the window strap with mighty hands. He gave a huge upward tug. He crouched; he changed his grip and settled his right foot and one knee more firmly against the panelling. Once more he hove powerfully, his shoulders hunching with effort and his face growing redder every second; but still the window would not shift an inch.

"Blast the man," said John, panting a little now. "What the hell can he have done to the bloody thing?"

"Perhaps he's put a nail through it at the bottom."

John actually bent down to examine the panelling under the little flap table. "Can't see anything," he said. "I'll have another go."

He wound the window strap round his wrist to get a better grip and, planting his feet wide apart, braced both knees against the panelling. I stood back a little. John was a big man and I felt I knew what was going to happen next. Crouching to get a better leverage, with his arms bent and his two great fists almost under his chin, John put legs and body into a long, shuddering pull. Every muscle of his back and shoulders seemed to be trying to burst his jacket, while his face turned from deeper red to purple, and a little line of bubbles began to appear between his lips. The window creaked but held firm. The strap began to groan, then suddenly, with a loud report, it parted.

John seemed to explode upwards like a land mine. His two fists caught him beneath the chin and drove on upwards towards the bracket lamp. The strap shattered the lamp into a hundred pieces. John's left knee smashed through the flap table, which promptly flapped down—spilling all his odds and ends of shaving and writing gear on to the floor. The man himself flew across the compartment like a boulder from an avalanche and crashed, in a heap of purple fury, into the lower panel of the door. For a second there was dead silence; then, with an insolent "chunk," the window slipped down nearly a foot and remained there, half open. The frosty air came pouring in over it and down on to the ruins below.

There were steps in the corridor: the door slid back and Alphonse's little bald head poked through.

"Oh!" he said sadly, then, "Ah, yes," and disappeared.

3

WE continued with our unpacking.

"I see what you mean about the top bunk," said John suddenly, straightening himself up to give me as steady a look as his breathless condition would allow.

"H'm," I replied innocently. "I'm afraid it *is* going to be a bit chilly in the lower bunk to-night. Still, I think I can let you have my Burberry to keep the worst of the frost off."

"Good God, no! I can manage all right," said John stoutly; but he cheered up at the thought, and ultimately accepted my offer with very little loss of face, thanks to his fundamentally frank and kindly nature.

"Look here," I volunteered later, when our unpacking was completed and we had wandered out into the corridor for a smoke. "You're taking things much too seriously."

John grunted doubtfully. He was as solid and admirable a citizen as one could wish for as companion in a foreign land. I felt proud of him and his sort. But still, neither of us would be likely to have a chance like this again, a complete holiday from the war for a day or two, and I was anxious to make the most of it.

"Just look at us," I said. "This is the first time I've been in plain clothes for over two years—travelling as we used to in peace-time. And you—why you've never been abroad in your

3

life really. There's no great difference to you between Buenos Aires, Hamburg and Liverpool Docks."

John turned and stared out of the window, but I went on, with growing enthusiasm.

"This train must be crammed with people just like ourselves. Spies, old boy! Crowds of 'em! Under the seats—poking their heads round every corner. We'll never have a chance like this again in all our lives."

"What do you suggest we do? Put on long, black beards and go spy-hunting?" John was by no means convinced, but he began to look less self-conscious, and a little humorous line appeared round the corner of his eyes.

"Well, first of all, let's try and meet someone who's *not* British to his eyebrows, and see what he's got to say for himself."

John looked mildly interested.

"Come on," I insisted. "Let's see who's in the compartment next to ours." I tried the handle as I spoke.

The door was locked; but immediately there was a click from within and it slid back to reveal a youthful pasty face, rather plump. Above the face, a slick of sparse hair was plastered back over a big, broad head.

"I beg your pardon," I said, a little taken aback at the suddenness of the results achieved. "I tried the wrong door."

"Don't mention it," said the other, in smooth and almost faultless English. Very smooth it was; he looked a very smooth young man.

He was lying on the lower bunk and, having opened the door, he thrust his head a little way out to see through the window, glanced down the corridor, then, with a wan little smile in our direction, he lay back in his bunk, shutting the door again as he did so.

John was inclined to be derisive. "So much for our young secret agent's first attempt at a contact. Pretty clumsy, I thought."

"I believe he was a German, anyway," I asserted defiantly.

"Pooh!" scoffed John. "Probably some inoffensive clerk from our people in Ankara. Feeling a bit train-sick, by the look of him, anyhow. Why can't you leave people alone?"

"I don't know. I still think he was a German, and I bet you he tries to get into conversation with us later."

"Well, he didn't look particularly keen. Perhaps it was your uninteresting appearance or maybe that vile purple suit of yours made him feel sick. Come on, let's go for a walk as far as the engine."

We strolled along to the end of the corridor and climbed out into the snow. Then we started to pace up and down beside the train.

It was much colder now and, over in the north-west, in the direction of Ankara, heavy clouds seemed to indicate more snow. Many of the other passengers were also walking up and down in pairs and threes, or singly. Most of them seemed to be people of the country—Greeks, Turks, or Armenians—with one or two solitary individuals, clearly foreigners to Turkey and probably connected with some Embassy or other, by the silent self-conscious way in which they strode briskly along —their stern expressions inviting no approach as they carefully avoided the other groups who were ambling about, chattering aimlessly.

Alphonse was there too, talking to the station-master and a porter, until the loud ringing of an outside telephone bell sent him hurrying into the station-master's office. When he came out he seemed worried; his sad little eyes carried a new animation as he started a vehement discussion with the other two. He broke off presently and passed us on the way to the dining-car.

"What's the news, Alphonse ?" we asked him.

"The line is still blocked and the snow plough is derailed down there as well now," he said, and hurried away on urgent little legs to the train.

We went on with our promenade for a bit. Then we asked the station-master, in French, whether it would be safe to walk up into the town of Kayseri. I doubt whether he really understood us, but he shook his head so it did not seem worth risking. The engine, by the way, had disappeared—possibly to go to the assistance of the snow plough. After a while the air began to get colder; we climbed back into our carriage.

As we came down the corridor to our compartment our pallid neighbour emerged and spoke to us. "It is much colder," he said. "I only hope the heating fuel lasts."

"Good heavens. I hadn't thought of that, had you, John?"

I was eager to accept any opening for a conversation in spite of the fact that we had already received this disquietening news from Alphonse. John merely grunted and turned self-consciously to the door of our compartment into which he disappeared, his burly back seeming to register embarrassment as well as disapproval.

We talked for a bit, the stranger and I. He turned out, as I had thought, to be a German, the son of a wealthy merchant from Samsun. . . . "And who are you?" he asked politely enough.

"Oh, I'm just an Englishman," I replied without encouragement. But he did not, as a matter of fact, appear anxious to hear any more. For a while we talked about Turkey and the Turks. I longed to ask him point-blank about his views on the war, but I felt I must go carefully for fear of frightening him away altogether.

When I returned to our compartment, John was reading a book which he had rather obviously picked up as he heard my steps approaching. We talked of this and that till dinner-time, when Alphonse once more stuck his head through the door to announce the meal. It was growing dark as we made our way along the corridor to the restaurant car, but we were pleased to notice that the little coal heating stove was still alight when we passed it.

My young German acquaintance did not come in to dinner; conversation between John and myself was, however, hampered by the fact that we were obliged to share our table with two strangers—Syrians, I think, but "foreigners," of course, to John. Since John therefore was once more pre-occupied with thoughts of ships and with the dark and tortuous "leads" of the Turkish coast, he replied to my attempts at a more general discourse in offhand monosyllables.

At last the two foreigners left the table and John immediately unburdened himself of what had been uppermost in his mind:

"I don't trust that Jesse," he announced, leaning over the table so as not to be forced to raise his voice. "He's probably spinning them all some bright yarn up there; and when we get to Ankara we'll find the orders all ready for us . . . drafted by Lieutenant Matheson—R.C.N.V.R." He emphasised the initials at the end with unusual bitterness.

"Oh, nonsense, John. Jesse's far more likely to be busy looking for girl friends, or learning up some 'cute dialogue' in Greek or Turkish and practising his appealing look." But John only shook his head in a knowing manner and refused to be convinced that Jesse was anything but a plausible young schemer. Since this conviction seemed in some odd way to please old John rather than to perturb him, I soon gave up all efforts to prove him wrong.

On our way back from the dining-car we saw a tray of food disappearing into the next compartment to ours. As we passed the door we heard the voice of the wily Alphonse talking loudly to our neighbour in fluent German.

"So much for Alphonse not speaking Deutsch," I remarked. "Young Fritz seems to have got him taped all right anyway."

"That Hun must be a regular customer on this train, or else he's very well off," observed John sourly. . . . "Maybe both."

For an hour or so we played cards and drank *raki*, the Turkish equivalent of absinthe. Then John decided to turn in. It was warmer now, in spite of the half-open window; perhaps because of the *raki* we had been drinking; perhaps also because more snow had begun to fall. At any rate, there was no need for John to put my raincoat over his single blanket, but he seemed pleased to have it handy in case it was required later on.

"Aren't you going to turn in now?" he asked. "I should; before it gets too cold to sleep."

But I was not cold yet, nor sleepy; I was full of the glow of *raki* and fantastic notions. For a moment I contemplated the snowflakes drifting in at the window. Then I glanced at the faint light shining through the frosted glass panel of a door beside me.

"No," I said, "I'm going to have a talk to the Hun."

John grunted and took up his book.

4

SOME of the compartments in this carriage were so arranged, in pairs, that there was a small toilet between them, from which a door led into each. The idea was that, if the occupants of either compartment wanted a wash, they went into the toilet, shut the door opposite leading into their neighbour's compartment, and so included the toilet in their own little section of accommodation. Alternatively, as frequently happened, they opened their own door only to meet their neighbour just opening his; each then apologised, hesitated, blushed, stood on one leg, half withdrew, then advanced again, until finally both retired, in various states of anxiety and discomfort, to wait in their own compartment for a few moments before the next ugly rush, which would decide the winner.

I opened our toilet door and tapped on the opposite one.

"*Herrein!* please," came in a weak voice from the other side. I went in.

Young Fritz was still lying on the lower bunk with a blanket and a heavy overcoat drawn up to his chin. He raised himself on one elbow as I entered and smiled a little nervously. He was very pale, I noticed again, and the single, shaded lamp just above his head threw long, streaky shadows down the lower part of his face. It was not an unpleasant face; almost pathetic in expression, if anything, and there was a quizzical droop to the right-hand end of his mouth—possibly the result of a childhood scar. It gave the lad a young-old look by which I felt I should always remember him. The room smelt foully stuffy. Only the reading-lamp in the lower bunk shone weakly through a haze of cigarette smoke.

"Good evening. I came to see how you were doing in here."

"Oh, it is courteous of you."

"Not a bit of it. Just idle curiosity I'm afraid."

"And your friend?"

"He's an anti-Nazi."

Fritz smiled again weakly. "And you not?" he inquired, still smiling, but with more amusement in his eyes.

I thought it best to be frank.

"Yes, I am," I said, "but I am also interested to meet one of our enemies in such unusual circumstances."

He said nothing, but lay back upon his pillow, and motioned me to the little flap seat near the window. I thanked him and sat down. He watched me gravely and, I thought, still a little nervously, as I took out a cigarette and lit it.

"Well," I began again, tossing the match on to the floor,

and treading it out. "Who do you think is going to win the war?"

He did not answer at once; but he showed no surprise at the directness of my question. "Of course Germany must win," he said slowly after a while. But he said it without any arrogance and quietly, as if thinking aloud, or perhaps he had been trying to find a way of framing his convictions so as not to give immediate offence. I encouraged him to go on. Soon he warmed to his subject, and before long I found myself listening patiently to the usual clap-trap about master-races and suffering minorities to which the world had by now become accustomed.

I found it intensely interesting though, to hear all this at first hand. "You sound very sure about the future," I remarked, more by way of filling in a pause, than because I was interested in disputing his conviction.

At that he became quite carried away with his theme. . . . "But, please," he almost pleaded and, raising himself on one elbow, continued with sudden animation. "Even a fool can see the way it is all going." I smiled as he went on, with growing excitement, to enumerate the recent triumphs of the German armies in Africa and Russia. I must admit that I was fascinated by the fellow. "This, then, is the way they really do think and talk, these Huns," I thought to myself. "How wonderful to have heard it all from the horse's own mouth." I sat watching him and listening intently. He developed his arguments with the utmost precision and conviction, but without a trace of ill-humour. I put in a remark or two occasionally, of course. It would have been impossible, even with one's tongue in one's cheek, to agree with him when directly taxed for an answer. In the end we reached a deadlock.

We left the war then and spoke of his home near Samsun. He told me his name too—Fritz Scheibel. Then we talked about Silesia, where his father's home had been, and of the Austrian Tyrol, which both of us had known in peace-time. Later on the talk turned inevitably to sense of humour. As far as I recall he tried to tell a joke—some futile pun with a very woolly climax which I missed completely. He laughed hugely, however, and then laughed at me for missing the point.

"What has become now of your great British sense of humour?" he asked, vastly tickled at his own astuteness.

"Oh, you'll never understand that," I replied tolerantly. "But I'll give you an illustration of the German lack of it, if you like."

"Please."

So I told him the story of a sailing race between German and British cadets at Dartmouth just before the outbreak of war.

The Dart is one of the trickiest rivers in the country for dinghy sailing—whenever there is any wind at all it comes in sudden gusts and awkward flaws, which only the cadets with several seasons of local experience are able to deal with. It had not been in the least surprising, therefore, that one of the German boats had capsized within a few minutes of the start. Of course we had all laughed at the unfortunate lads as they floundered forlornly amongst the sails and rigging of their overturned boat; we would have laughed even more heartily if they had been our own cadets. Then suddenly, to everyone's acute embarrassment, the German officer in charge of their party had lost his temper. He turned white with passion and began to rave and curse at his boys. He had even threatened them with bloody reprisals as soon as they returned on board the German training ship.

"And why not?" observed Fritz. He regarded me gravely for a moment; then added, in a tone of patient piety: "That is German discipline—the secret of German greatness."

"No doubt," I assented dryly. "At any rate our people tried to calm your officer down. 'After all,' they said, 'it is only sport'."

"I can imagine his answer."

"His answer was that 'A German officer is not allowed to make a fool of himself *even in sport!*' "

"And wasn't he surely right?" asked Fritz calmly.

I smiled at that but could think of no suitable reply. Instead I asked him a question that had bothered me from the first. "Are you unfit for service?" I said. "Wouldn't you rather be a soldier, than in a neutral country? You seem so keen on your army and its magnificent victories."

"No, I do not like to be a soldier." He was not in the least put out by the question. "I do not wish for fighting—physical fighting, I mean."

"You sometimes talk as though you approved of it."

"No, I hate it," he insisted; "it is wasteful and beastly. But in Germany it is not necessary for all to fight. All are soldiers, if they fight or not."

"Including the Gestapo, I suppose?"

If I had known what effect this remark would have had upon him, I might have left it unsaid. He seemed to curl right up into himself. He cast a furtive glance at the door. He was shaken. He looked suddenly quite young again, younger than before but not eager nor boyish—just frightened. "You talk of things you do not know of," he said at last in a thick, low voice, all his self-assurance gone. I apologised and went on watching him.

"How old are you?" I ventured at last.

"Thirty-eight."

I was astonished and I must have shown it.

"Is that such an impossible age?" asked Fritz petulantly.

"I thought you were at least fifteen years younger." I was all at once furious with him. I felt cheated. To think that I had been listening to a sermon on German greatness from a flabby Hun many years older than myself! I remembered the remarks of Ensor and the upright, the honourable Hilton. I felt ashamed, but there was no sense, even so, in losing my temper. It had been entirely my own fault.

"I must go now," I told Fritz, rising to my feet rather awkwardly. He seemed surprised—even a little frightened, like a child about to be left in a darkened room. But his expression only increased my irritation. It looked grotesque on the face of a man of thirty-eight.

"It is still quite early," he said reproachfully. He turned suddenly and produced, from beneath his pillow, a bottle of what looked like brandy. "How about a drink, anyway, before you go."

"No, thanks." I was suspicious, now, as well as ashamed.

"This is good Turkish cognac."

"I don't want a drink." He looked hurt; and the oddly self-righteous ring of my own remark made me smile in spite of myself.

"Have I not amused you then? You came into my compartment to be amused, did you not?" he asked, with a faintly sardonic lift to his eyebrows.

This was too much. I blushed and felt uncomfortable. Then I thought of that silly story I had told him about the German cadets at Dartmouth, and my discomfiture was complete. What did it matter that my pre-war connection with the college had been purely fortuitous and in no way connected with my subsequent mobilisation in the naval reserves? Fritz Scheibel would assume, from what I had said, that I was a naval officer and, therefore, that I was in Turkey on some sea-faring business. On both scores he would be right. My God, what a fool the man had made of me!

I thought of trying to pretend that I was an Assistant Naval Attaché or something; but realised at once that I would almost certainly make a mess of it and increase any suspicions Fritz might already have . . . besides, I had not yet been told what our official alibi in Turkey was to be.

"You have amused me exceedingly."

"None the less, I am sorry that you refuse good cognac on a night like this," he insisted, with a pleasant smile.

"Don't worry," I said, also smiling, but sick of him and anxious to get away. "Perhaps we shall meet again . . . we may then have a very different war picture to discuss." I tried to talk naturally, but failed. The remark was wholly lacking in poise, and I knew it.

"In Turkey, people are always meeting again," he answered, "but they do not always speak to each other."

I left him then, and I heard him lock his door to the toilet as I opened ours.

John was asleep, but my entry wakened him. He sat up and shivered, looked at me oddly and then lay down again, drawing his blanket closer round his neck. "Damn you for waking me up," he growled. "I'll never get to sleep again in this cold." I threw my Burberry over him.

"Thanks," he mumbled through his coverings. Then I put my hand on the radiator under the table—it was only just warm. Outside the snow had stopped and the sky was icy clear and flaming with stars. One could feel the cold lapping in over the top of the window and see a sparkling powder of frost all over the table and floor and on the foot of John's bunk. I shivered and rubbed my hands furiously together.

"What did old Fritz have to say," muttered John, yawning into his pillow.

"Nothing much," I replied. "His name *is* Fritz as a matter of fact."

"Of course it is—they all are," mumbled John impatiently, as he rolled himself over to face the wall.

I left it at that. I was thoroughly depressed and worried about the whole business. I knew that I had been childishly irresponsible over my conversation with the German and, at the end of the interview (making the whole affair appear somehow worse) . . . unpardonably ill-mannered. I climbed into my bunk and put out the light.

Strangely enough I went straight to sleep, and when I woke up there was Alphonse's comic little head poking through the door to make some slightly involved statement about breakfast.

5

ALPHONSE was trying to explain that there would be only black coffee and biscuits for breakfast. John merely glared at him savagely till he popped out of sight and slid the door to with a bang.

I threw off my blanket and dropped on to the floor. It was bitterly cold. Although I was dressed in thick underclothes, trousers and sweater, I felt the cold bite through me. The little table by the window was covered with a rime of frost in the middle of which stood a glass of water frozen solid. I toyed with the idea of trying to hitch a towel or something into the gaping window-frame; but this would have blocked out the light and anyway I had nothing to hitch it with . . . and anyway it would blow down . . . and anyway . . . and anyway I was standing there freezing. With a violent shiver I hurled myself back into my bunk and pulled the blanket over me.

A little later the good Alphonse, either from kindness of heart or in the hope of improving the Hilton liver, brought in our coffee and biscuits on a tray. He informed us that during the night there had been more than thirty degrees of frost and that all the heating fuel had been used up. I could see now that there was frost all over our radiator.

Then came the news of the Japanese attack on Pearl Harbour. Apparently the station-master had just heard the announcement on the Turkish radio; but few details about the attack had been given, and nobody seemed to be taking it at all seriously. Perhaps we had been assured too often that Japan was neither strong enough nor well enough organised to present us with a serious military problem. Still, the attack had at last been launched; and at last the newspapers would be able to talk freely about their beloved "global conflict," a term at which they had been nibbling impatiently for some time. It would vary the monotonous diet of "ever-increasing flows," "ever-widening scopes" and "remains to be seen," I reflected, without feeling very much real interest in the news. To myself (and possibly even to John, in spite of his pose of gloomy apathy) it was more fun to lie and dream of great deeds among the Aegean Islands than to indulge in uninformed speculation about the defence of the sweltering Malacca Straits.

The morning wore on. About noon John rolled out at last and tottered into the toilet. I heard him lock the door into Fritz Scheibel's compartment; but I did not hear him unlock it when he came out again.

"Haven't you left old Fritz's toilet door locked?" I asked.

"To hell with Fritz," said John.

"Still, it's a bit tough—locking him out of his toilet," I suggested. I was not keen to try conclusions with the Hun a second time; did not want to have any more to do with him if I could help it. But John was still feeling liverish.

"Not going to have any bloody Huns using my washplace," he growled, and got back into bed. "Anyway, it'll do him good to take a walk down the corridor—pasty-faced little worm."

I said no more and a little later we both got dressed and went down to the restaurant car, hoping for lunch.

The meal, when it arrived, consisted only of a few scraps of cold meat and salad with stale bread; crude black bread it was, peculiar to Turkey, who was very short of wheat in those days. But the air in the dining-car was much warmer and there was still a little *raki* and *cognac* left. So we sat there quite happily for a while. The sun shone brightly through large windows upon a scene of considerable gaiety. Most of the other passengers were in there too; Levantines of all sorts, Greeks, Turks and nondescripts; but there was no sign of Fritz Scheibel, nor did we see him again till we reached Ankara.

About 1.30 p.m. there came a sudden loud whistle and next moment the train began to move. There was great excitement among the passengers and we hurried back to our compartment from which we hoped to watch the passing landscape in greater comfort. We were disappointed in this, however. The wind now flew in at the window with such icy violence that the compartment was uninhabitable; so, after stowing all our baggage under a blanket on the top bunk, we returned to the dining-car where we remained for the rest of the journey.

Once or twice we saw a convoy of military vehicles—American and British vehicles, crawling along the rough road which more or less followed the course of the railway line.

"I wonder what on earth's brewing up here," I said presently.

"I've no idea," grunted John, who appeared to have something else on his mind.

"All this transport looks very fishy. D'you think there's something in the wind for these parts and that our operation is part of the general plan?"

"There's certainly *something* in the wind, but I don't know what it is any more than you do." John relapsed into silence again, then. . . . "I had a word with the Consular shipping bloke at Adana, while you and Ensor were messing about."

"What did he have to say?"

John looked round hastily, the dining-car was much emptier, and the nearest people were well out of earshot.

"A lot," he stated with considerable satisfaction. "He told me quite a bit about the coast between Adana and the Dardanelles . . . and about the neutrality rules. . . . One thing he told me was that if, by any chance, these craft come from the Black Sea, they won't be armed with anything heavier than machine-guns: they may not even have those."

"How's that?"

"The Turks won't allow any offensively armed ships to pass through the Bosphorus or Dardanelles. That was a part of the Montreux Convention, it seems."

"What else did he tell you?"

"He told me something about international law that I'd never heard before. . . . Apparently it's legal, so long as the first contact is made outside territorial waters, for a warship to chase an enemy right into neutral waters and finish her off there."

"That sounds interesting; but as for the ships being unarmed, I don't see that that makes very much difference. They'd never stand a chance against E-boats or destroyers or aircraft in daylight anyway."

"I suppose not," agreed John . . . "nor against the shore batteries on Leros and Rhodes," he added glumly. "But as a matter of fact," he went on, brightening a little, "there isn't much chance of our meeting E-boats or destroyers north of Rhodes . . . they're all too busy watching for our own light raiding forces in the gaps between the outer islands . . . we won't meet them; that is, *if they aren't expecting us.*"

John glanced at me sharply, almost accusingly. I knew that he was thinking of my affair with Fritz Scheibel.

"That's our only chance," he said presently. "Secrecy—absolute water-tight secrecy."

"Dark nights and bad weather would help," I ventured, but John only frowned at the suggestion.

"That all depends on whether we're going to use the inshore channels or not," he growled. "I'm not taking any ship in there in the dark, that's certain. . . . C. S. A. Adana says that only the Turkish lights are kept burning these days, not more than half of the essential ones in fact—only six in all. The Greek lights are extinguished."

"As long as you can keep really close to the shore—within a couple of cables—you can see all right on the darkest nights," I observed. "It's only when you open to half a mile or more that you begin to get foxed. . . . I know, because I've tried it in peace-time."

"I expect you've done a lot of funny things in peace-time," remarked John acidly.

This happened to be true; though not in the way that John

had meant it; but I saw no use in continuing the argument in the face of his prejudice, so I changed the subject.

The plateau of Anatolia continued snowbound and featureless. The train jogged across it at a steady twenty-five miles or so per hour. We passed several places where the snow had been piled high on either side of the tracks by the snow plough. After tea (very weak tea) it grew dark, and for many hours we sat playing cards or reading, unable to see out because of the lights which were on in the dining-car.

Soon after ten o'clock, Alphonse told us we were getting near Ankara, so I struggled along the corridor of the wagon-lit to get a glimpse of Turkey's capital.

When I looked out I could just see the dull glow of a city in the distance, but shortly afterwards the track curved round into a small valley at the end of which was a wide cluster of lights. I went back into the dining-car.

"Come on, John," I called, "we're nearly there."

He followed me to our compartment, where we both started packing up our belongings.

Then John got suddenly worried about his appearance, and whether or not one could notice he had not shaved since the evening before.

Poor John; as the second-in-command of our little gang, he always bore the direct brunt of old Mathews's frequent tantrums, which usually reached the rest of us with a somewhat reduced impact on that account. I therefore smiled now at his obvious anxiety.

"You look perfect," I tried to reassure him.

"You never know who may be there to meet us," he fussed. "Might be the Old Man himself."

"Yes, and a few diplomats with their wives." I took him up enthusiastically. "We might have a party."

"Oh, hell!" cried John in alarm, taking me seriously. "D'you really think so? I'd better shave anyway." And just as the train was beginning to slow down, he disappeared in a fluster into the toilet.

When we reached the station I got out and soon, above the crowd, I caught sight of the fiery head of old Commander Mathews, bobbing down the platform towards me.

"Ah! Good boy," he boomed, when he saw me. "Glad you

got here all right in the end. Had a pretty bad time I expect."

"Oh, not too bad, sir," I replied . . . "and full of excitement."

"Where's Hilton?"

"He won't be long, sir. I think he's still shaving."

"Shaving? What the devil for?" ejaculated the Old Man. "Does the fella think we're going to attend a diplomatic dinner-party or something."

"Oh, I think he just wanted to clean up a bit in case you were here to meet us."

"Well, I damn well am here, and I've got a car waiting outside," retorted the Old Man testily. "He'd better not be long."

We stood there chatting for a few minutes; the Old Man rather impatiently, and I trying to keep his mind off John's shaving. I did not at first notice a repeated knocking and rattling from the carriage beside us, for I was busy watching the carefully graded expressions of gratitude and resignation chasing each other over the features of the cunning Alphonse, as he stood at the receipt of blood money by the carriage door. I saw Fritz Scheibel clamber out, and noticed, from Alphonse's passionate appreciation, that an even larger tip than usual had changed hands. Then Fritz, with a slow, uncertain little smile in my direction, slipped away into the crowd and disappeared.

Now the rattling and the knocking suddenly forced itself on my attention. It had become a pounding and a furious battering, accompanied by loud calls and violent imprecations.

"God spare the crows. What the devil's that row?" asked the Old Man, whose impatience had almost got the better of him; then we both peered in at the half-opened window to see the door of the toilet shuddering beneath a terrific rain of blows from within. Suddenly there was a splintering, tinkling crash, and a massive fist shot through the glass. This was followed by the furious red face of John Hilton, whose savage bellows died abruptly as he observed the red wig and ferocious aspect of old Mathews in the carriage window. Alphonse, who up to then had seemed quite oblivious to the racket, gave an anguished howl, leaped into the carriage and scuttled round to the compartment door.

"What the hell are you doing in there, Hilton," roared the Old Man.

"I'm—I'm sorry, sir," stammered John. "I got locked in. It must . . ."

"So I can damn well see, you bloody idiot," burst in the Old Man in a fury. "And how the devil am I going to run this job with a bunch of half-wits who get themselves locked in the lavatory before we even start?"

It was only by a superhuman effort that I managed not to laugh. Poor John! He'd been so desperately anxious to make an impressive arrival at Ankara. How magnificently he had succeeded! He now opened the door, which had in some strange way become locked from inside our compartment, and struggled out, still purple with rage and embarrassment. He appeared ready to fell Alphonse on the spot, but that little man, sure of his ground, stood defiantly in the compartment door and refused to give an inch till he had been supplied with John's full passport identity. At last we got away and followed the Old Man out of the station.

John was beside himself.

"If ever I catch that yellow-bellied little bastard outside Turkey," he fumed, "I'll break his bloody neck like a match-stick."

"Are you sure it was Alphonse who locked you in?" I asked soothingly.

"Of course it was him and a bloody fine cut out of the damages he'll get into the bargain. Unless . . ." he paused, then went on again, looking about him with a puzzled expression on his rugged old face, "unless it was that pest-ridden Hun, trying to get his own back."

I, too, had been thinking of Fritz, and wondering whether this might be the second time in twenty-four hours that he had made a prize fool out of one of us with such masterful ease. Remembering his glance in my direction as he left the train, I also began to look round among the crowd, half expecting to see his quizzical gaze bent upon us from behind some pillar. He was nowhere about, however, and I turned to follow the others, smiling a little to myself, but at the same time, resolving never again to discuss sense of humour with a German.

6

AFTER breakfast next morning we all drove up from the
Ankara Palace hotel, where we had spent the night, to
the British Embassy. The Old Man led the way into the Naval
Attaché's office, which had been lent to him during the owner's
temporary absence. As soon as the door was closed, old Mathews
looked at us both very sternly and said: "I suppose S.O.I.
Med. has told you what this party's all about?" We shook our
heads, then gave him a short résumé of what we *did* already
know, namely:

(1) That we were to smuggle some craft (size and nationality
unspecified) out through the enemy blockade of the
Aegean.

(2) That the channels between the Turkish coast and the
enemy-held islands were exceedingly narrow.

(3) That only half the lighthouses (i.e. only the Turkish
ones) were working.

(4) That if the enemy caught us outside neutral waters they
were allowed, if they liked, to chase us right into Turkish
waters to destroy us.

(5) That the ships might be unarmed.

(6) That we could expect no assistance from naval craft
(*and that we were, in some odd way, to blame for S.O.I. Med.
having even brought this last point up*).

And John might have added that he was not in the least bit
happy about the "whole bloody business," which would have
been quite untrue; he was revelling in it, at heart.

The Old Man heard us out, then sat himself down at the
N.A.'s desk and said: "Right," in a tone of finality, and went
on. "Then all I need tell you is what ships they are. . . .
Well, the first three are an 11,000-ton ice-breaker and two
large tankers. . . . All Russians!"

"A Russian ice-breaker, sir? We didn't . . ." John Hilton
gaped at old Mathews in astonishment, unable even to finish
what he had been going to say. The latter, however, continued
coolly: "Yes, she's a huge lump of a ship; very conspicuous in

daytime with her great spoon bow. She'll have to go down by
night of course."

John made no reply to that. He was obviously dumb-
founded at the news and the difficulties which it implied. It
was clear that, although he had growled at me at Lydda
about the "young fellas'" ignorance of merchant ships, he had
never really expected that even he would be required to handle
one on this job.

"The position is," went on old Mathews, "that the Russians
are in a panic to get their big ships out of the Black Sea before
the Germans occupy the whole of the Russian coastline (they're
somewhere round Taganrog at the moment). . . . The ice-
breaker and two tankers are on their way to the Bosphorus
now."

It was a most dramatic turn of events. Coasters and *caiques*
might not have been very difficult to cope with; but huge
merchant ships . . . right under the enemy's nose. How on
earth were we to smuggle them through his patrols and past
his observation posts? And Russians . . . what kind of crews
would they have? How would we talk to them? What sort of
discipline were they under? Did they have a proper Master,
or were they commanded by a sort of Soviet? A hundred
questions of this sort chased themselves through my head, and
my excitement grew.

"The trouble is that we don't know anything like enough
about the Turkish coast yet." Old Mathews was speaking
again, and I cut short my silent conjectures to pay attention
to what he was saying. "However, Matheson's just made one
voyage down it by daylight."

This also was interesting news; we had had no idea that
the party was going to start so soon. I noticed that John felt
some misgivings on this score. The Old Man then told us how
Jesse, in a small British-owned general cargo ship disguised as
a Turk, had steamed right down the coast without any serious
interference, except in one place where she was examined by
an Italian patrol craft.

"He got away with it all right," said old Mathews, "but I
don't know the full story myself yet. He's only just arrived
back in Istanbul; and he passed through Ankara while I was
away."

I wondered whether we might not obtain local knowledge of the coast from some of the Greek or Turkish coaster skippers, but apparently that was not going to be easy.

"They don't move by night," said the Old Man shortly, ". . . gave up night sailing when the Germans came."

Old Mathews brought out a chart and motioned us to gather round it. It was a general chart of the eastern Mediterranean, coloured all over in red, blue and green chalk.

"Now look here," began the Old Man. "All these islands coloured red are garrisoned by the Italians, these blue ones by Germans, and the green area is Turkish. Territorial water extends nominally to three miles from anywhere on the Turkish coast, but that's not very much help for two reasons. First, because some of the islands are a mile or less from Turkey . . . and, secondly, because I'm quite certain that the enemy would attack you wherever you were—you'd never be able to prove that you were in territorial waters anyway."

"Aren't there Turkish coastguards all the way down?" I asked.

"No, there aren't. Just a few look-out posts manned by soldiers," he said shortly. "And even if there were, the Turks couldn't take the word of a single coastguard against the official report from the captain of whatever had sunk you . . . in any case you'd be sunk by then, so it wouldn't help us much if they did." He gave an impatient snort and turned back to the chart.

"Looks like we'll have to go straight out to sea and down the middle then," suggested John.

"Impossible," retorted old Mathews. "The ice-breaker's only got a speed of twelve knots, and the tankers can't do more than ten . . . even with the fourteen hours of darkness we're getting at this time of the year, you couldn't get farther than Kos in one night. . . . You'd be caught right in the open at dawn, somewhere off Leros; they'd get you at once."

"Presumably the ships aren't armed," I put in.

"No, they're not . . . not much use if they were, anyway."

"And half the lights on the coast are out," from John.

"Yes."

"How are the tankers loaded, sir?" John again.

"Light ship . . . no cargo."

Old John, by the awkward but determined expression on his face, was obviously working himself up for a long and vehement speech.

"Well, sir, I mean . . . Well, if you don't mind my saying so, sir, from a merchant seaman's point of view that is . . ." he paused and looked uncomfortable. "Well, I just don't think it's possible, sir," he ended firmly.

"Go on, Hilton," growled the Old Man. "Might as well know just why I'm a complete bloody fool, I suppose."

John screwed himself up and began again doggedly. "These tankers aren't like destroyers, you know, or any other warships for that matter. . . ."

He paused again to examine the chart.

"What I mean is this," he went on after a moment. "Some of these places look pretty narrow. . . ."

Poor John's face began to grow very red. He seemed at a loss as to how he should continue in the face of the Old Man's ferocious expression. The latter must have seen this, for he controlled his impatience a little and the hint of an encouraging smile crossed the corners of his mouth.

"Go on, Hilton, I won't eat you, for God's sake . . . you're the expert in this party on merchant ships. . . . We'd better hear what you've got to say."

John cleared his throat and began again. "You'll no doubt be wanting us to make this passage by night, sir?"

"Of course. Damn it! I've just told you so." The Old Man was unable to keep the edge out of his voice.

"Well, in peace-time, sir . . ." The Old Man began to glare at him dangerously. "I mean, these narrows, sir. . . ."

And there the poor fellow gave it up and, relapsing into moody silence, he stood gazing despondently at the chart.

I felt sorry for poor John. There was a lot of sense in what he was trying to say, and if he had not been so painfully shy, he would have said it and then stood by his opinion. He ought to have been given a fairer hearing.

But old Mathews's impatience had got the better of him.

"What's the use of telling us how you'd make the passage in peace-time," he snorted. "This damn well isn't peace-time, and in war-time risks have got to be taken. I quite agree with everything you've implied Hilton; but I've been into the whole

thing very carefully with Matheson and others and . . ." He
saw the hurt, obstinate look which flashed across John's face.
"All right," he put in. "I know Matheson's only a yachtsman
and hasn't your knowledge of merchant ships; but he's a keen
and capable chap just the same."

"The position is this," he summed up, driving his point
home with a smack of his right fist into the open palm of his
left hand. "Getting the ships down is going to be risky and
difficult however we set about it. But, down they've got to
come. . . . Is that quite clear?" He gave each of us a pene-
trating look. "They've got to, see?"

"It's a problem," he went on more evenly, "over which we've
all got to put our heads together and then get on with it."

Old John accepted the situation with a nod; but I could see
that he felt disgruntled. He was no fool over anything to do
with ships, nor a coward by any means, and he felt that he
had been called both by implication. "It may not look half
so bad," he conceded at last, "when we get down to it in
detail on the large-scale charts."

"It doesn't look bad now," retorted the Old Man. "Only
difficult."

He put away the charts and locked the cupboard containing
them. Then he stumped off to arrange for our train tickets to
Istanbul.

Ankara is not an inspiring city at first sight; it seems to lack
the true character of a city. There is no great river and, of
course, no harbour, nor any natural contact with the outside
world. We found the usual jumble of squalid houses and
muddy streets, dominated by a small steep-sided mountain,
rising out of the centre of the city. The only other remarkable
sights in Ankara were a railway station that looked like a
Gaumont cinema, an airfield without any aircraft, a garden
suburb and one or two modern hotels. We caught the night
train to Istanbul that same evening, December 9th: at
breakfast-time next morning we reached Scutari and the railway terminus of Haydar Pasha. After many days we had
come at last to the very edge of Asia; upon the other side
of a brilliant strip of blue water lay the first great city of em-
battled Europe.

II

MOONLIGHT ENCOUNTERS

7

THE sun had already risen and, as we hurried across the Bosphorus in a ferry, it shone glaring down the wooded fjord to strike colour out of the mosques and minarets of Constantinople, which stood out like almonds upon a magnificent pink and yellow trifle. Or a Christmas cake . . . yes, maybe it was a Christmas cake, for on Galata quay, near the entrance to the Golden Horn, stood a gaudy figure reminiscent of those with which a Christmas cake is frequently adorned. "There's Matheson," said the Old Man, and started waving furiously.

I was astonished at Jesse's appearance. When last I had seen him he had been dressed in the sober uniform of a Lieutenant R.C.N.V.R.; but the figure I now beheld looked more like a caricature of an American playboy as depicted on the musical comedy stage. Jesse looked gay and irrepressible in a bright check suit, grey felt hat, red tie and a pair of black-and-white "co-respondent's" shoes. He saw the Old Man waving, and waved back. The ferry was still fifty yards from the quay, sidling in towards it.

"Have you got a car?" yelled the Old Man.

"Yes, over behind the shed, sir," Jesse shouted back.

"Bring her alongside somewhere. We've got a pile of stuff with us."

Jesse hurried off to bring the car nearer to where the ferry's gangway would be. I heard a muffled snort and knew that John was standing behind me registering disapproval of Jesse.

"Got a girl in the car, I suppose," he grunted. This was quite possible. Jesse always had a girl; often more than one, and it was unlikely that he would have spent a week or more in Istanbul without having collected a companion from among the lovely little Greek girls that one saw about in the streets and on the ferry.

It was not surprising that girls fell for him. He was tall and slim, with dark, rather satanic good looks, unquenchably cheerful and a champion ski-runner into the bargain. He came, moreover, of a wealthy family and had been quite famous before the war as an ocean-going yachtsman; also as the author of a book on deep-sea navigation.

In due course the ferry berthed. We struggled ashore with our bags to find Jesse waiting for us beside a large, black car with a British Embassy chauffeur. There was no girl in evidence, and a few moments later we were driving off up the steep hill from Galata to Pera, the district in which the British Embassy was situated. On our arrival we went straight up to an office on the first floor which had been allocated to old Mathews for the duration of the tanker operations.

The Old Man was anxious to hold a preliminary conference at once; so all the relevant charts were got out, and for half an hour or so we pored over them, while Jesse recounted his experiences on the voyage he had just made down to Mersin, in the coaster *Vana*.

"As she was supposed to be a Turkish ship," he began, "we naturally did the whole passage in daylight. The Turks have agreed with the Huns not to sail their shipping by night without previous warning; so any craft seen moving on this coast by night is liable to be attacked."

"Did you keep in territorial waters all the way then?"

"No, I followed the normal Turkish shipping route round Cape Baba and straight down the middle of the Mitylene Channel to the Gulf of Sandarli, where I anchored the first night. Next day I steamed across the mouth of the Gulf of Izmir, through the Khios Strait, round to Kuçadasi, through the Samos Strait there, and anchored off the mouth of the Meander River—right there," and he pointed to it on the chart.

"What was it like at Khios? Are both these islets in the channel Turkish?"

"No. The one in the middle of the Strait's Greek. That's to say, German now; but they tell me the light's extinguished, so perhaps they've abandoned it altogether. Anyway, there's plenty of room between the Eastern Island (which is Turkish) and the Turkish coast . . . over a mile and plenty of water."

Poor John looked dubious but said nothing.

"And what about patrols?" I asked.

"Well, I didn't see any in the daytime; but there's a rumour about a couple of armed motor-boats in the Khios Straits at night."

"*They* wouldn't do us much harm," said John.

"That's not the point, Hilton," snorted the Old Man. "Once you've been seen you can be shadowed and dealt with at leisure. Everyone knows the Turks've got only one large tanker and that she's down in Syria at the moment. As for an 11,000-ton ice-breaker, well, even a Greek fisherman would know her for what she was."

"I suppose that's so," agreed John.

"Are there any other patrols?" asked the Old Man, turning back to Jesse.

"Well, the only one I saw, sir, was the chap who boarded me. That was on the second night when I was anchored off the Meander."

"Tell them about it."

"It was bright moonlight at the time," Jesse began. "*Vana* was lying in seven fathoms, about a mile and a half off shore— here." He pointed at a spot on the chart.

"I'd turned in early," he went on, "and about midnight the old skipper called me on deck. As soon as I came up I saw what looked like a trawler circling round us about a cable or so off. She shouted through a megaphone in Turkish, and my skipper answered her."

"What did they say?" asked John.

"Oh, just asked our name and port of destination; and my skipper told them *Vana* and said we were bound for Mersin."

The Old Man nodded approval.

"Then the other guy sang out that he was going to send a boat," went on Jesse. "Up to now we'd taken her for a Turk; but, just as she turned to pass under our stern, the moon shone on her ensign and we saw she was an Iti."

"A bit awkward, eh?"

"Yes. Just imagine my embarrassment," drawled Jesse. "Anyway, we had a play all figured out for that one, and believe it or not, it worked. The old skipper could talk Turkish at least as well as an Italian, and the fact that the crew were mostly Greeks wasn't unusual in a Turkish ship. I was the only suspicious character on board, so I went below and stood by the sea cocks in case of accidents."

"They didn't find you then?"

"No. They just had a bit of an argument with the skipper and drank a bottle of his vodka and then got the hell out of it. They were still around when we got under way again at dawn, but they didn't interfere with us after that."

Even in Jesse's casual tones it sounded a pretty ticklish affair, and we said so.

"That rules out a daylight passage for the ice-breaker, you see," put in old Mathews.

"She's due in the Bosphorus the day-after-to-morrow night, you know, sir," Jesse informed him. "The Soviet Embassy sent us a chit about it yesterday evening."

The Old Man whistled. "Is she, by Jove! Then we've got to make up our minds quick. Any news of the tankers?"

"Not yet, sir."

"Right. Now, what's the name of this ice-breaker—let's get her settled first."

"*Kirilovka*, sir," replied Jesse.

"Yes, that's it. Now you, Hilton—you're senior officer of this party. You'd better have first go." John came forward in silence and together they turned to the charts, while Jesse and I looked on from the other side of the table.

The problem was now discussed in great detail from every possible angle. In the end it was agreed that *Kirilovka*'s best chance of getting down safely would be for her to make the most of her 12 knots speed, keeping as close as possible to the Turkish coast throughout the first night and endeavour to reach Rhodes before anyone knew that an allied ship was moving.

The moon, which had been full on December 3rd, would now be in its last quarter; a condition which suited everybody. The Old Man was satisfied, because most of the night would be dark; while John was pleased because: "If I leave the Dardanelles about sunset, I'll be down to Khios Strait soon after moonrise and have a little light to help me get through those narrows. . . ."

"It'll be nearly dawn when you get to Samos," warned Jesse.

"And a good job too," replied John impatiently. "I shall need a bit of light to get through there and all."

"Well, that's settled then," said old Mathews, straightening up from the chart table. "Of course, once you're at sea, you're free to take whatever action the circumstances may dictate and you can count on me to back you up."

"Thank you, sir," said John. "Of course, I know you'll do that."

The Old Man picked up his black felt hat, badge of the diplomat, of which he was very proud.

"Before we go any farther, I'll just drop round to the Soviet Embassy and see what they've got to say. . . . They'll probably want you to go aboard after dark, Hilton."

John nodded. Now that most of the details had been settled in a neat and seamanlike manner, his former doubts had been put away. He became positively good-humoured. His eyes began almost to sparkle.

The Old Man moved towards the door; then turned and surveyed us all sternly.

"Now, before I go, all of you; don't forget about secrecy. It must be absolute . . . asleep or awake."

"How about the Turks, sir?" asked John.

"Oh, they'll play all right. They won't split on us to the Huns. But this city's the headquarters of all the intelligence organisations in the world just now, and don't any of you forget it. Hilton's only chance of getting down is for him to catch an enemy completely by surprise."

Jesse and I murmured our acknowledgment of this pronouncement.

"What'll I need to take with me, sir," asked John.

"Oh, just your light baggage, the charts . . . and some Turkish money, in case you get into any trouble down the coast."

"And a bottle of whisky?" added John with ponderous jocularity.

The Old Man smiled and left the room.

We were billeted (if the word can decently be used to describe such truly sumptuous surroundings) in the Park Hotel. This was a magnificent establishment—large, up to date and far more luxurious than the gloomy old barns we had seen in Cairo and Alexandria. It stood upon a hill facing the Bosphorus and boasted a very smart and colourful clientele. The concierge, with the personality and appearance (and also the income for all I know) of a famous film star, must have been intimate with half the interesting and important figures of Europe.

It was amongst all this splendour that we ate our lunch—upon a sunny veranda with the sparkling blue Bosphorus spread before us and the pine-covered hills rising beyond. It was amongst all this magnificence of wealthy Levantines, gay White Russian demi-mondaines and sour-looking Herrenvolk, that we each smoked a provocative cigar—provoking no one, in fact, to anything but amusement. And it was amid the sensuous luxury of an expensive honeymoon suite on the first floor that we all three finally slept away the remainder of the afternoon.

We dined that evening in a quiet, secluded restaurant, owned and managed by three middle-aged White Russian ladies, who also served at table. The dining-room was small and panelled in dark oak. In one corner of the room a Hungarian string quartet played superbly. The food was such as one remembered only dimly from pre-war days in Vienna or Stockholm —rich, plentiful and varied. There was red wine to drink and *vodka* as well and good French brandy with our coffee. We ate enormously and without haste.

When we could at last eat no more, we sat back in our corners in contented silence—ready to spend the rest of the evening listening to the Hungarians and watching the people at their supper. Then I noticed Fritz Scheibel. He was sitting in a corner by the door, talking earnestly to an elderly man in pince-nez spectacles. The light was not full upon him, but I could recognise him easily by that quizzical droop to his mouth and the young-old expression on his face. I turned to John.

"D'you see who's sitting over in the corner behind me?" I asked.

John glanced over my shoulder absently; then I saw his eyes narrow and he looked away. "Your boy friend again, eh?" he said grimly, and immediately turned to Jesse who had just asked for the bill. "C'mon," he said shortly; we all got up to go, Jesse leading the way out.

Fritz Scheibel glanced up as we passed his table. He recognised me at once, and half rose with that weak little smile of his, as though he meant to speak to us. Then abruptly he sat down again and there was the hint of an awkward flush about his neck as he turned to his companion. I imagined that he must have caught an angry glare from John behind me, and I looked away quickly as well.

We had arranged to meet the Old Man after dinner at the house of some friends of his, who lived in the hills north of the city. They were a British woman, whom the Old Man had known since boyhood, and her twenty-two-year-old daughter who, to my joy, seemed to take a greater liking to old John than to the more obvious Jesse. But she could not restrain herself from unmercifully mocking at him and his pompous manner; until I began to feel heartily sorry for the honest fellow; he seemed to be taking it all so seriously. The Old Man didn't help matters by suddenly butting in with, "Shut up, Lavinia; or he'll go and lock himself in somewhere. He did when he saw me in Ankara," which made poor old John blush painfully and turn to gaze out of the window. Fortunately the sight of the first snow of the winter, falling gently among the trees outside, provided a good opportunity for changing the subject. After that the talk turned to the usual war gossip, which kept us going till the midnight news.

I will always remember that midnight. The portentous booming of the Old Man as he discussed the latest staff blunder, the good-humoured violence of Mrs. B——, the bright chatter of Lavinia, and John, sitting glum and uncomfortable, bolt upright in the middle of the sofa. The light streamed out of undarkened windows on to the falling snow and fir trees. Inside us was the glow of hot soup and a glass of good whisky. There was a fire of logs smouldering on the hearth; and the day had been full of excitements. Small wonder, then, that Jesse and I, at least, felt in good heart and happy.

The Old Man looked at his watch. "Two minutes to midnight," he said, and got up to switch on the radio. We all watched the magic green eye begin to glow, then split up and grow bright just in time for the last reverberations from Big Ben to come pulsating heavily into the room (like the drone of a receding bomber, I suddenly thought). Next the clear, unhurried voice of the announcer saying, "This is London calling Forces everywhere. Here is the news."

There followed those momentous headlines—*Repulse* and the great *Prince of Wales* had been sunk.

I thought at once of Fritz Scheibel, and wondered whether he was listening to the same news in a broadcast from Germany. For me it was the most dramatic moment since the night I lay alone in the cabin of a trawler, in the North Sea, and heard Churchill's speech on the fall of France.

We sat on in silence, and I could not tell what the others were thinking. The silence continued; there was little to be said in the presence of such staggering events. It was John who spoke in the end.

"No good sitting down under it," he pronounced gruffly but stoutly. "Time we took off our gloves and went at 'em bald-headed."

Somehow this meant nothing and yet everything and was so much John Hilton that we burst out laughing; but we felt none the less completely restored in spirit.

For a long time, that night, I lay awake thinking about the news and Fritz Scheibel and wondering how events in the Indian Ocean would ultimately affect us. How big a part could our insignificant little special service party, with its pretentious "Force 'W'" for a title . . . how telling a part could it possibly play in the pattern of Total World War?

8

"WHAT's it to be? The dames?"

It was our second evening in Istanbul (John Hilton's last for some time), and Jesse was marching us down the Rue de Pera, past the various night-clubs with their glaring electric signs. His friendly inquiry sounded suspicious. I felt sure that sooner or later we should find ourselves faced with one of Jesse's own girl friends, one of his "steadies," and be obliged to spend the rest of the evening watching that gallant rogue enjoying himself. John, apparently had also had some experience of this little trick of Jesse's.

"Whatever's best," he replied guardedly.

"O.K. then," said Jesse, turning suddenly up a narrow side street.

"Now remember—no Germans, Jesse," warned John.

"O.K. No Germans," agreed Jesse patiently, stopping before what looked like a small bar. "There's a sweet little Russian girl in here, and if she's talking to any Huns, we'll high-jack her out of it. Will that please you?"

"Not much unless she's got a sister," replied John, full of suspicion, "but I suppose there's no harm in just having a look at her," and he followed us reluctantly through a little swing door with a sign above it bearing the single word LOTTIE.

We entered a narrow hallway with a bar at one end and, to one side of the bar, a flight of three steps leading down on to a medium-sized dance floor beyond. At the bar were a few high stools, and upon the one nearest to the steps sat a queer little girl in a black beret and dark blue raincoat. She was leaning well back against a wooden pillar, which also acted as a banister post for the steps. Close up to her face, between her two hands, she held a coffee-cup . . . idly, pressed against her teeth, as though her mind were far away. Jesse went across to her, but she did not move until he spoke.

"Hello, sweetheart. How's tricks?" he greeted her.

The girl looked up slowly. Upon her face there was a large-eyed, serious and wholly childlike expression of inquiry; her head was cocked a little to one side like a young robin's as it perches upon the gardener's spade. Her coffee-cup remained

5

in its previous position; she made no move to put it down; but, after a moment or two, a slow smile began to creep into her eyes as she continued to stare at us all gravely. From her quaint expression and dark, bobbed hair, the girl might have been no more than sixteen; nor had she taken any trouble at all over her appearance—no lipstick, no make-up, just a plain, little white face with upon it that whimsical, almost elfin look of inquiry. She seemed a most unusual type to find hanging about in bars . . . she might have been an English schoolgirl in her 'teens.

I confess I was surprised. This was not the sort of young woman that Jesse usually collected. He confined himself normally to high-spirited blondes with rather more obvious selling points about them . . . "oomph" he called it. I wondered what exactly he saw in this quiet waif; what they talked about and what *she* thought of *him*.

Behind the bar stood a large, handsome woman of about forty, with jet-black hair and flashing eyes . . . presumably Lottie herself. "Good eefening, Jesse," came out of her in a rich, jovial voice. "Won't you all sit down?" and she pointed to the nearest table by the wall. We hung our overcoats on some hooks near by and did as she suggested. "Aren't you going to sit with your friends, Nadia, darling?" she added, to Jesse's little girl.

"Yes, sure. Come and sit with us," invited Jesse, ". . . before your stockings fall down," he added, grinning at her slim legs that hung limply over the edge of the stool.

Nadia put her coffee-cup on the bar and, with an angry glance at Jesse, started to hitch up one stocking, which had slipped; then she wriggled to the edge of her stool and slid down to the floor. One saw now that beneath her raincoat, which hung loosely open, she wore a simple black dress with a white collar. Her stockings were cheap cotton ones, many times mended. On her feet were black walking shoes with crêpe rubber soles. As she stood up and then advanced towards us, I noticed her slim lithe figure and her legs that were graceful but not too thin. She stood before us for a moment, hands on hips, coat swept back, her feet apart in a hoydenish pose. Her eyes were half serious, half smiling, as she gazed at Jesse doubtfully.

"Are you going to be rude to me, Jesse," she said quietly, and in good English, with a slightly American inflexion. She spoke clearly, and there was a musical lilt in her voice which lightened the seriousness of her tone. Jesse had already risen and was drawing up another chair. "I certainly am not, unless you want me to be," he replied with a wink. She frowned but sat down nevertheless. Jesse introduced us. Nadia gave each of us a polite little smile and then turned again to Jesse.

"Four *vodkas*," said John to the waiter, who had just arrived.

In due course the party warmed up, but Nadia was always quick to put Jesse in his place. She liked him, I thought— might even be fonder of him than she cared to admit. One just couldn't make out her true feelings. I soon realised, however, that she must be a year or two older than I had imagined.

The bar in which we sat had a gay Viennese atmosphere about it. A jolly-looking Austrian barman kept the radiogram going, while Lottie moved from table to table, speaking and laughing with everyone and occasionally having a drink. It seemed, from the talk, that many of the guests were Austrian or German; but none of them took any notice of us, nor we of them. We soon began to enjoy ourselves hugely. Nadia entered more and more into the spirit of things; became gay with sudden laughter now and then. Old John thawed completely, and insisted on holding Nadia's hand, which she good-naturedly permitted; but she kept a sharp eye on any liberties attempted by Jesse.

All at once a hush fell upon the whole company and faces were turned towards our table as there came floating up from the dance floor the first haunting bars of a tune that I had never heard before. The tune was *Lili Marlene*, that a year or two later was to become world famous. Nadia stopped talking to listen and to hum softly. The rest of us fell silent.

"How I love that melody," sighed Nadia, when it was over.

"Memories?" I asked, hoping to get some clue to her; but she pretended not to hear me. She turned instead with a bantering smile to old John, who was having some difficulty in getting his handkerchief from his left side jacket pocket without losing hold of Nadia's hand.

We did not dance at first. John was a very clumsy dancer

and hated making an exhibition of himself: so, as this was really his party, his farewell party, we let him run it in his own way.

John preferred to spend the rest of the evening in drinking beer and, by eleven o'clock, he was easily the dominant figure in the room. He had mellowed by then into a ludicrous picture of semi-paternal roguishness and benignity. He called Nadia "my child" and "kiddie" and insisted on holding her hand whenever it was available. She, on her part, played up to him with seeming affection; but I knew that she merely thought him safe and homely and hoped that Jesse was jealous. Only once did Nadia's attention wander for a moment from John's elephantine blandishments. Unfortunately, however, it was in the middle of one of his most elaborate speeches that she began to stare absently across the room.

"Hey, wake up, my child. Did you hear what I said?" cried John reproachfully.

Nadia started and turned to him with a quick smile, "What's that? I'm sorry, John. . . . Yes, of course I am listening . . ." she added hastily. But John, full of beer and *vodka*, was hurt. He edged his great bulk round to scan the crowd. "Huh. Competition, eh?" he grunted pugnaciously, and I saw a deep flush spread across his already inflamed countenance as he half rose from his chair with a growl of annoyance. Following John's eyes I caught a glimpse of Fritz Scheibel's plump figure making for the door; just before he reached it he cast at us, over his shoulder, a quick appraising glance, then disappeared.

John swung back to Nadia frowning. "Was it that fat little swine you were looking at?" he asked angrily.

"Yes, John, why do you ask?" she replied coolly.

"D'you know him, then?"

"Yes, that's Fritz Scheibel. He's a German. He comes here quite often," said Nadia with deliberate patience.

"H'm," grunted John sulkily. He took up his beer and drained it.

"C'mon, be your age, John, for-crying-out-loud!" broke in Jesse. "You don't own the kid, and this is a neutral country."

Just then, to my relief, the orchestra struck up a Viennese waltz, and Jesse whisked Nadia away before John could reply. When they returned, John was as jovial as before, and Nadia sat down beside him as though the whole incident had been forgotten.

At last there was no more music; it was time to go. A taxi was found without difficulty; John and I stood back to allow Jesse to see Nadia home. She dragged us all in, however.

"Come on all of you," she said. "You can drop me in Ayas Pasha and then go on down to the Park."

After three or four minutes only, the taxi stopped outside an apartment house. Nadia was out on the pavement in a flash; then, with a quick smile and a wave, she was gone. The taxi drove off. "Heigh-ho. No dice again," sighed Jesse, settling back again in the cushions.

"She's a quaint little witch though, ain't she?" he said again, still thinking of Nadia, as the taxi turned down the hill out of the square. "Always the same. . . . But, oh boy, can she dance?"

That, then, was the key to Jesse's interest in the girl. Jesse himself was a brilliant dancer, so, if Nadia's dancing happened to suit him, it was not surprising that he enjoyed going out with her. I wondered how far he had succumbed to her personal charm, or she to his for that matter.

"How long've you known her, Jesse?"

"About a week."

"Well, what's her background? D'you know that?"

"I'm not very well up on it," admitted Jesse. "It seems she's got mostly Russian blood in her, but I believe she's Turkish by birth. She never has any money; doesn't seem to want any; never even carries a bag, as a matter of fact—just a kid's purse in her raincoat pocket."

"D'you suppose she's working for anyone?" I asked, thinking of the Old Man's warning.

"I haven't an idea," replied Jesse cheerfully. "You know what these Security birds are. It's their business to suspect everybody. Some of them say she stinks; others tell you she's harmless."

"And what d'you think yourself?"

"Personally, I'd say she was harmless. I believe she just don't give a damn for any of us, Germans, Russians or British. Figures we're all rogues if not fools. Maybe she has something there, at that."

"I didn't like her knowing that little rat of a Hun," put in John, suddenly turning savage.

"Aw, hell! She knows everyone," expostulated Jesse. "And everyone knows her. Don't get sore just because you ain't her only little love-bird, pop."

"Sore, be damned!" roared John, flaring up in beery truculence. "I'm just not going to have any bloody Huns spying on me a few hours before . . ." he paused, spluttering, as he realised that he was being overheard by the driver; then ". . . and don't you youngsters damn well forget it, see!" he ended lamely.

"Roger—out," drawled Jesse, in imitation of an American radio operator acknowledging a signal. Old Hilton subsided into his corner with a few gruff asides and went on picking his teeth.

"But hasn't she ever asked you any awkward questions or anything?" I inquired, still puzzled and, I had to admit to myself, considerably intrigued about the girl.

Jesse laughed. "Yes, once. She asked me why my mother hadn't been more careful about speaking to strangers."

"That was a smart one," chuckled John, cheering up wonderfully. We had arrived at the Park by now, and old John was gallantly paying the taxi driver. "She certainly didn't seem to have much time for you to-night," he added, beaming with ponderous self-satisfaction. "Looks like you're slipping, Jesse."

"Guess so," replied Jesse good-humouredly, and tipped his hat on to the back of his head as he barged through the swing doors into the hotel vestibule. He threw an outrageous wink at the disapproving magnificence of the concierge behind his desk; then sauntered across to the lift, and we all piled in.

9

NEXT day John installed himself in old Mathews's office with charts and sailing directions. Jesse and I were there too for a time, but chiefly as onlookers, while John and the Old Man worked out the final details of the plan for *Kirilovka*.

The Old Man, having discussed everything with the Russians the day before, was ready to answer the questions which the methodical John had written down in a small note-book. The first one was:

"How do I stand with *Kirilovka*'s Master. Which of us has the ultimate authority?"

"I've got that as clear as I can," replied the Old Man a little doubtfully. "As far as C.-in-C.'s concerned, the Master of the ship is always ultimately responsible. But the Russians say they've instructed their Masters to obey your orders unconditionally so, from what one hears of Russian discipline, you shouldn't have any trouble. I'm afraid I can't give you a better answer than that."

"And the Turks know when I'm sailing, don't they, sir? They *have* been warned?"

"Good heavens, yes. They're in on the whole operation . . . it's entirely legal, of course, for a merchant ship to use the protection of neutral waters; and the Turks will be as helpful as strict neutrality will allow. The only trouble is that we know for a fact the Huns won't respect that neutrality; that's why we have to insist on all this secrecy."

"How do we know they won't, sir?"

"Well, as a matter of fact," answered old Mathews, grinning, "we've already violated Turkish neutrality once ourselves, so we haven't really got a leg to stand on." This was a surprising statement.

". . . Yes, our Fleet Air Arm boys made a slip, nearly a year ago, when they went and torpedoed a merchant ship full of Vichy French, while she was at anchor just outside Adalia Harbour. Incidentally a second torpedo hit the harbour mole itself and blew part of it away; so, although we've since been forgiven, the Germans know that any infringement of theirs would have to be winked at by the Turks."

John looked a bit puzzled by this admission.

"Don't worry," said the Old Man. "The Turks'll help us all right so long as we don't compromise them. But their ability to do so will depend a lot on your keeping to a strict time-table. You see, they can't issue a general warning at once to all their coastal batteries to watch for you and let you through; there are too many German agents about who'd get wind of it. They'll have to warn each section of their defences a few hours before you pass it."

John nodded and went on to the next question:

"What about communications, sir?"

"*Kirilovka* will be in direct touch with Alexandria by W/T as soon as she leaves the Dardanelles. C.-in-C. Med. will pass your signals back to us by ordinary cable. We ought to get them within six hours of your making them."

Again John looked doubtful; and the Old Man added cheerfully:

". . . the delay is acceptable really; because there isn't a damn thing we can do for you if you get into a mess; we've got no ships up here. Still, it would be nice to know what had happened to you; we might be able to get the Turks, as a special favour, to go along in due course and pick up the pieces."

Poor John was not receiving much encouragement; but he did not look in any way put out. He cared far less about the malice of the enemy now that he had been given a free hand to choose for himself the route which, from the navigational point of view, he considered the safest and the most seamanlike. He had only one more question to ask:

"What are the chances of meeting one of our own submarines, sir?"

"Oh, God; I nearly forgot that. I'll let you have the recognition signals this evening," answered old Mathews. And thereafter the pair of them settled down to work out exact courses and distances for use by the Turks in warning their gunners along the coast.

That evening Jesse, John and I had dinner with the Old Man, who was living in rooms on the top floor of the Embassy. John Hilton and he had spent a large part of the afternoon with the Russians in the Soviet Embassy. But now, with everything settled, they were both in excellent spirits and disposed to relax in good food and Turkish red wine.

"The Russian N.A.'s coming along himself to-night," said old Mathews, getting up from the table to fetch cigars. "He's going to drive us down soon after midnight."

"Decent of him," said John. "Will he come off to the ship as well?"

"Oh, yes. We'll give you a good send-off," boomed the Old Man. "Niko'll introduce you to the Master. He wants to make sure himself that everything's on the top line for this operation," he paused in the act of handing John the cigar box. "You two had better come along as well," he said to Jesse and me. "Put you in the picture for the tankers."

"Niko," by the way, was the name by which we found it easier to refer to Admiral Ivan Nikolaevski, the Russian Naval Attaché. He also was a big man, not much more than forty-five years old, moderately stout, always calm and courteous, and usually smiling.

The port had been round once and the loyal toast drunk. Now it came round again, the cigars with it. We drank a toast to John Hilton, and he had just finished replying to it in a long and rather halting oration, bulging with bawdy good humour, when Admiral Nikolaevski was shown in by the steward.

The Admiral seemed also to have dined well; so had Borionov, his secretary, who accompanied him. They both joined us heartily in several more toasts . . . *Kirilovka*, the Russian Black Sea Fleet and so on. By the time we reached the car it was after midnight and we were all highly pleased with ourselves and with each other.

Borionov was a very high-spirited young man, who spoke good English, but rather too much of it. He was: "delighted to meet us; so happy to work with us; longing to enjoy the night life with us; eager to take us to Russia; desolated at the idea of our having to leave so soon" all the way down the steep, winding, back streets of Pera to the Bosphorus. He and I were sitting in the front together and, though I was in the mood to enjoy this spate of good fellowship, I was more anxious just then to savour the excitement of this midnight drive, through tortuous cobbled alleys and down pitch-dark lanes, to the first of our rendezvous with the Russian ships.

The fog of urgent mystery melted for a while beneath bright arc lamps in the Turkish customs house, where we were forced to wait for half an hour along with a crowd of peasants, pigs and chickens; but it fell around us once again as soon as we shoved off from the quay and went puttering out in a small motor boat upon the black, swift waters of the Bosphorus—dark and freezing cold they were with snow-flood from the north.

We edged slowly upstream towards the Black Sea entrance. Lustre-paths, like fluttering white fingers, were seeking after us upon the water, but never reached us quite; and soon a mist came filtering down the fjord. We plugged along quietly, straining our eyes and ears. The boatman slowed his engine; our bow wave dropped to a ripple, and we waited for a while just stemming the current.

All at once a sharp word from the boatman sent the engine belting full astern, with a flurry of wash alongside. Next moment the gloom ahead grew darker quickly, bulging black towards us, curving over us. Then we grated hard against a high, black wall of iron plating. There was a thin cry from overhead, answered by Borionov in Russian, and down came a jumping-ladder with a clang, rattle and thump of wooden rungs against the iron hull. There were the muffled silhouettes of one of the mates and two sailors on deck as we came inboard over the rail, then a quick word or two of greeting and we all hurried aft and up a ladder on to the poop . . . Borionov leading. A door crashed open; bright light shone out from a cross alley-way and we trooped, blinking, into a large saloon.

At the head of the long table stood the captain (not a very old man), with his chief engineer and several others beside him. On the table was *vodka* and some plates of raw salt herring, onions, a great mound of caviar and some biscuits. The mate who had seen us aboard came clumping in behind us, slamming the door. In a round of greetings and introductions we sat down.

Jesse and I stuffed ourselves with good things while the Admiral was presenting John and the Old Man to the company. To our great amusement and admiration John produced a copy of Hugo's *Russian Grammar* (which he had bought in Alexandria) and began at once to attempt conversation in their own language with his future shipmates. This was a remarkable concession on John's part—even though his method of speaking to his new friends consisted only of pointing to certain phrases in his book such as:

> 11. I am learning Russian.
>   Have you been learning English?

Unfortunately, both John and the Russian with whom he was attempting to converse had those thick squat fingers common to most professional seamen, so that what the Russian read was:

> 9. Don't complain to me.
> 10. Warm yourself; don't laugh.

John turned the page and tried to point at "1. How do you do? At last we have met you!" But the Russian read "6. It is a pity that we have no Uncle," and excused himself politely but firmly to go off in search of *vodka* for his guests.

Attempts at further conversation were abandoned in favour of drinking. There was a largeness to the friendly joviality of these Russians—an eager, almost childlike pleasure in welcoming us. Others came in and joined the party shyly, but by no means awkwardly—more with an easy eagerness to meet friends and strangers and to welcome both. One could feel at once that the moment was purely communal and natural to them all. Ship's discipline was there, but stowed away neatly for further use when required, like Saturday's cold sausages when there are guests to Sunday dinner.

Soon it was time to say good-bye. *Kirilovka* had not stopped when we boarded her, and since then she had been forging slowly down the Bosphorus towards the Marmara; she was already nearly abreast of Scutari. The Old Man and the Admiral rose.

"Well, good-bye, Hilton," rumbled old Mathews. "You've got a fine ship. Look after her."

"See you don't catch cold," put in Jesse, "they tell me you're liable to get snow north of Khios—four-day blizzards, too."

"To hell with that for a game of soldiers!" returned John with decision. "If it comes on to snow, I'm standing out to sea to heave-to and turn in."

We shook hands again all round, then thumped old John soundly and hurried out.

For a moment, in the glare from the alleyway door, I caught a glimpse of one or two Turkish sentries standing armed about the deck. These followed us into the boat and we bore off. Smoothly, then, the bulk of *Kirilovka* fell away, grew shapeless, melted, and was gone upon a deep slow rhythm of her idling screws.

10

DURING the following day no news reached us either of *Kirilovka* or of the tankers that were expected from the Black Sea. This was in no way disconcerting. We all hoped that the tankers would not arrive until after John had returned by air from Syria with a full report on his voyage. As for *Kirilovka*'s silence, we knew that she was spending the day in the Sea of Marmara and would not even pass the Dardanelles until that evening at sunset. About the middle of the forenoon the Old Man went over to the Soviet Embassy, so Jesse and I strolled off to have a look at the sights of Istanbul.

It was a beautiful sunny day again, and quite warm, so we decided to buy sandwiches and eat them on one of the Bosphorus ferries. While we were buying our lunch, Jesse suddenly thought of taking Nadia with us. He rang her up. Yes, she would be delighted; she would be ready in ten minutes. So we got a taxi, fetched Nadia from her flat, and all drove down to Galata quay at the mouth of the Golden Horn.

A wide curving arm of water which cuts back from the northern side of the Bosphorus, like a curved dagger plunged into the heath-grown hills of Thrace—that is the famous Golden Horn, about which the city of Constantinople is built. Across the mouth of it stretches Galata bridge, the only bridge

connecting the old city of Constantinople on the southern side
with the newer districts of Galata and Pera to the north. All
along the outer side of Galata bridge lie the ferries—sometimes
half a dozen or more large steamers. They ply in many directions; up and down and across the Bosphorus, and out along
the shores of the Sea of Marmara.

This morning they all seemed crowded, but we managed to
squeeze aboard one of them. We did not ask where it was
bound. We were in the mood not to care. Nadia was wearing
her black beret and blue raincoat of two nights before. Her
stockings were not as yet coming down, but one felt that at
any moment they would. Wrinkled stockings, with Nadia,
were more a part of her attitude to life than due to any sloven-
liness of mind. She was very gay, laughing and jabbering
with the crowd around us, which, in turn, was a very friendly,
holiday sort of crowd for a winter's forenoon. There were
several family parties; fat parents in tight-fitting finery, with
four or five children, who shot off in all sorts of directions, were
shrilly recalled, threatened, smacked, kissed and released to
shoot off again to the ship's side or between the legs of people
standing.

Nadia was no longer on the defensive against Jesse; she was
frankly delighted at having been asked to come with us . . .
at being treated as a friend more than as a cabaret girl. I felt
convinced that Nadia really hated the life of the bars; and I
wondered again why she had chosen such an existence when her
whole manner and appearance proclaimed her rebellion against
it. Had Lottie some hold over her? From their attitude to each
other this seemed unlikely; but one never could tell with
women.

For nearly ten minutes the ferry remained alongside the
jetty, while people continued to surge aboard, filling up every
corner of the deck and saloons. Other ferries arrived and
departed around us with thunderous churnings of paddle-
wheels and bumpings and the creaking of six-inch hawsers.
There was a blaring pandemonium of Oriental music from their
many loud-speakers. To our unaccustomed ears this music
seemed to have no beginning nor end, nor refrain, nor even
much appeal. Our own ship's radio suddenly joined in, drown-
ing the others. Then, with a great stir and a heave and some

crashing thumps into neighbouring ferries, we barged away
from the jetty and clear of the Golden Horn.

We headed straight out to sea towards a little group of
mountainous islands about ten miles to the south-west.

"Why didn't John come along?" asked Nadia suddenly, in
the benignly scolding tone of a mother who has mislaid one of
her brood.

"Sorry, Ma," replied Jesse. "He got his pants wet yesterday
and had to stay in bed."

Nadia's stern and unquestioning reception of this remark
made us both laugh. We half expected her to turn and exchange
family worries with one of the plump mothers beside her. "He
is a very good, kind man. He must be more careful," she
asserted reprovingly.

"I'll tell him," said Jesse, and Nadia nodded.

As we got nearer the islands, we saw that there were four of
them, pine-covered like the shores of the Bosphorus, and each
with a small village on the southern side.

We disembarked at the second and climbed to its summit,
where Nadia was keen to collect fir cones for her stove at home.

We stayed on the island all day. During the afternoon we
collected as many fir cones as could be carried in Jesse's jersey.
Like children, we also threw a large number at each other, and
Nadia was even persuaded to climb a tree. This she did with
surprising grace and a singular neatness in managing her
clothes. Later we walked for a mile or two along the cliff top;
then scrambled down a steep pathway to the sea. It was so
sunny and warm that we almost decided to bathe; but thought
better of it when we put our hands into the icy water. Finally,
we had tea in a small café by the ferry landing.

The boat we caught back to Istanbul was a more magnificent
one, but it contained the same families, unstable as uranium
atoms, but gyrating more slowly now—similar music (a woman's
voice singing in a nasal minor) and, in addition, a small bar
from which we bought *raki* and cups of coffee. We sat wedged
together, happily sipping our drinks and chewing peanuts or
flicking some at the children who came clamouring round us.
We had been happy together all day; no bickering between
Jesse and Nadia, no awkward questions except the one casual

inquiry after John. We would have liked to change ferries and paddle on up the Bosphorus; but by the time we reached Galata it was already night—gay and brilliant in patches, with those pitch-dark cobbled side streets cutting the city into squares and slabs of brightness, like chunks of coco-nut icing.

John, I reflected, as we plodded up the hill, would just be leaving the Dardanelles. The night was cold and clear; only a few filmy streaks of mist lay among the trees by the water's edge. I wondered how John was faring. Then I glanced at Jesse and saw at once that he had no thoughts for anyone but Nadia. They looked very happy and unsophisticated as they strolled up the hill arm in arm. Nadia glanced up, now and then, with her quick little elf-like smile and a teasing remark. Jesse was bending over her; off his guard, not so dashing, very boyish in his delight in Nadia.

"Can't we go and dance somewhere?" I suggested presently, not because of any personal desire for gaiety just then; but I was worried by the spell of enchantment that seemed to have fallen upon both Nadia and Jesse. It was so unlike Jesse to allow himself to be deeply moved by any girl; I felt sure that the mood would pass and, in passing, bring unhappiness to one of them . . . probably to Nadia. This at least was what I told myself and, at the time, I honestly believed that my mind was free of any personal bias in the matter.

"Aw, shucks. We're always dancing," complained Jesse. "Why don't *you* go and dance?"

But Nadia, perhaps because she suddenly realised that she was in danger of losing complete control of her feelings, was all for going to some gay restaurant for dinner.

"Where d'you want to go then?" asked Jesse, a trifle sourly.

"Let's go to the Excelsior," replied Nadia with enthusiasm. "Lilli or Helene might be there." So off we went to what might, by its appearance, have been a very ordinary European night-club. We found there a young Greek girl called Lilli, who was immediately asked by Nadia to join our table.

I have said that Excelsior resembled an ordinary night-club. This is true: It did—save in one particular only, its bewitching orchestra. The leader, a great brutal-looking fellow called Koronin, who played the 'cello, drew from that instrument such music, such heavy flowing curves of pure melody as I have never heard again to this day. Even Lilli's trivial chatter could not dull the magic woven by the huge gorilla, hunched there oblivious, playing sadly to himself alone.

As soon as we were settled round our table, I asked Nadia to dance.

"Yes, come on," she cried eagerly, getting up, but neglecting the customary fiddling and smoothing of the clothes that most girls seem to find necessary.

On the dance floor Nadia became transformed; the hoyden in her vanished. As if of themselves her slender legs moved on; the music seemed to enter her veins, and she gave herself languorously to it; her winsome face lost its childlike mien as her body seemed to surge and wander with Koronin along a pathway of wild remembrance.

It was a very happy party. The music and a superb dinner made me feel as though we had suddenly been transported from the realms of war-time reality into an enchanted land, a land in which it was possible once more to believe in fairies, to forget about spies, to look upon Nadia and even upon the friendly Lilli without any cynical doubts. Jesse, after a few drinks, became again the frank, high-spirited boy that he was at heart; his speech and manner lost all trace of conceit . . . a conceit which had always been due more to doubt about his own personal brilliance than to a belief in it.

We both danced with Nadia once or twice; but later on I found it more thrilling almost to watch those two dancing together. Jesse had the lithe grace and perfect timing of the athlete. While he was dancing he forgot himself utterly; he seemed lost to all but the music and the nearness of Nadia, who lay in his arms like a petal . . . like part of him. Together and as one they followed the winding thread of Koronin's music. They became a floating descant to the 'cello's air. The other dancers left the floor to sit and watch them also. The talk died down, and into the tango which Koronin played there came a new magic, borne between him and these two young people.

The music stopped suddenly. Jesse and Nadia swayed on for a moment and then fell apart, a little bewildered, like people roughly awakened from sleep. Then a storm of applause burst round them and they were both blushing as they picked their way back to our table. Jesse, I thought, had never looked more genuinely moved; for a moment I was almost able to believe that my fears for Nadia had been groundless . . . that Jesse might at last have found a girl so different from his usual playmates that all his feelings for her were different too. . . .

I I

NEXT morning there was still no signal from John.
Old Mathews was a bit crusty. "You had too much to drink last night," he snapped at Jesse. "Montolieu, the security officer who's been attached to us for this job, has sent in a report saying that you were seen behaving indiscreetly in a restaurant in the town."

But it was not Jesse's behaviour of the evening before that was really worrying him; it was the enforced waiting for news of John. *Kirilovka*, of course, would not break W/T silence unless she were spotted, so the lack of news was in some ways encouraging. But it never really is, and so . . . "You should learn not to mix your drinks . . . or your women," the Old Man growled again. Jesse said nothing.

All that forenoon we sat about; Jesse and I fiddling with the charts and making scrappy conversation, while the Old Man tried to concentrate on letters, then Fleet orders, then a book and then letters again.

"Where had he got to by dawn?" the Old Man's voice was suddenly more alive. He looked up, at the same time sweeping away a piece of note-paper at which he had glared for some little while without writing anything.

For the twentieth time we measured off twelve mile spaces through the islands, counting out the hours "—seventeen hundred—eighteen hundred—nineteen hundred in the Mitylene Channel. . . . Twenty—twenty-one—twenty-two—twenty-three—midnight just entering Khios Strait (moon sets at one-twenty). One—two—three—four—five—six—just beginning to get light in the Samos narrows. Seven. . . ." I put the dividers down and looked across at old Mathews. He took up his pen again and scratched out the name after "Dear" at the top of his letter, then started doodling on the blotting-paper.

6

"Might have been misty," he observed absently, but without conviction, and then: "Let's see; what's the time? Eleven-thirty. An immediate signal to Alex would be deciphered in about an hour, I suppose. The Turkish cable office are pretty good over our stuff; they'd probably get a priority cable across here three hours after it was dispatched from Alex . . . allow an hour for all delays at both ends. Yes, we ought to have heard something by now if he'd had any trouble at Samos."

Old Mathews looked down at his blotter; then impatiently screwed up his sheet of note-paper and, starting on a fresh one, scribbled away furiously for half an hour or more, while Jesse and I measured and fiddled and laid off courses and measured again and again in silence.

After lunch, the Old Man went round to the Turkish Naval Headquarters, more for something to do than in the hope of hearing any news. Communications in Turkey are most un-reliable, and it had been very difficult for the Turks to impress their coastal troops with the importance of sending back prompt reports about *Kirilovka*. They had been forced to strike a most uncertain balance between the risk of warning the Germans as well as their own people, and the even greater risk of a Turkish battery commander opening fire upon a suspicious-looking ship without lights.

During the afternoon Jesse, rather foolishly, wandered into Montolieu's office, which was next door to ours. From the sound of violent battle which ensued, and from what Jesse told me on his return, it seemed that Montolieu had let him have a few home truths about his carelessness over Security. . . . It appeared that Montolieu had complained bitterly about the company we were keeping.

"Guess I'm wasting my time anyway," said Jesse presently. "Nadia just won't play ball."

I felt that this grudging admission was no more than a face-saver in case he should ultimately be forced to give the girl up; but I was pleased to hear it none the less so I let it go without comment.

At four-thirty the Old Man returned looking very cheerful indeed. *Kirilovka* had just been reported from Samsun Dagh; she had passed through Samos Straits at six-fifteen that morning without incident!

At once the tension gave way to excitement and eager speculation. Jesse and I grabbed a pair of dividers each and got hopelessly entangled in each other's measurements.

"Here, let me have a go," boomed old Mathews, bundling us both out of the way and sprawling across the table himself. "Seventeen—eighteen—nineteen. . . ." He began all over again. ". . . she must have been doing twelve knots all right. . . . Yes, now where would he have been at noon to-day . . . seven-fifteen—eight-fifteen. . . ." He measured on past Mandelyah Gulf and into Khios Strait, ". . . through there about 10 o'clock. We ought to have heard from him by now if he's had any trouble." He measured on: ". . . ten-fifteen. . . . There you are; he would have got round Cape Krio by noon all right."

The Old Man straightened up, beaming, and started pacing about with his hands in his pockets, all thoughts of letter-writing and Fleet orders forgotten. For more than an hour we went on arguing and measuring every likely variation of John's route. Had he passed outside or inside the Island of Symi? Did he hug the Turkish coast as far as Cape Marmarice, or did he cut straight across past the northern tip of Rhodes? Turkish ships might take either route.

On the way back to dinner at the Park, Jesse and I argued vehemently about John's possible decisions and his chances. The operations had begun, had come to life. All other concerns faded at once into the background of our minds; so we were in no mood for gaiety of any sort that evening, and after dinner we went straight to bed.

I woke up with a bang. The telephone between Jesse's bed and mine was ringing furiously.

"Hello, who's that?" said a gruff voice at the other end. I told him.

"Oh, this is Commander Mathews. You fellows sleep too much. Gadding about all night I suppose. Have you had breakfast?"

"Not yet, sir."

"Well, you'd better shake it up a bit. Things are beginning to move down here." He rang off.

"There must be a signal in from John. That was the Old

Man on the 'phone," I said to Jesse, who had got out of bed.

Jesse tottered towards the bathroom door. "So what," he mumbled grumpily; but he was awake now, and it didn't take us more than ten minutes to get shaved and dressed. It was not quite nine o'clock when we walked into the Old Man's office. He was poring over the charts, with the untidy remains of his breakfast on a chair beside him. As we entered he looked up; then took a couple of signals from the table and held them out.

"Read those," he said shortly, and turned back to the chart. Both signals were short and very clear.

IMMEDIATE. My position 7 miles 145 degrees Castelorizzo. Course 097. Speed 12 knots. Visibility good. Sea smooth. Wind South West, force 2-3. Two suspicious dark objects bearing 115 degrees distance 4 miles. Time of origin—0018/13 December.

and the second one:

IMMEDIATE. Am being attacked by gunfire from 2 E-boats. Altering course North. Time of origin—0048/13 December.

We crowded round the chart.

"This is where he was," said old Mathews, pointing, with one leg of the dividers, to a pencilled cross on the chart.

"How far's that from the Turkish shore, sir?"

"About six miles—half an hour at twelve knots."

"Any islands handy?" We bent over to look more closely. No; only the enemy-held group of Castelorizzo. There were a few deep inlets on the Turkish shore near by, but these would be very tricky to pick out from seaward at night. John wouldn't have attempted it.

"Why no torpedoes, I wonder?" said the Old Man, trying hard to sound casual. "Enemy must have been caught on the hop with only gunboats handy or no tubes loaded."

"Tough break for John," observed Jesse. "One big bang and you're in the water, when it's a fish . . . it's easier." He left to our imagination the picture of what it was like to be ruthlessly peppered with 20-mm. shells and machine-gun bullets. We imagined it in silence for a while. The old atmosphere of tenseness returned to the room. Idly we continued to measure and mark and pore over the chart, and finally stood gazing at it grimly, as though we expected a sudden burst of tracer to come streaming out of it near those awkward little lumps of rock and desert at Castelorizzo.

About ten o'clock there was a knock at the door and a messenger entered with two more signals. "Ah!" The Old

Man snatched at them, and his face took on a grimmer look as he read each signal through carefully. "All right," he growled at the messenger, who withdrew at once.

The first signal was timed nearly twenty minutes after the last of the previous two:

IMMEDIATE. Enemy closing and attacking incessantly. Starboard lifeboat on fire. Time of origin—0107/13 December. and:

IMMEDIATE. One enemy aircraft attacked with torpedoes. Missed ahead. Intend beaching East of Hypsili. Time of origin—0119/13 December.

Again we all studied the chart. John must have been less than two miles from the coast when he made the last signal.

"Seems to be a fairly clear bay just there," observed the Old Man. "If he does beach her, we might get her off all right later, provided the weather doesn't break."

"Is there a salvage company in Turkey?"

"Yes, we're lucky about that. The manager of it's an Englishman called Rees—good chap—I'll get on the 'phone to him." The Old Man picked up the 'phone and asked the Embassy switchboard to get him a number; then he replaced the receiver and waited.

"Poor fellow! Twenty-five minutes steady machine-gunning and no come-back," remarked the Old Man absently. "Wasn't dead when he made those signals, though," he added gruffly, a moment later.

"Still kicking," put in Jesse.

The 'phone rang, and the Old Man answered it: "That you, Rees? Ah, good morning! Can you spare a moment to come round to the Embassy; might have a job for you. . . . What's that? No, not on the 'phone. . . . Right. Good-bye," and he put down the receiver. We returned to our chart and to our discussion of John's chances. "I suppose I'd better tell the Russians something about all this," said the Old Man suddenly. And once more he picked up the telephone receiver.

Within half an hour both Captain Rees and Admiral Nikolaevski were in the office, whereafter Jesse and I took no further part in the discussion. "Yes, if we're lucky," I heard Rees say. "There'll be no current to speak of in there and fairly good holding ground." The Admiral looked glum and said very little. One wondered how heavily the responsibility for *Kirilovka*'s safety was placed upon his shoulders by his own government.

The discussion about possible salvage had been progressing less than ten minutes when there was again a knock on the door and another signal was brought in. When he had read it the Old Man passed it on to Admiral Nikolaevski.

"Looks as if we may not need your assistance after all, Rees," he said, still in an anxious voice, but with what looked like a gleam of hope in his eyes. Captain Rees took the signal from the Admiral, read it and passed it on to me. It had been dispatched nearly half an hour after the previous one:

IMPORTANT. Enemy have withdrawn. Ammunition possibly expended. My damage one lifeboat jettisoned on fire. Some damage to bridge structure from heavy machine-gun fire. No casualties. My position 082 degrees 11 miles from Castelorizzo. Course 083 degrees. Speed 12 knots. Time of origin—0142/13 December.

"Wonder whether they'll leave him alone now or not?" said old Mathews, in a definitely hopeful tone. But we could not believe that they would. At best this was no more than a respite; a chance for a hurried survey of the damage, a chance to get the crew busy and the burning lifeboat over the side, to check the course; then back to the front of the bridge to sweep the horizon, listening—listening with every nerve astrain for the first, faint, distant murmur of aircraft or E-boats' engines. "They are bound to send more," John must have been thinking. "How many miles to Cyprus? More than two hundred. No hope of air cover before morning!" It might be all over by now, we reflected. One could imagine an aircraft gliding in unheard—the whistle and swish of a stick of bombs and the tearing roar of destruction; no time to make a signal or even to shout a warning.

The Old Man started pacing up and down again. After a while Captain Rees got up, with a murmured excuse, and left. The rest of us continued to sit in silence, waiting for a further signal. There was a tenseness in the room almost equal to the strain poor old John and his chaps must have been feeling . . . out there in the darkness of the night before.

"The moon would not have risen till some time after that last signal was made," remarked the Old Man, stopping suddenly half-way to the window and turning to Jesse with an inquiring look. Jesse consulted the almanac. "About three hours' later," he confirmed. "At o—four—o—seven."

"If they sent a second wave, it might have failed to find him." The Old Man's face brightened slowly as he made the suggestion.

Yes. If only he had decided at last to edge close in under the Turkish coast; against the towering blackness of Cape Kheldoniah he might have been missed. We doubted whether even an aircraft and E-boats could so shake old John's obstinate pride in his seamanlike prudence; but at least the idea was feasible; we had found a possible way out for John, and after a while our spirits began to rise. When Admiral Nikolaevski left, soon after noon, there was a distinct look of relief upon his face.

Jesse and I stayed at the Embassy for lunch, and sat on in the Old Man's office afterwards. When no further signals had arrived by tea-time we all began to feel fairly optimistic about John's chances.

"He must have been spotted from Rhodes yesterday afternoon," said the Old Man. "Just measure up and see where he was."

"Somewhere just north of Rhodes town at four o'clock," I told him, when I had measured it off on the chart. "He would have passed less than ten miles off, if he was following the normal Turkish shipping route."

"That's it then. They must have spotted that *Kirilovka* wasn't a Turk; they could probably even see she was an ice-breaker. So they sent a small party to intercept her at Castelorizzo."

"Too easy altogether," drawled Jesse. "They'd figure that a big ship'd never attempt to pass between Castelorizzo and the Turkish coast in the dark."

"Yes, so they waited for Hilton to leave territorial waters before attacking him."

But by six o'clock, since no further disturbing news had come, our hopes had grown into a firm conviction that *Kirilovka* must somehow have got through. For an hour or two more we discussed every possibility at great length. We felt so sure of John's safety, that we even smiled at the idea of the poor old boy ducking and dodging about the bridge and trying desperately to give instructions from his Hugo's *Russian Grammar*.

12

IN the morning, sure enough, there came a final signal from John announcing his arrival at Famagusta in Cyprus. To celebrate this there was an exceedingly gay lunch-party at the

Nikolaevskis' private residence on the Bosphorus. As far as I can remember we were invited at twelve-forty-five, sat down to lunch at about three-fifteen and finally left the table with some difficulty at five-thirty. But, as Niko and the enchanting Mrs. Niko told us with a deprecatory smile, this was only an impromptu celebration. As soon as John returned, they assured us, we would have a real party!

For the next few days Jesse and I had nothing to do but enjoy ourselves. This consisted of my accompanying Jesse and Nadia on various expeditions—to the bazaars and mosques of the old city; on more ferry trips up and down the Bosphorus; to queer meals and entertainments in many outlandish "joints." And every outing ended at Lottie's about six-thirty in the evening.

They seemed to be falling in love, these two; but how could one tell? Little Nadia, brought up in a city of exiles and opportunists from every part of the world, must have become fairly shrewd, and even fastidious, to have retained so much individuality; it seemed unlikely that she would fall easily to Jesse's rather obvious charm. And Jesse was hard-boiled, too. I had seen him in similar situations before—all out for love while it lasted, but glad of a change when it came.

After a day or two the aimlessness of our existence began to pall. There was too much gipsy music—you listened to it in every bar and in every restaurant and night-club; there was too much *vodka* about as well and nothing else to do but drink it. One evening we sat for some time over a single round of drinks. (Nadia refused hers and would not let Jesse buy a second round.) They quarrelled mildly over this, then:

"Let's get out o' here," exploded Jesse. "This music kind of pours down your neck like soup." And off they went, leaving me to stroll back to the Park by myself, quite glad of the chance of an early night.

"You're late again," observed the Old Man sternly. "What on earth are you two getting up to every night. I can never get hold of you at the Park. . . . Where's Matheson? Still in bed I suppose. . . ."

Just then a messenger came in with some papers and I was

relieved at being spared the necessity of thinking up an answer to the Old Man's last question . . . relieved because I had not seen Jesse since the night before.

For ten minutes or so the Old Man was busy signing letters and reports. While he was still engaged upon this task, Jesse came quietly into the office. He looked a little bewildered . . . less sure of himself. This may only have been because he had not shaved; none the less I felt instinctively that things had by no means gone according to plan with Nadia . . . that he might have learnt something new about life. I decided, however, not to ask any questions for fear of shaming him into some boastful invention.

"Get yourself a new razor, Matheson," said the Old Man, looking up suddenly. That was his only comment upon Jesse's unobtrusive return to the fold. Shortly afterwards the messenger left us, and the Old Man got up from his desk.

"Well, now, there are two interesting bits of news in to-day's signals," he said, handing me a small sheaf of them. "The first is that Hilton's due back at Haydar Pasha station at eighteen hundred this evening. . . . I want you two to meet him."

This remark cleared the atmosphere completely. As soon as John returned we would be able to get on with the active planning of our next operation, and the time would hang less heavily for all of us.

"The second bit of news is that the Americans have come up about a small tanker they want us to take down along with the Russians."

So that was why the Old Man had been spending so much time in the United States Embassy during the last few days. We had been wondering what was afoot, but he had refused to tell us anything before now.

"This tanker's registered under the Panamanian flag," he went on, "and owned by a chap who was born a Russian, naturalised something else and lives here. She's been trading around these coasts for some years; but since Panama declared war on Germany, a few days ago, they've made an order requisitioning all their ships, so the Yanks, who are acting for them, are trying to get hold of this one."

"Sounds a mess, sir," remarked Jesse, "and liable to take quite a time to sort out."

"Yes," agreed old Mathews. "The owner's got the Huns backing him for all they're worth, and the Turks aren't at all keen to lose a tanker from this coast . . . the ship's name's *Olinda*, by the way, and she isn't requisitioned yet; but the Yanks are working on the Turkish Government in Ankara . . . we'll probably hear by this evening whether they've had any luck or not."

At six o'clock Jesse and I went down to the station to meet John. The train arrived about twenty minutes later and out

of it climbed John, looking red and gloomy as of old. There was a different wagon-lit attendant, and I was amused to see John give him a magnificent tip and hurry towards us, showing considerable embarrassment.

We both greeted him effusively.

"John!" cried Jesse in ringing tones. "We women are proud of you," and, taking John's arm, he began to shove him through the crowd towards the ferry landing.

We asked him about the train journey back.

"Oh! Not too bad. No trouble from the wagon-lit bloke this time, anyway," he answered grimly. "Brought all my meals in to me."

"What! Have you been on your back ever since you left Tripoli then?"

"No. On my front."

We must have looked puzzled.

"Splinters," explained John gloomily. We showed concern. "Wood splinters," he added, ". . . in my bottom."

"How did it happen?" asked Jesse with an altogether indecent show of eagerness.

"Sitting against *Kirilovka*'s engine-room telegraph, trying to get a bit of cover during the shooting . . . bloody three-o-three ripped through the deck under me. . . . Ooh!" John groaned as he sat down too suddenly upon one of the hard wooden benches in the ferry. He turned quickly to take his weight off his behind. We couldn't help laughing at him. Just the sort of thing that would happen to poor old John, to come through an action like that almost unscathed . . . except for splinters in his bottom.

Admiral Nikolaevski and the Old Man were waiting for us at the Embassy. John (who refused a chair) embarked upon his story at once.

There was little doubt, from what he said, that he had reached Kos without his presence on the coast being suspected by the enemy. He had seen no patrols in the Mitylene Channel, nor at Khios. At Samos there had been no sign of life on the enemy shore, and he had steamed from there direct to Kos Strait, where he had passed a couple of fishing-boats in the middle of the channel.

Early in the afternoon, when *Kirilovka* was between Cape Krio and the Island of Symi, a Junkers 52 had passed over him fairly low; but it flew straight on and landed at one of the airfields on the Island of Rhodes. He considered that it was probably a troop carrier on a routine flight, whose pilot would most likely not have noticed anything unusual about *Kirilovka* from above. He had stood on, passing south of Symi. On the Island of Seskli, at the southern end of Symi, he had noticed what looked like an enemy observation post; a soldier had come out of a little camouflaged hut to look at *Kirilovka* through binoculars. Feeling that he had probably been reported from Seskli, John then steered straight from Symi past the northern end of Rhodes to Cape Suvelah. Although this involved passing less than ten miles off Rhodes town, he had felt that such an action would be likely to disarm any possible suspicion and would in any case allow him to make the most of *Kirilovka*'s speed.

His description of events south of Castelorizzo was laconic.

"Got just about fed up with it after nearly half an hour," he said. "Crawling about the bridge on all fours, trying to keep me head down. Had to poke it up now and then to check the ship's course. . . . What made it so bloody tiring was having damn-all to shoot back with."

"What guns did *they* have?" asked the Admiral.

"Twenty-millimetre and machine-guns," said John. "They must have been using some armour-piercing as well as H.E., judging by the damn great holes in the plates and funnel."

"Any casualties?"

"No. It was amazing. The Mate got a bullet slap on his wrist-watch. Didn't seem to care a damn, except about having his watch smashed. They're the most extraordinary people, your Russian sailors, sir. . . . Seemed to think it was all a joke." Niko smiled and bowed slightly.

"I'm glad you didn't have to beach her," said old Mathews. "It would have taken a long time to get a salvage vessel down there. The weather might have broken before that."

"Yes. I was going slap in for the beach. I don't suppose I was more than half a mile off when they suddenly stopped firing and turned away. They may have been worried about international law or they may just have run out of ammo."

"It is more probable that they lacked ammunition," said the Admiral, in rather precise English. "They would not be much concerned about law, even if they did not know they had the right to continue the chase."

As old John went on talking, in his slow despondent voice, there grew before us, in spite of his reticence, a vivid picture of those two anxious days and particularly of the final action. We imagined the still, flat, sea with the black mountains of Turkey spreading across the northern horizon and *Kirilovka* pounding steadily into the darkness to eastward. We felt the tingle of sudden alarm at the first sight of those two black shapes, which should not have been there; imagined the quick turmoil in John's mind. . . . Then the growing red chain of tracer and a hailing fury of explosions all over the bridge. We could almost see the ship turning slowly, so very slowly away . . . a second hail of shells and machine-gun bullets . . . splinters

flying in all directions, whirring and hissing about their heads
. . . the lifeboat on fire.

"Surprising they didn't come back and finish you off,"
commented the Old Man. "Did you get in under the coast
there, off Cape Kheledoniah?"

But poor, solid old John seemed more concerned just then
about the splinters in his bottom. "No, sir. Didn't seem worth
it," he said shortly, and the discussion then turned to plans
for the next voyage . . . the voyage of *Olinda*.

Old Mathews had spent most of the afternoon at the American Embassy. Apparently there had been "vigorous diplomatic
exchanges" with Ankara over the small Panamanian tanker.
The difficulty had been to persuade the Turks that the Americans were in a position *legally* to requisition *Olinda*. This had
at last been accomplished, but the formalities had now to be
completed through the Turkish Admiralty Court in Istanbul.

Old Mathews was still snorting with impatience over the
business. The struggle to obtain possession of *Olinda* had been
going on for many weeks before our arrival in Turkey. It had
involved a maze of plots and counter-plots, offers of fantastic
prices for purchase of the ship and counter-offers to the owner
from the Germans. The Old Man had only just been brought
into the field, but he was already fed up with "all this hanky-
panky."

"Time we showed 'em we mean business," he boomed.
"Now, come on. Whose turn is it for the next passage?"

It was mine.

"Right now, let's see if we can't improve on Hilton's method.
The Huns aren't likely to be caught on the hop like that
again."

"If I make the passage in short stages, by night only, it ought
to be possible to slip down without being spotted at all," I
said. "That is, unless the Germans make a thorough air-search
of the coast to see where we're lying up by day."

I pointed out that the coast was steep-to and clear of shoals
for most of its length. One could almost have made the whole
passage with one foot on the beach.

"Yes, and the other in the grave," jeered Jesse.

"Look at some of these creeks and places," I went on, ignoring

Jesse's remark. "You could hide away up there in daylight, and no one'd ever know you'd been there."

"Tie up to a blade of grass, I suppose," put in John, with friendly sarcasm.

Admiral Nikolaevski looked interested in my idea, but he kept aloof from the argument, and it was the Old Man who interrupted with:

"They'll certainly use aircraft to search for you. After all the ill-feeling there's been over *Olinda*'s requisitioning, and all the publicity, you can be sure they'll make every effort to intercept her. No . . ." He paused to give added effect to a suggestion which was really a decision. "What I think is that it ought to be possible to *disguise* a small ship like *Olinda*."

John looked dubious. "What's her tonnage then?" he asked.

"I'm not sure, but less than the Russian anyway."

"What speed will she do, sir?" I also felt a bit doubtful.

"About eight knots, I expect. She'll probably have a reduced crew on board. Men are difficult to find these days. That's another point in favour of doing your short stages *in daylight*."

Here was certainly a very different problem to the one presented by *Kirilovka*. The Old Man was possibly right about our being able to disguise the ship for a daylight passage; on the other hand, she would be even easier, if she were small enough, to smuggle down unseen by night among the rocks and islands along the coast. Bad weather, a little snow perhaps, and moonless nights would all help. Keeping a look-out into snow or rain is a wearisome, uncomfortable business, and I could not imagine the enemy, especially the Italians farther south, being particularly keen on it . . . not unless they knew exactly when to expect us. But the Old Man was adamant.

"*Vana* got away with a daylight passage, but *Kirilovka* was attacked; so we'll try another one by day this time. Must ring the changes, you know. . . . All you'll have to look out for is not to anchor at night in a place where there might be enemy patrols."

"What sort of crew has *Olinda*?" I asked.

"At the moment only the Master, the Mate, two engineers and a Bosun. All Russians. . . ." The Old Man noticed a slight bridling on the part of Admiral Nikolaevski, and added hastily:

"that is, Russians who have been living in Rumania on what they call a Nansen passport . . . not proper Soviet subjects."

But the Admiral still looked embarrassed. He presumably held no brief for renegade Russians, who had escaped or been driven into Rumania many years before.

"It appears that this discussion no longer truly concerns me," he observed politely; then, turning to John: "My very hearty congratulations and thanks, Commander Hilton, for your services to the U.S.S.R."

John smiled and blushed; then the Admiral included us all in an invitation: "My wife and I would be most honoured if you would all dine with us next Wednesday evening, to celebrate this first success."

We murmured a grateful acceptance and the Old Man escorted the Admiral out.

"Will that mean full evening dress?" asked John anxiously, as soon as the door was closed.

The Old Man returned.

"Now what were we talking about? Oh, yes; *Olinda*'s crew; she needs at least a dozen more. We may manage to pick up one or two locally, and I'll make a signal to Sea Transport, Egypt, for the rest . . . they might even be able to raise a few Britishers for you."

"How about the radio operator? It'd be worth having an Englishman for that."

"*Olinda* has no W/T," announced the Old Man with finality.

No W/T! Then, as soon as we were clear of the Dardanelles, I would be entirely on my own . . . free to choose any method of smuggling *Olinda* down, which the weather or the presence of enemy patrols might suggest. I thought again of the inshore route; then my mind went back to schooner days in the South Seas and elsewhere . . . sneaking in through the reefs at Mangareva; midnight struggles among the rocks and shoals of the Galapagos Islands; forcing the pass at Hao against a strong race; feeling our way round the Nova Scotian banks in clinging fog. Here was something I knew how to do, and would far rather have attempted than to risk being caught out, like a sitting duck, in broad daylight . . . in a ship which had become so well known to the enemy.

Meanwhile, however, the Old Man was in charge of the planning side of the operation, so I locked away my own ideas in the back of my mind, where they remained throughout the rest of the meeting . . . laughing and wrangling among themselves, like naughty children imprisoned in the back of the car, while mother goes in to return a call from the vicar's wife.

III

GAY STRATEGIES

13

ALL through Christmas and the New Year we continued to wait. It was a Christmas such as I have seldom known; more parties, more all-night dancing, more drink and more confusion than ever before. And, from those days, only a few bright scenes, as well as one or two moments of jangling discord, stand out like flowers upon a hedgerow . . . like tin cans winking from the still depths of memory's green harbour. But there was also a plot, a general trend that linked them all together, and sent us adventuring on at last . . . down to the Dardanelles and out upon the dark waters to the South.

.   .   .   .   .

All through these weeks we were preoccupied with *Olinda*. . . . She must be disguised. We must find a Turkish ship for her to impersonate. There were photographs in the Naval Intelligence files. We studied them.

"What about this one, *Orak*? . . . bridge and machinery aft like *Olinda's* . . . about the same size . . . Turkish general cargo vessel."

"The owners are strong anti-Nazis." From "Security" Montolieu.

"That might be useful later," observed the Old Man, thoughtfully. "Where is she?"

"Iskenderun . . . on the south coast; but she usually trades between Smyrna and Istanbul."

"That's fine. Can we get sime more photographs of her?"

.   .   .   .   .

Olinda is lying in the Bosphorus. Jesse and I try to catch a glimpse of her from our window; but she is hidden from us by trees.

"Montolieu's got a flat down by the shore there."

"Aw, that long streak of misery gets on my nerves . . . always snooping. Say listen: last night in the Casino, there he was slinking round like he always does. Then he starts staring at one of those big mirrors—like he was in a trance or something.

... I go up to him and ask what's eatin' him. There's someone there I haven't seen before, he says ... wonder who it is ... looks like a Hun, he says. Yes, it was himself he was looking at. Can you beat it ... the man's nuts. ..."

"Still, we'd better go down to his flat and have a look at *Olinda* through glasses. ..."

.   .   .   .   .

John and Jesse are friends these days. ... All John's surliness has vanished; the imminence of further operations has put him in the best of spirits. He shares the Old Man's flat at the Embassy. He is very much the Second-in-Command and the accepted authority on blockade running in Russian merchant ships. He is looking forward to showing the youngsters how it should be done.

"And don't you take any notice of what you're told—about creeping down through those straits in bad visibility," he pronounces importantly. "I've seen 'em."

"No sense in wasting thick weather if we get any."

"You keep your ships off the rocks. That's your job." John is emphatic.

"They have lovely stewardesses on board the Russian tankers." From Jesse.

"We'll have our hands full without any of that nonsense," retorts John, but grins a trifle sheepishly. ...

.   .   .   .   .

Christmas Day. This day had its ups and downs for most people.

The B.B.C. announced the recapture of Benghazi by the British and the rout of the German armies all along the eastern front; then later, the fall of Wake Island and Hong Kong. The Free French, however, had pounced with loud "huzzahs" upon the tiny islands of St. Pierre and Miquelon, away over on the very coast of Newfoundland. And Haiti, God bless her, had cocked an official snook across four thousand miles of ocean, by declaring war upon Hungary, Rumania and Bulgaria all at once.

For the world at large then, Christmas day was a day of light and shade; but for Special Party, Force "W," waiting for

the Turks to make up their minds, it was a day of boredom . . .
of arrested motion. . . .

.   .   .   .   .

Jesse and I strolled one evening with Nadia down those
pitchy side streets, till we came out by the water's edge. There
was a new moon in the sky, and the weather was clear with a
blue smell of frost upon the air. We strolled along for a mile,
before the houses began to thin. Then we passed through a
final village to find ourselves out on the bare heath with the
Golden Horn winding bright beside us and round the nearest
hill.

I felt worried as we walked along; but not entirely on the
grounds of security. The Old Man had made no further sug-
gestions about whom we should choose or not choose as our
friends. In any case I was the last person who had any right
to question Jesse's pleasure in Nadia's company. . . . I would
have chosen no other companion myself. Nevertheless I felt
worried and also a little depressed. I suppose, to be honest, I
still felt that Jesse did not really appreciate Nadia; that she
must be just another "dame" to him.

We climbed the shoulder of the next hill. Beyond it the
water ended in a wide, silvery pan and on its nearer shore
there stood a mosque, all alone. It was built of white stone
that shone in the moonlight. The dome was of blue-grey slate,
and there were minarets at each corner—silver lances tipped
with steel. The Mosque stood all alone. Jesse and Nadia
wandered towards it, but I remained upon the hill. There
was no profit in following them farther . . . they were completely
absorbed in each other, so that conversation between us had
ceased.

Alone, after a while, I strolled away.

.   .   .   .   .

John is doubtful. . . . "It'd take a couple of months in a ship-
yard to make *Olinda* look like *Orak*."

Olinda is a tanker with the usual "flying bridge," a heavily
built and supported gangway, running across the tank tops, all
the way from the poop to the forecastle head.

But, to old Mathews, the larger and more cumbersome the

obstacle, the greater the satisfaction in battering it down. . . .
The louder and more cheering the bang when it finally tumbles.

"Come, come Hilton. All we've got to do is to hack away
that flying bridge . . . after that it's just a matter of painting."

John still looks doubtful.

Later the same day. . . .

"What about the masts?" *Olinda*'s got one and *Orak* two . . .
and cargo derricks as well."

"We'll get some rough spars and give *Olinda* a false mast and
derricks."

"*Olinda* hasn't got any cargo hatches like *Orak*. . . . She has
a flat tank top covering her whole foredeck, with small "lids"
in it . . . an aircraft would notice that."

"We'll build up two squares of packing-cases on her tank
tops . . . then we can lash tarpaulins over them. That'll look
like hatches all right."

"What about the funnel. . . . *Olinda*'s is longer?"

"God dammit. We'll soon lop a chunk off the top of the
bloody funnel."

We imagine the Old Man charging aboard *Olinda* and laying
about him with an axe. John is still dubious, but he sees what
the Old Man means. . . .

.   .   .   .   .

Late one night. . . .

It came as a surprise to me that this could be Goebbels
speaking. . . . That misshapen little wretch was usually seen,
in photographs, with his huge mouth agape; one only imagined
him ranting—screaming invective. Yet the voice I now heard
was melodious, calm and deeply touching. He spoke of the

Fatherland, looking upon it now on Christmas Eve: *"wie schoen es ist, wie weiss . . . wie wunder-weiss und schoen"*; and there flowed through those simple words such music and such emotion as must have set every German in the world aflame with passionate patriotism.

I tried to shake off the spell of that voice. "Propaganda," I told myself cynically, as I got into the lift. "Propaganda. . . . Yes, but whose? Which of us was right about Goebbels . . . we or the Germans?"

When I came down again, there was dance music on the radio from Hamburg.

.   .   .   .   .

"What we want is an oxy-acetylene burning plant . . . must have a burning plant," says the Old Man with relish. "Montolieu . . . where can we get a burning plant?"

Montolieu is uncertain.

"Must have a burning plant," insists the Old Man, ". . . burn through all the stanchions under the flying bridge . . . wait for a decent roll of the ship . . . then 'splash' . . . finish . . . how's that?"

John is cautiously approving.

I go one day to a small ironmonger's shop in a side street of Pera, and there I buy a burning plant for cash (nearly one hundred pounds sterling). I also buy three cylinders of oxygen.

Outside is one of Montolieu's Greeks, looking rather self-conscious, because he is supposed to be disguised as a porter. He has a handcart with him. Together we trundle the burning plant away.

There follows an exciting afternoon. An R.E. sergeant, on the Military Attaché's staff, is instructing me in how to use a burning plant. The Old Man wants to learn, too. He is inclined to make wide, triumphant gestures. These are dangerous, because he is still holding the burner.

.   .   .   .   .

Nadia walked in alone. . . . She saw us in our corner and waved. For a moment she hesitated by the bar, then came towards us smiling.

John immediately looked flustered, half got up to welcome her, glanced hastily round, and then sat down again. "I don't think we ought to have Nadia over here," he mumbled. "Not after what Montolieu's been saying."

"Aw, nuts," said Jesse.

"Well, anyway, if she asks any awkward questions," growled old John, "remember that our cover is a Boom Defence job down south. They understand about that in Turkey, because there's a British Naval Boom Defence party helping them with their own booms in the Bosphorus and Dardanelles."

Nadia came up to us. "Hello, stranger," she greeted John gaily, obviously pleased to see him again. "Where have you been for so long?"

"Booming." It was Jesse who answered her. John scowled at him furiously; then turned to smile at Nadia as he rose heavily to offer her his seat.

"I had to go back to Syria on some duties connected with one of our Boom Defence parties," he declared, but much too laboriously, as though Nadia had been a brother technician.

"Yes, booming," said Jesse. "John is always booming at someone.

Nadia looked perplexed, then giggled; old John smiled weakly. . . .

. . . . .

After Christmas . . . very, very secret agents bought an assortment of rough spars for use in constructing false masts and derricks for *Olinda*.

One dark, wet night Jesse and I got into a motor boat belonging to the Boom Defence trawlers. Then we towed all the timber out of the Golden Horn and round into the Bosphorus.

In the blackness and driving sleet we could see little of *Olinda* or her crew. The end of a line was hurled down to us, and we made it fast to the floating spars; then shoved off again.

The timber was secured on *Olinda*'s deck, ready for use later. We saw, from Montolieu's flat next morning, that it had been well concealed between her bulwarks and the tank tops. . . .

. . . . .

And one evening . . .

The road from Therapia to Pera clung for several miles to the shores of the Bosphorus, which lay smooth and glittering in the light of a chubby new moon. As we drove along, I tried to judge the distance to the other side of the fjord, and noticed how difficult it was to make out the ships at anchor against the darkly wooded hills. Then the road dived into a tunnel of trees and began to climb through a forest; away from the water's edge and up on to the open hills beyond.

Nadia was excited; it was not often that she was treated like a little queen by three men, two of whom, at least, preferred quite obviously to share her company than to rake around for partners of their own. Her mind had a darting, flame-like quality; it flickered out occasionally through the cracks in a covering of native caution, and licked eagerly, avidly at life. It was like a spring crocus peeping through a crust of late snow.

Ahead of us now the road, cut by hills and hollows, lay in silvery moonlit strips between the valleys. Nadia was determined to be thrilled with everything; with the moonlight drive; with being the only girl among three men; and especially with Jesse, who already had one of her hands in his and was stroking it assiduously, behind a smoke screen of ceaseless banter, most of which was directed at John's solid back, bulging over the edge of the seat in front. . . .

·　　·　　·　　·　　·

In the office. . . .

"Why d'you have to go on running after Nadia if she won't 'play ball' as you call it?"

"She likes me to go on pitching to her, I guess. . . . Wouldn't be fair not to . . . then she'd have to start in pitching, wouldn't she?"

"All you Yanks think a bloody sight too much of your chances with women," grumbles John.

"Oh, yeah?" Jesse's voice is dangerously quiet. "And where d'you get this 'Yanks' stuff from anyway? I'm Canadian and proud of it."

"Well, I'm damned if Canada has any cause to be proud of *you!*" retorts John.

"No? . . . Say, it's time somebody showed you just where

you head in." Jesse takes a step forward and his jaw sticks out aggressively.

"And who's going to do it?" asks John ominously.

"Guess, I will."

"You, and who else?"

At any moment they may come to blows. But it is Jesse who recovers his sense of humour in time to prevent serious trouble.

"O.K. O.K.," he says easily, "seems I'd better scram outa here before someone says something unfriendly to me."

John, in a fury, tries to get in the last blow: "As second-in-command here, I order you to keep clear of all foreigners, including the women, from now on. . . ."

But Jesse has left the room.

Later in the forenoon, Jesse stood poring over the morning paper, which was spread upon the table before him. In one hand he held a cup and saucer. He pointed, with the uneaten portion of a bun, at a second cup on the table beside him.

"Your tea," he mumbled, with his mouth full. I took the cup and strolled across to the window. I felt that things were beginning to get out of hand; that an effort must be made to restore the calm.

"John worries too much," I remarked casually. "Makes him nervy these days."

"Yea. He's had it," agreed Jesse without looking up.

"He's a good old egg, though. No sense in arguing with him."

.   .   .   .   .

At Montolieu's flat. . . .

"No good disguising *Olinda* here in the Bosphorus of course. We've got to think of a quiet spot to hide her in for a few days before she leaves. . . ."

"The Sea of Marmara and the whole of Thrace is a Turkish Military Zone. There wouldn't be enemy agents there."

"We'll anchor her in some deserted part of the Marmara for a day or two, then . . ."

"Won't that give the Germans time to get ready to intercept her?"

"There's no reason why they should expect her to go down

at all. They think we only want to keep her out of German hands. . . . We're putting out a story that we're going to sell her to the Turks, as soon as we get hold of her."

Later the same day. . . .
"Wouldn't the Turks really buy *Olinda?*"
"No, they'd rather not; by international law she'd still be an enemy ship, and they don't want to risk having a row with the Germans, who would still be entitled to attack her . . . but they don't mind helping us by allowing the negotiations to start; so as to give us time to smuggle *Olinda* away while they're still in progress. . . ."
"Wouldn't it be easier just to leave her here?"
"Risky these days. . . . The Huns might walk into Turkey any time now. Besides, she's needed down south."

.   .   .   .   .

On New Year's Eve. . . .
There were no tables vacant, so Jesse went on across the dance floor to a smaller room in which a long bar occupied the whole of one wall. Round the other three walls ran a luxuriously padded settee, and the walls themselves consisted of a succession of large plate-glass mirrors. The bar was also crowded, but we managed to find room in an angle of the settee.
Early on New Year's morning John went home and later on Nadia came in and joined us. Then Jesse got up to fetch a round of drinks from the bar.
On his way back Jesse winked, then nodded sideways to a part of the bar which was hidden from me by a pillar. I leaned forward until I could see round the obstruction. There, upon a high stool, sat Fritz Scheibel. I thought I recognised the man beside him too.
A bar stool near Fritz became vacant. "Come on," said Jesse. "Let's get our feet in the bucket," and we sauntered across to the bar. A Greek sitting on the near side of Fritz slid from his stool. Nadia took it and Jesse sat down next to her. I stood behind.
Fritz stopped talking to the other German and glanced round as Nadia wriggled herself on to her stool.
"Good evening," he said pleasantly. That quick little smile

fluttered round his mouth for a moment when he turned a little farther and saw me standing there.

"Good evening, Fritz," replied Nadia calmly. "You have been away."

"Not for long."

Jesse was wise-cracking with the barman about some *cognacs*. When he turned back he grinned maliciously. He pretended he had not noticed Fritz before.

"Who's your fat boy friend, honey?" His voice was harsh and over-loud.

"Don't be silly, Jesse. You've seen Fritz before, many times."

"Our friend is not always able to see very well in the evenings." Fritz was unruffled, smiling.

About 3.30 a.m. Jesse began to yawn. "C'mon, my dear," he said, taking Nadia for granted. "Time you and me went home."

Nadia looked at him quietly, but without smiling. "I would rather stay here a little longer," she said.

"So you don't want to come home with me, is that it?" The drink in Jesse suddenly came to the top.

"Please, Jesse. Don't let's have any more scenes," implored Nadia. "It is Christmas-time . . . we ought to be happy . . . all of us together."

"Meaning you want to get back to your fat friend in the bar, I imagine. . . . O.K. C'mon then," growled Jesse, flinging away. "We'll go back in the bar . . . the fat slob better not make any passes though, or . . ."

"No need to get annoyed." The drink was in me too. Stupidly, unforgivably, thinking of John and imitating Jesse's voice, I added: "Just because you ain't Nadia's little love-bird either."

"Be quiet—both of you." Nadia was in a rage herself. "At least the German boys know how to behave in public . . . they don't quarrel like hooligans." She was furious with both of us; suddenly blazing at us . . . there was colour in her face. She looked fine.

Then it went horribly wrong; everything. . . . Jesse rounded on her.

"Is zat so!" he flared. "Now let me tell you something. We Britishers don't quarrel neither . . . not over bar-girls, anyway."

Jesse was fairly "high"; but even so it was brutal. There was deliberate venom in it.

Nadia went very white; a look of deadly hurt flashed through her eyes; her mouth opened, drooping pathetically. I thought she would burst into tears; but her expression changed. Her eyes went hard—narrowed; and her mouth closed firmly. "She may hit him," I thought, and drew back to give her room. But she stood quite still, glaring at Jesse in murderous silence.

"Jesse, that was a beastly thing to say," she told him at last, and her voice was quiet.

Jesse's face sneered at her. He glanced down, then: "Your stocking's coming down," he stated coldly. Then he turned on his heel and strode out of the Casino.

.   .   .   .   .

On New Year's day. . . .

"Look here," said the Old Man. "I've just heard from Montolieu that the Huns may have actually connected you personally with *Olinda*. . . . I don't know if you were spotted buying that burning plant or what. If you were, I suppose it might have made them a bit suspicious. Anyway, we'll have to get you out of the way for a few days . . . make it look as though you've gone off on some Boom Defence job; otherwise when you do leave, they'll know exactly where you are."

"Why only me?" I thought to myself, and the Old Man must have seen what I was thinking.

"Matheson's O.K. He's been messing about here all along, so there's nothing unusual about his staying here. . . . And Hilton's only just come back from the south."

"When will you want me to leave, sir?"

"Oh, I don't think we need actually send you anywhere. The Huns would soon find you and start wondering what you were up to . . . besides I want to keep you handy in case *Olinda* is suddenly released. . . . Montolieu's got a better scheme, I think."

.   .   .   .   .

Montolieu's flat, like himself, was discreet and colourless. He regarded everyone and everything with elaborately cultivated suspicion. After three days of miserable incarceration with him,

I felt like screaming every time I saw him, with his head a little on one side, carefully, suspiciously lifting the lid off the special hot plate on which his breakfast was always served. With aching malice I longed for the day when he would lift that lid to find a plump little black bomb ticking away merrily on the plate. I felt that I would accept the death with relief.

And every morning, at exactly 9.22—

"Well, I must be off now . . . hope Mehmet is making you comfortable . . . don't hesitate to ask for anything you want. . . . What? . . . Oh! I really must remember to get a bottle . . . terribly sorry, old chap; never touch the stuff myself, you see . . ." then a nervous little giggle and ". . . no accounting for tastes, is there?"

That was every morning at exactly 9.23; for it took him precisely one minute to go through the act . . . every morning.

.   .   .   .   .

Press and Propaganda. . . .

The case put up by the American Government in support of their claim to the tanker *Olinda* has caused considerable surprise in Istanbul shipping circles. . . .

It is clear that certain interested parties are endeavouring to influence the course of justice . . . they should remember that Turkish Justice is well known to be unequalled by that of any other great nation in its impartiality and . . .

Perfidious Albion . . .
German arrogance . . .
Legitimate Turkish aspirations and the vital interests of her people. . . .

Whatever the outcome of this most undignified attempt at double dealing and intimidation . . . it should be noted that the German hold upon the Aegean is now complete . . . penalties for deliberate infringement of the Laws of peoples and . . . national honour . . . criminal elements . . . overwhelming German superiority. . . .

What was the use of our elaborate attempts at secrecy and security in the face of all this fuss. I was heartily bored both

with Montolieu and with his gloomy servant. The view across
the Bosphorus had begun to cloy. The colour of the blue fjord
and the trees beyond looked fanciful . . . unreal as a picture
post card. And I was sick to death of sitting, with my eyes glued
to binoculars, in the hope of observing some new point about
Olinda's appearance.

·   ·   ·   ·   ·

Snow. . . . For two whole days it snowed steadily, and
during the night of the second day there was a strong wind
which shook the house and set the snowflakes driving.

In the evening John came out to see me. When he left, it
was pitch dark and still snowing, so there could be no harm in
my walking a little way with him. The wind had risen to gale
force, and we were obliged to struggle up the hill towards the
bleak expanse of Ayas Pasha. As we reached the top, a violent
squall swept round the corner of the houses, tearing at our
ears and hair, and dashing a cloud of icy snow crystals into
our faces.

"Just the night for a quick dash through the Khios Strait,"
observed John laconically. "You ought to be at sea, my lad,
not loafing about in Istanbul."

I laughed; but my heart quailed at the thought. I remembered the remarks I had frequently made about using bad
weather to get through the narrows. I felt like recanting on
the spot. The violence of the enemy is understandable, and
his reactions can often be predicted; but the violence of wind
and weather is soulless, blind and far more terrifying.

·   ·   ·   ·   ·

At last a scribbled note. . . .

. . . expect the final hearing to be on January 6th, so you
can come out of prison for to-day. Take your bags back to the
Park. Make it look as though you've just come back from somewhere. Montolieu will fix it.

L. T. M.

8

14

As we were walking along, a large, grey saloon car swept by, travelling very fast. Neither of us had heard it approaching from behind, and it was only by luck that I happened to look round in time to hurl myself and Jesse off the road. It roared past us, accelerating, with its wheels almost touching the grass bank.

"Well of all the . . ." began Jesse, picking himself up and glaring after the disappearing car. Then, with a shrug, he recovered his bag of clubs and we started off again. "Looks like the Turks have it in for us too."

"Those weren't Turks. I believe I recognised the man beside the driver."

Jesse raised his eyebrows. "Fritz?" he asked, a slow smile beginning to spread across his face.

"No. One of the Huns staying at the Park."

"Oh—oh!" observed Jesse. "Going to get tough with us are they?"

We reached the club-house and saw at once that there was far too much snow for golf. It lay an inch or two thick over most of the fairways and only those patches of rough, which contained the longest heather and scrubby bushes, stuck through it here and there.

The club-house was locked and deserted, so we decided to go for a walk round the course.

There was a broad band of footprints leading down the first fairway, across a stream and up the opposite hill. We kept to these for fear of getting bogged, and Jesse set the pace with long ski-runner's strides.

When we reached the third tee we paused for breath.

The hill upon which we stood was the end of a spur of high ground, whence one could see for a great distance to east and west through north. To the westward there was another small ridge of high moorland; beyond it must lie the Golden Horn. To the northward the hills rose steeply to a greater height, and craggy peaks lifted above the forests of Therapia. Round to the eastward, a mile or two away, the moor went tumbling down into the valley beyond; then rose again, thick with pine forest, farther off. Between those two ridges lay the Bosphorus, though one could not see the water itself. Nearer still, skirting the edge of the golf-course, ran the main road up which we had walked the two or three miles from Pera. It wound away to the north-eastward, and up the hill, till it disappeared among the trees on the way to Bebek and Therapia.

It was a brilliant day; the wind of yesterday had died. I took off my coat, threw it over a patch of scrub near the tee, and lay down upon it. Jesse perched himself upon the sand-box. He had been unusually quiet all morning and he still looked thoughtful—almost depressed.

"Not worrying about Nadia, are you?" I asked.

"Nadia? Why should I?" he replied with a frown.

"I like Nadia; and, what's more, I'm certain she doesn't belong in these surroundings. Wonder what story there is behind it all."

"I ain't worryin'," observed Jesse dryly. I was surprised by his bitter tone. But possibly his quarrel with John explained it. He looked away and began to stare moodily across the heathy slopes before us. For a few minutes, in silence, we both watched the cloud shadows chasing each other across the moors and forests, and diving down the hill-sides into the Bosphorus valley. Suddenly his gaze became more intent and I turned my head to look in the same direction. Next moment I had raised myself into a sitting position and we both watched in silence the rapid approach of a large grey saloon car—down the road from Therapia.

When it reached the point where the road turned away slightly to skirt the golf-course, the car slowed down as though the occupants were searching the countryside for something. Jesse slipped off the sand-box and got down among the heather beside me. The car crawled past, about half a mile off, and disappeared behind the hill.

"Funny," said Jesse quietly, "wonder what those Huns were looking for."

I made no reply, but instinctively we both scrambled to our feet, and started off down the steep hill-side towards the third green, which lay at the bottom of the valley.

It was late afternoon when we finally returned, muddy and dishevelled, to Pera and the Park Hotel.

As we crossed the hall on our way to Jesse's room, we saw
two men sitting on the sofa. They were two of the Germans
whom we had often seen in the Park. Normally we and the
Germans had ignored each other; but now these two were
glaring at us with a stony, unblinking stare, which I felt was
more than our bedraggled appearance deserved. We felt their
eyes following us into the lift.

After tea, as we were walking across Ayas Pasha towards the
Embassy, I chanced to look round and noticed that the two
Germans from the hotel were following a short distance behind
us. I mentioned the fact to Jesse. We strolled on down the
Rue de Pera and, when we turned in at the Embassy gates,
we saw the Germans disappear into a cake shop opposite.

The Old Man was in a most jovial mood. He took us up to
his rooms and poured out drinks for us all, including John,
who was sitting by the fire with a book.

"We'll fix 'em this time," proclaimed old Mathews. "I've
just heard that the owner's lawyer has had his last objection overruled, and he's been forced to wind up his defence.
Olinda ought to be finally ours and ready to sail within a
week."

"The Huns have been keeping an eye on us to-day," I
announced, but not with very much conviction. Now that we
were back among the homely surroundings of Pera, we had
begun to feel a little uncertain about the whole golf-course
incident.

The Old Man burst out laughing when we told him of the
afternoon's happenings.

"My God, what a panic!" he roared. "The poor old Huns
were probably just watching for a chance to pick up a few
cheap golf balls.

"Not much chance of finding golf balls in the snow,"
remarked Jesse, a bit nettled at the derision in the Old Man's
voice.

"Oh, to hell with you!" scoffed old Mathews. "You'll have
us all wearing false beards and masks in a minute." Then,
changing the subject firmly . . . "Anyway, what d'you think
about this?" and he handed me a foreign-looking message
form on which was written, in a Continental hand: "*Akhtari*

and Tarkhan arriving Bosphorus January 8th." "That's from old
Niko . . . just came across about half an hour ago." No wonder
the Old Man was in such excellent form. It looked as though
all three ships, *Olinda, Tarkhan* and *Akhtari,* would be able to
go down at the same time . . . each by a different route. Soon
we were busy again with charts and almanacs, and before long
a complete plan had been worked out.

John in *Akhtari* and Jesse in *Tarkhan* were to leave the
Bosphorus as soon as the tankers arrived on the night of
January 8th. They would then steam at slow speed across the
Marmara, so as to pass through the Dardanelles and reach
Tenedos just before sunset on January 9th. It had already
been discovered, upon inquiry by signal, that *Akhtari* could in
fact do eleven knots and *Tarkhan* at least ten; so John was to
follow his old track inside Mitylene and Khios, while Jesse
was to take the shortest route outside those two islands. Both
ships were to spend the first day at anchor in secluded bays
south of Izmir. This was another Turkish military zone;
heavily guarded and therefore secure from enemy observation.

Meanwhile I was to leave the Dardanelles in *Olinda* at dawn
on January 10th and proceed in daily hops down the coast.
If *Olinda*'s disguise proved ineffective, she still had the protection of Turkish waters to fall back on, and her presence on the
coast would create a useful diversion for the passage of the
two larger and more important ships.

After leaving the first day's anchorage south of Izmir, *Akhtari*
was to take two more nights to get to Castelorizzo, anchoring
in the Gulf of Doris by day. *Tarkhan* was to spend three nights
covering the same distance, and to anchor near Budrum and
Fethieh.

As soon as everything was settled, old Mathews straightened
up from the chart-table and passed round his cigarette-case.

"The Huns here are as mad as hornets," he chuckled.
"They're swearing that they've got U-boats and aircraft ready
all down the coast; but that's all my eye, of course—'war o
nerves' stuff. Their C.-in-C. Aegean's got other things to
worry about than tankers and the prestige of a few seedy
German diplomats. . . . Still, they're watching us like
hawks," he admitted grudgingly . . . and they've got eyes
everywhere."

"So we've noticed, sir."

"Oh, stuff!" The Old Man burst into laughter again. "All that nonsense on the golf-course was just your imagination. . . . Montolieu's been getting under your skin."

But as we left the Embassy we saw our two shadows emerge from the cake shop. They followed us down the street and into a restaurant. After a quick glance in our direction, they sat down at a table near the entrance.

We smiled at the sight of their serious expressions; for the Old Man's ridicule had somewhat restored our self-confidence.

"What *is* this?" Jesse wanted to know. "What are they aiming to do . . . put us off our meals by making faces at us?"

I grinned at the suggestion, but Jesse's last remark had suddenly given me an idea.

Just then one of the waiters, a chap we knew quite well, approached the Germans' table with the menu. As soon as they had ordered, the waiter came over to us.

"Can you make some sandwiches quick?" I asked him. "We've got a train to catch." The waiter looked unenthusiastic, to say the least; but in the end he went off with a dubious shrug of his shoulders and a promise to do his best. He returned later with two large dishes for the Germans.

As soon as the food was set before them, they fell upon it with characteristic voracity. The mask of stern Prussianism dropped from them at once, as their healthy stomachs took clamorous charge, and they began to stuff themselves hurriedly with as much as their forks could carry. Jesse and I watched them with growing amusement until the waiter brought our sandwiches; then we rose to leave.

The look of comical dismay upon the faces of the Germans as we passed their table made us laugh outright. One of them sat gaping, with his heaped fork half-way to his mouth.

"*Mahlzeit*—enjoy your dinner!" drawled Jesse, over his shoulder as we reached the door. The other German pushed his plate away with an angry snort and, rising, called for the waiter and the bill. We led them from bar to bar for an hour or more, taking care only to enter those in which food was not served, until we finally managed to lose them in a crowd

which suddenly gathered in a side street to watch an old Greek
being set upon by his infuriated wife.

15

"SIT down, I'm busy," boomed old Mathews, and picked
up the 'phone to ask for another number. He was in a
towering rage over something.

It was 9.30 a.m. on January 7th. I had just arrived at the
Embassy and, as I entered the room, I had heard the tail
end of his previous telephone conversation, which had gone
something like this . . .

"No."

"No, I tell you" (*shouting*).

"I tell you he got permission from the police to go on
board."

"The Turks can go to ——!"

"Nonsense!"

"Pah!"

"!—!—!" and crash down went the receiver.

He now got on to his new number.

"Who's that?" he snapped. "I want to speak to the Naval
Attaché." There was a pause during which old Mathews
snorted once or twice and said, "Hello," violently, a few times
more. Then someone came on the other end of the line.

"Good morning, sir," rumbled the Old Man. "This is
Mathews from Istanbul. They've arrested that Maltese storekeeper of ours . . . the one with a Turkish passport."

The voice at the other end made some observation.

"I can't tell you over the 'phone," replied old Mathews.
"It doesn't matter very much anyway; but could some of the
high-ups be approached about him?"

The Old Man's telephone conversation ended. He put down
the receiver and sat for a moment looking thoughtful. I could
see that he was worried at last. He frowned at his blotting-
pad, and started to draw upon it idly with his pencil.

"This is getting beyond a joke," he growled at last. "First
young Matheson gets into trouble with our security people
over some Russian girl, and now one of *Olinda's* crew has to

be pulled in by the Turkish police for attempting to leave the country without a pass. . . . I suppose the Germans are behind most of it." The "Russian girl" was presumably Nadia, although we had heard that she was technically a Turk. So Montolieu had objected to her personally! What on earth had Jesse been up to now, I wondered.

About ten o'clock Jesse put in an appearance. He was looking dull-eyed and, once again, he was poorly shaven.

"Where the hell have you been all day? D'you realise what the time is?" snapped the Old Man. Jesse said nothing, and the Old Man returned to the silent contemplation of his blotter. All at once he picked up the 'phone and asked for an extension. . . . "That you Montolieu? Can you come up for a moment?" Then he replaced the receiver.

"Montolieu keeps insisting," growled the Old Man, "that the Huns know more about our plans than we imagine."

He snorted.

"Always got some bee in his bonnet, that fella; still, I suppose we ought to hear what he's got to say."

Montolieu came in—that is to say there was a discreet knock; then the door opened slowly, just enough to allow Montolieu's slender frame to creep round it and into the room. Deliberately he closed the door again. All his actions and his appearance gave one the impression that Montolieu hoped he was not going to waste his time; hoped we were ready at last to defer to the master-mind. One felt that he had been waiting many years for this moment (before the war he had been a shopwalker in a large London store). He now turned towards the Old Man, and a faint, pitying smile grew upon his face as he advanced towards us.

But before Montolieu could begin to speak, old Mathews, who had been watching the pantomime of his studied entrance with ill-controlled impatience, burst out with: "Now, look here. What the hell makes you think the Huns suspect anything . . . that's just what they'd like us to believe isn't it—that they're suspicious? They may know next to nothing. . . ."

Montolieu opened his mouth to interrupt; but the Old Man boomed on without a pause, having apparently forgotten that he had sent for "Security" Montolieu in order to hear "What *he* had to say."

". . . They may just be trying to make things awkward for us in the hope that we'll give them a clue with some damn-fool attempt to put them off the scent." He glared meaningly at the unfortunate Montolieu, who was still standing in the middle of the room looking intensely irritated. ". . . Some clumsy manœuvre," continued old Mathews, "that would show them just exactly what it was we wanted them *not* to believe."

At last Montolieu had a chance to speak.

"We're convinced, sir, that they've heard about the burning plant that was bought the other day."

"I know you are. Well, what d'you want us to do?" he sat down abruptly at his desk with a gesture of resignation. "You'd better fix it all up between you anyway. I haven't time to go playing pirates and smugglers all over Constantinople. . . ."

Montolieu turned to me patiently.

"Whatever happens," he said, "we'll have to make sure the Huns don't know you're on board *Olinda* when she sails . . . otherwise it would give them a pretty strong line on what the burning plant's going to be used for and where *Olinda*'s going."

"They'll guess where she's going anyway, won't they? . . . Where else would she be likely to go, once she's left Istanbul, except out through the Dardanelles."

"Surely you've heard that we've put round a story about selling her to the Turks," retorted Montolieu. "The Turkish Naval staff are helping us by letting it leak out that they're getting a new oiler for their Fleet Anchorage in the Marmara Islands."

". . . and you're hoping that when the Huns find out in the morning that *Olinda*'s left the Bosphorus, they'll think she's gone to the Marmara Islands?"

"Yes, that's it," interrupted old Mathews gruffly. "Actually, of course, *Olinda* will be at Erekli, on the northern shore of the Marmara here, disguising herself." He got up and pointed to Erekli on the chart, then strolled across to the window, looking thoughtful. Suddenly he swung round and strode briskly back to his desk. Then he looked at me, smiling.

"If your disguise is good, you ought to have an easy passage." The whole tone of his voice had changed in a moment to one of bold assurance. "Personally I'm convinced that the disguise *will* be effective. . . . Now let's see. . . ." The Old Man was himself again, full of drive and determination. ". . . your crew are all on board; at least all except one of the Maltese, and he'll probably be there too before sunset. . . . The ship'll have steam by then as well. . . ."

I was a little startled at the suddenness of all this. It was the first I had heard about the arrival of *Olinda*'s crew. I felt I really did not know quite enough about things . . . about the other tankers, for instance, that were going to leave the next night, January 8th, and . . .

But the Old Man rattled on, eager, aggressive.

"How long will it take you to paint ship, get that flying bridge, cut away and the jury mast stepped?" One could almost hear him say, "You liar," at the end of the question.

"That'll depend a lot on the crew, sir. What do they look like?"

"Oh! The usual Sea Transport crowd," he replied airily. "They'll be all right, I expect. . . . One or two Arabs of course . . . jolly good sailors, I'm told."

"I suppose we *could* do the job in twenty-four hours with all hands. But that's assuming we don't strike any snags."

"Of course you could," snapped old Mathews. "There mustn't *be* any snags; that's all. . . ." (It was never any use to argue with the Old Man once he was personally convinced that everything was settled. Besides, he usually turned out to be right in the end.) "Good. Well now, you and Montolieu must fix up the drill for to-night. . . . Let me know afterwards what's been arranged; and don't forget you've got to be on board the ship by twenty hundred at latest. . . ."

Soon after lunch that day, the sky clouded over and the wind rose in angry gusts with flurries of rain and sleet. By nightfall it had freshened to a blustering half-gale from the westward. The air grew hourly colder. I shivered, in spite of a heavy coat and scarf, as Jesse and I left the Park and started off down the hill towards the Bosphorus.

Looking back, a moment later, I saw two men coming down a hundred yards or so behind us; but it was not possible, in the darkness, to see who they were. When I looked again, a car had slowed alongside them, and the two men on the pavement were talking across to the driver as they walked along.

Before we reached the Bosphorus, the wind lulled a little and it began to snow. After a while I glanced over my shoulder again. The two men behind seemed to be nearer, as though they had increased their speed so as not to lose sight of us in the snow. Behind them, now, the car came crawling—close to the pavement. The two walkers passed under a street lamp, which shone full upon the face of one of them.

It was maddening that we were committed to a rendezvous with the Old Man at 7 p.m. What a riotous, hilarious dance we could otherwise have led these liverish-looking Herrenvolk —in and out of taxis and all round the town. But Montolieu had arranged a most complicated time-table in which the Old Man (who secretly enjoyed complications) had concurred; so there was no option for us but to hurry on and hope for a chance to get rid of the Huns later. Soon we reached the tramlines, which run along the edge of the Bosphorus, and there we found a crowd of people waiting for the six o'clock to Bebek.

These trams were of the most common Continental type— single-decked, with two separate coaches coupled together. An entrance at either end of each coach led on to a platform, surrounded by a bulwark, where the driver stood or where passengers were allowed to stand when the driver was at the other end. When the six o'clock tram arrived, Jesse and I just managed to scramble on to one of the two centre platforms. Our shadowers showed what seemed like unusual delicacy by climbing on to the rear platform.

As soon as the tram started, we began to edge our way through the closely packed people towards the outer side of the platform, so as to be able to keep a watch upon the roadway as we went bucketing and jolting along. The snow was falling steadily now and the air was not so cold. Occasionally a few flakes whipped in under the canopy of the tram and settled for a moment on the people packed there; on the black veil of a peasant woman; on the rough cap of a Turkish soldier; on the moustache of an old man in a black velour hat, an old man with fierce eyes glaring at nothing in particular. The snowflakes melted quickly and formed into drops. One of them clung to the old man's moustache and hung there, trembling with every jolt. A beam of light shone out from inside the tram upon the old man's face and set the trembling drop a-glitter.

Over on our side we were packed so close that no one could move. We all swayed together with an occasional stagger and shuffling of feet as the tram jerked over points, from single to double track and back again. For three or four miles Jesse and I travelled in silence, then:

"Did you see Nadia home that night at the Casino?" asked Jesse casually.

"Yes. She was in rather a state. I've got an idea the poor kid had been hoping to marry you and get out of this place." But I was not very keen to go on discussing Nadia with Jesse. I felt sure that we would soon fall out if I did.

"Marry me?" echoed Jesse, then coarsely: "Hell, one doesn't *marry* that kind."

As if in sharp retort, the tram suddenly slammed across some points and halted so abruptly that Jesse was toppled into the arms of a portly Turkish dame in furs, who had been trying to catch his eye for some time and was by no means annoyed at the upset.

When Jesse had regained his place and a fair proportion of his poise, I turned to him again. "What *kind* exactly is Nadia then?" I asked .

"Just an ordinary bar-girl," he replied shortly, ". . . no different from any of the rest."

I was about to make some angry reply to this remark when, fortunately perhaps, there was a violent jerk and the tram started off again. By the time I had disengaged myself from the old man in the black velour hat, whose ferocious expression neither lightened nor deepened, the opportunity to reply had passed. In any case the whole subject was driven from my mind, for a few minutes, by the sudden realisation that the old man, in spite of his fierce eyes, was blind.

Presently, though, I could not resist bringing up the subject of Nadia once again. "She certainly *is* different from the others . . . and I don't believe she eats proper meals either . . . she's far too pale."

"You should worry," growled Jesse. "All Nadia needs is a good scrub and someone to dress her . . . and that someone ain't going to be me, let me tell you."

I made no answer. Jesse was just being childish. He seemed to be trying hard to convince himself, and me as well, that Nadia had never meant anything in his life.

We rattled along for another mile or so until we came to a part of the route where the tracks passed through a wood. Here we began to watch the road on our left more closely. Ah! There it was, just before the next tram stop—a car parked on the opposite side of the road and facing back towards Pera. Old Mathews would be in that car, and this was where we must leave the tram.

I had forgotten about the two men on the rear platform; but, just as I was about to jump down into the roadway, I was suddenly reminded of them by the sight of another car, crawling up astern of the tram, instead of passing it on the outside, in the normal way. I hesitated; then I began to barge my way back across the platform.

"What's eatin' you now?" inquired Jesse impatiently. Then he also saw the second car, and shrugged his shoulders. "Hell!" he said. "What's wrong in that? Can't other automobiles use this road as well as ours. . . . You'll have the Old Man hoppin' mad if you keep him waiting." But I shoved back all the same into my previous place on the outside edge of the platform— squeezed up against the old man in the velour hat, who con- tinued to glare with impassive ferocity at nothing. I noticed that the drop of water had at last been shaken from the end of his moustache.

The tram started again. About half a mile farther on it swung suddenly on to a double track. A moment later it stopped alongside a Pera-bound tram, which had been waiting to move on to the single track itself. "I'm going now," I said to Jesse. "Good-bye. See you in Syria . . . expect you'll be there before me anyway; you always have the luck," and, cocking one leg over the low bulwark, I stepped across on to the platform of the tram next door, just as the latter was beginning to move. Five minutes later I got down into the roadway a few hundred yards from where the Embassy car was still standing.

16

THE Old Man had come alone to meet me.
I knew also that Montolieu had made special arrangements for a single customs sentry to wait for me at a deserted point on the Bosphorus coast, and escort me out to *Olinda*. I was not surprised therefore when, after a drive of only ten minutes or so, the car turned down a dark lane which ended at the water's edge.

A small motor boat lay alongside a wooden jetty. On the jetty stood a Turkish soldier. The snow had settled upon the peak of his cap and upon the shoulders of the rough cape he wore. He held a short rifle carelessly, with the butt resting between his feet, as he waited. In the boat a single figure, seen dimly in the darkness, was leaning out over the bow to keep hold of the jetty. The motor boat's engine could just be heard, muttering softly above the gurgle of swift water passing. The Old Man bid me a gruff "Good-bye and good luck," as I clambered in after the sentry. The boat shoved off.

By now it was snowing heavily, so that we, in the boat, could hardly see ten yards ahead of us. We therefore went feeling our way down along the beach till we came to a small jetty, abreast of which I knew that *Olinda* was lying. Then we struck out, slanting across the stream, and the shore faded quickly into the snow and gloom astern.

There followed an age of anxious waiting. Then suddenly we had arrived—bumping in gently alongside the high, black wall of *Olinda*'s hull. I grabbed the ladder and swung myself up on to the deck. My bag was hove up after me. The motor boat bore off and was swallowed at once in the seething darkness. For a moment I stood listening to the last faint mutterings from the boat; then abruptly a figure loomed up beside me. It was heavily muffled and I could not make out, in the darkness, a single feature; but I sensed more than saw that it was an Arab.

"Captain?" I suggested hopefully.

"Yes, c'mon, please!" he replied, in that quick little scream-ing voice which is peculiar to natives of the Middle East.

He led me aft and through a door facing forward at the break of *Olinda*'s poop. We stepped into a long, dark corridor. My guide shuffled past various cabins and past the entrance to the engine-room. Next, on the inboard side, came a large door, and from this door a bright light was streaming into the alleyway. I entered, with snowflakes still scattering from my clothes, what was obviously the ship's saloon.

At a table laid for supper, above which hung a multi-wick oil lamp, sat four men. One of these men, an enormous fellow sitting at the head of the table, was clearly the Master. He must have been six feet four inches tall and immensely broad.

I remembered that the Master was a Russian, so I dis-counted the innocent, childish look in his blue eyes and upon his great, broad face. Since he was also as bald as an egg, it was difficult to tell his age—between forty and fifty perhaps; but the most conspicuous feature in his face was a set of the largest false teeth I had ever seen. They kept slipping down across his mouth, and must have made eating very difficult.

The Master got to his feet as I entered and introduced me, in passable English, to the chief engineer—a slight elderly man with a thin, cultured face, intelligent eyes and a trim, grey beard; he looked the image of Lenin grown old; his name was Feodar Pavlovitch. Next came the second engineer, a lithe, black-eyed, little fellow, who had the keen, pointed face and olive skin of a Spanish nobleman. This one darted a fierce inquisitive glance at me and then went on with his supper. The Mate was an old man with white hair. He, too, was fairly tall; but he stooped a little, and upon his face was an expression of patient suffering, as though he accepted without pleasure the burden of a thousand worries. "Dinner-time," announced the Master abruptly, with a grin that was spoilt by his teeth suddenly snapping shut in the middle of it. I sat down and started on a large bowl of soup, which Feodar Pavlovitch had just set before me.

"These officers only speak Russian?" I inquired of the Master, by way of keeping the conversation going.

"Also little Turkish and Feodar Pavlovitch . . ." a slow,

rather enigmatic smile crept over the face of the chief engineer at the mention of his name, ". . . he spickin' some French sometimes."

I went on with my soup. So did the others; Feodar delicately; the Mate slowly, without much appetite; the second engineer, whose name was Ivan Oreshkin, in quick, eager gulps. As soon as Ivan had finished, he got up, looked round with a swift flash of a smile, and went out. We heard his feet clattering down the iron rungs of the engine-room ladder; then a snatch of song and some bangs and rattlings as he took up again his interrupted work. After supper I went up to the bridge; a little later the Master joined me.

By midnight it was snowing less heavily and, over the ship's port side, the hazy loom of the city's lights struggled out to us across the water. I thought of John and Jesse and the tankers *Akhtari* and *Tarkhan*. To-morrow night these two great ships would come stealing into the Bosphorus just as *Kirilovka* had come stealing three weeks before. I wondered whether Montolieu would invent another complicated plot for getting John and Jesse aboard their ships. The thought of worthy old John being chivvied round Istanbul at dead of night made me smile. I imagined him being finally decanted into the motor boat, grumbling, embarrassed and very resentful at being obliged to "play hide and seek with a lot of damned foreigners."

Shortly after midnight the visibility improved to nearly half a mile and *Olinda* sailed.

By the time she reached the Marmara the sky had cleared. The wind, working round to the north, blew bitterly cold; it came singing across the hills and down the Golden Horn at us, tearing at our hands and faces as though carrying a dust storm of powdered ice. All the stars in heaven were blazing. Upon silent white roofs in the city there lay a sheen. Black spires and minarets, too steep for snow, stood out against the hills. Only the lighthouse on Cape Seraglio seemed alive— sweeping round, flaring and dying; then flaring and dying again.

About 8 a.m. that day, January 8th, we reached the tiny port of Erekli, on the northern shore of the Marmara. Most of the ship's company were still hard at work, as they had been all night, upon the alterations to *Olinda*'s appearance. Feodar Pavlovitch had been directing operations with the burning plant upon the flying bridge, and the Mate had been occupied with the rigging for the dummy spars. The Master and I, of course, had been on the bridge watching the ship, like a perambulating beehive, pounding her busy little way across the Sea of Marmara.

Erekli looked a most primitive place—far smaller and more remote than Adana; but I noticed, through my glasses, as soon as we anchored, the precipitate arrival of a section of Turkish soldiers on shaggy ponies. They remained on the foreshore all day, and presumably all night as well.

By 11 o'clock in the forenoon, all the frames which supported the flying bridge had been cut. It only remained to saw through the two wooden ends and lever the whole structure over the side. We intended to do this on the way to the Dardanelles. The hands had already started on the painting, and we now began to cut the funnel and to lay out the spars, ready for stepping as a false mast with its derricks.

I had received rather a shock when I found that the total ship's complement, referred to by the Old Man as "the usual Sea Transport crowd—one or two Arabs, of course," actually consisted of the following:

1 Conducting Officer	English
1 Master	Russian
1 Mate	Russian
2 Engineers	Russian
1 Bosun	Russian
1 Cook	Chinese

9

2 Greasers	Chinese
1 Storekeeper	Maltese
1 Storekeeper's mate	Maltese
6 Sailors	Arab
1 Wolfhound bitch	Alsatian

This was about half the number that *Olinda* normally carried; and how on earth were they going to get on with each other anyway? they had no common language—I discovered, however, that both the Maltese, who had British passports, were roughly bilingual in English and Turkish. This sounded useful, though they were not a very prepossessing pair. The storekeeper was a little fat man of fifty-two, with one repulsively blind eye. He was voluble but lazy, and at first I thought him rather a nuisance. The other Maltese, who was his nephew, seemed quite a useful chap, though also apt to be found hurrying busily from nowhere to nothing, when there was a heavy job in progress.

The only other members of the crew whom I met that day were Ah Fong, the Chinese cook—fat, obliging and unfailingly cheerful, for ever offering cups of tea and special little cakes of his own invention—and Malu, the Master's wolfhound bitch. Malu was a terror, particularly to the Arab sailors whom she would chase unmercifully when they were silly enough to show any nervousness. She lived in the Master's cabin behind the wheelhouse, and no one could enter it without him. During the day, Malu would patrol the decks and bark furiously at any boats in the neighbourhood, or attack anyone who tried to come on board.

In the afternoon the sky clouded over again, and there was more snow, which continued intermittently until well after dark. We had to stop painting; but the rest of the work progressed well. By evening we had the funnel top ready for the final heave; so a pair of wooden skids were rigged, from the taffrail, against the lower half of the funnel. The jury mast, too, was all ready for stepping. It was to be lashed to the foreside of the wheelhouse, and roughly stayed with three-inch manila rope. I spent a troubled night in the spare cabin under the wheelhouse for, after several years in the Navy, I had become unused to the "fifth column" methods of the treacherous bed-bug, and there seemed to be more of them in this cabin than was reasonable.

Next day, January 9th, about half-way through the forenoon, the Russian tankers passed us on the southern horizon. We all watched them for a long time. I tried to determine which of them was John's and which Jesse's, and to guess at what thoughts would be passing through the minds of these two very different individuals.

At 3 p.m. we sailed, for I wished to reach the anti-submarine boom at Chanak by 2 o'clock next morning.

When we had cleared the nearest headland and altered course for the Dardanelles, there arrived the moment we had all been awaiting with considerable excitement. The hands collected on the tank-tops; the two ends of the gangway were sawn through; we all shoved and struggled furiously at the frames, till we had edged the ungainly structure bodily to the ship's side; then, with a bedlam of encouraging cries in six different languages (including Malu's), we toppled the whole thing into the sea. It entered the water with a mighty commotion and sank ungracefully, to a chorus of cheers and derision from all on board. Next came the funnel-top. This also required a final cut, then a quick heave on a pair of guys, and it followed the gangway with a clatter, a clang and a beautiful "splosh!" In a spirit of exuberance we tackled the mast and derricks and the dummy hatches; last of all we painted, upon the funnel and on either bow, the Turkish white crescent on a field of red.

Long before dark it was all finished. *Olinda* was gone from the sea, and *Orak*'s illegitimate sister was about to make things awkward for everybody.

As it grew dark the land to the north and south came up to meet us, to close upon us, and to shepherd us gently westwards. I glanced up at the sky; it was overcast but not actually snowing. Soon, however, a few light flakes began to float past. The wind, a moderate westerly, had been freshening slowly all day.

John and Jesse would have left Tenedos by now. They would be half-way to Cape Baba. Just the night for John on the inshore route; he'd be able to see well enough, but ought to be able to remain invisible himself, if he only kept close in to the cliffs. Jesse would be out to seaward; but he was less given to worrying anyway. I knew he would make his course and distances by the most advanced and complicated of modern methods. Provided he did not mislay a decimal point or two in the process, he was likely to arrive at his anchorage intact and on time.

As for myself in *Olinda*; my only problem—the language difficulty—had been temporarily solved; for the Master, Mate and Bosun had agreed to take the wheel in turns. I had spent a few hours the day before in working out with the Master the few necessary helm and engine orders in Russian, and had also memorised the Russian numerals up to three hundred and sixty (three hundred and sixty-nine, in fact). I now stood, in splendid isolation and muffled to the eyes, upon the standard compass platform or "monkey island." My charts and a flash-lamp were on a roughly made outdoor chart-table beside me.

Just before midnight we entered the Dardanelles at Gallipoli. It was snowing fairly steadily now; but we were still able to see the shore on either side. A leadsman stood by on deck in case of need. The engine-room was warned to be prepared for a sudden ring astern.

At 1.45 a.m. we anchored near the pilot station at Ak Bashi, a mile or two east of the boom, which was marked by a single green flashing buoy. It was not long before we heard the put-tering of a motor boat, and a few moments later the pilot launch came alongside; so I went to my cabin, intending to remain there until the pilot left us on the other side of the boom.

I looked through the scuttle, expecting to see the hands go forward at once, and to hear the sounds of the ship weighing. I waited for ten minutes, but nothing happened. Then sud-denly there came the unmistakable noise of the motor boat's engine once again, and I saw the pilot launch stand away from the ship's side, *with the pilot still in her*. A moment later the Master came to my cabin with a slip of paper. On it was a message:

Following received by telephone from British Embassy Istanbul begins *Akhtari* torpedoed and sunk off Cape Baba *Olinda* is to anchor close east of Dardanelles and await further instructions Ends.

Beneath the text was the signature of the cypher clerk and the stamp of the British Vice-Consul at Chanak.

17

"Good job *Olinda* not sailing," said the Master, with his toothy grin. This was a natural enough remark; no doubt we all felt a certain sense of reprieve. But, by the time we were plodding slowly back into the Sea of Marmara, a strong feeling of anti-climax had set in. I wondered whether Jesse had managed to get through in *Tarkhan* or whether, being slightly astern of *Akhtari*, he had been able to turn round and regain the shelter of Tenedos Island. I thought of poor old John and hoped.

We anchored in a bay just east of the Dardanelles, on the southern shore of the Marmara, and I was able to put the rest of the day to good use in going over all the charts once again. I made sure that I was familiar with every cove and beach, in case *Olinda* were forced to run for shelter. I also went round the ship with the quiet old Mate, and with that cultured greybeard Feodar Pavlovitch, who explained the machinery to me in halting French. I found out from Feodar that *Olinda*'s double-bottom tanks had a capacity of 800 tons of water and that it took nearly two hours to fill them, and six hours to pump them out.

"Better start off with them full," I told him. "Then, if we're forced to beach the ship at any time, we can refloat her by pumping out ballast." He agreed and went off to see about it.

Soon after breakfast, a clamour of excited voices brought me out on deck again to join in the general rejoicing as *Tarkhan* came steaming slowly in through the Dardanelles. Ten minutes later she anchored near us in the Bay.

During the night the weather had improved; so it was not long before we had our working-boat in the water and two Arabs pulling the Master and myself over to *Tarkhan*. Soon we were being offered *vodka* and salt herrings by the Master of *Tarkhan*, to an accompaniment of lively persiflage from a completely unshaken Jesse.

"I figure I was about five miles astern of the clumsy old Boffin" (*John presumably*) "when . . . 'whoosh!' . . . up she goes in a shower of sparks and flames as high as the sky . . . you can see *Akhtari* stagger and kind of sit back on her bum in the middle of it all. . . ."

Jesse went on to tell us of how he had turned *Tarkhan* at once, and steamed back to shelter inside Tenedos Island. At dawn he had re-entered the Dardanelles after a short argument with a Turkish boarding vessel.

". . . Asked for my papers, the wet sap . . . dripping wet; they all were—all of them in the boat . . . told him I'd burnt the papers . . . then he asked me who I was . . . I told him Mrs. Roosevelt; but he didn't get it . . . so I said Henry Ford . . . he wrote it all down in his log, I could see him. . . ."

None the less the boarding vessel had insisted on signalling for instructions before allowing *Tarkhan* to re-enter the Dardanelles; Jesse and the rest of them had spent a most uncomfortable two hours waiting for the reply, feeling themselves a very easy and tempting target for torpedoes.

Back on board *Olinda*, I speculated on the probable fate of poor old John; but it was not until the next afternoon that we received any news of him. This came to us in a somewhat spectacular manner: an old-fashioned-looking craft, which I recognised as the official security yacht, *Evangelistria*, came steaming in from the eastward. She was a steady old dame, with bowsprit, brass funnel, counter stern and a bridge which looked rather like a combination of an old-world summer-house and a trellis-work arbour. We had often see this *Evangelistria* lying at Therapia in the Bosphorus and had wondered how old "Security" had managed to justify her permanent allocation to his department. As she steamed past us now, we were suddenly startled by a stentorian hail from her bridge.

Then there was a flash of red, and I raised my binoculars just in time to see old Mathews settle his wig upon his head and then cram his black hat on top of it.

(We found out long afterwards that it was the necessity of going through this same performance every time he went to sea, which had finally made the old boy abandon the seafaring profession. According to this story, there had been a dramatic scene on the bridge of a destroyer in a gale of wind, when the Old Man's cap and wig had flown from his head in one piece. They had landed upon that of a young ordinary signalman, who had been so startled that he had sprung to attention and saluted, then burst into hysterical laughter. . . . Whereupon he was promptly put in the first lieutenant's report for "aggravated insolence.")

Now the Old Man took up a megaphone. "I'll be back before dark," he bawled. "I'm collecting Hilton and the ship's company of *Akhtari* at Chanak. Come on board, both of you, as soon as I anchor."

Jesse and I waved an acknowledgment of the message from the poops of our respective ships.

About 5 o'clock the same afternoon, *Evangelistria* returned, so Jesse and I went over to her in *Tarkhan*'s motor boat. Her deck was crowded with Russian seamen and, in her saloon, we found the Russian officers, John, the Old Man and Montolieu.

The change in poor old John was shocking. His face was grey with fatigue and he hardly spoke, even when the Old Man tried to drag him into the general conversation. His clothes, too, were tattered and dirty, and there was a wooden despondency about him which nothing would shift. Food and a few drinks revived him a little; but his story came haltingly. He was clearly sick of the whole business.

It was a submarine that had got him. He told us that he could see her quite clearly, less than half a mile away. He had also heard the torpedoes approaching (on the surface, he said), and seen their tracks.

Akhtari had been within a mile of the coast when attacked. One torpedo had struck in the engine-room; the others farther forward. By a miracle there had been no casualties, and the ship sank slowly, giving them plenty of time in which to lower and man the boats. But it was when they reached the shore that their troubles had really begun. The Turks had opened fire on them, from the cliff-top, with machine-guns and rifles. Owing to the darkness no one had been hit; but they had spent a nerve-racking quarter of an hour crouching amongst the rocks while John's interpreter, Osman, tried to parley with the soldiers.

At first the soldiers had only answered by shouts and a fresh hail of bullets. In the end, however, the whole ship's company had been frog-marched up to a nearby command post, where the officer in charge could not be persuaded that they were other than German saboteurs, landed from a U-boat. He had refused to accept the story of *Akhtari*. It was difficult to believe that none of his sentries had seen her when she passed so close to the shore; but distances at night are very deceptive, so we were inclined to think that she had, in fact, been a good deal farther off.

The most disturbing inference to be derived from John's story was that the warning to expect the tankers had clearly not reached that particular spot, for John and his crew had been kept in cold and evil-smelling cells all night, while the interpreter had suffered a very thorough interrogation, by third degree methods, on suspicion of being a fifth columnist. Nor was it until next day that orders had come through for them to be released and sent on to Chanak. The journey had lasted twenty-four hours, and the first ten miles of it had been done on foot over the mountains; the remainder in open trucks and carts in which they had been frozen nearly stiff.

"Was the U-boat surfaced when you first sighted her?" asked Jesse.

"Yes. She was sitting there waiting for me. I hadn't a chance."

"It certainly sounds as though the Huns were expecting you," observed Montolieu gravely, although he had doubtless heard the whole story at least once already.

"Of course they were. And I know who bloody well told them—the Turks at Ak Bashi."

"What makes you think that? They wouldn't have had time anyway," the old Man's voice was reasonable. He was trying to calm John down.

"Why wouldn't they, sir? They may have direct W/T communication with U-boats through a German agent. You never know with these foreigners. They did their best to hold me up anyway."

"Did they? How?" asked Montolieu coldly. This was a Security matter, and he seemed to feel that John showed undue temerity in voicing such opinions. But John was in no mood to be cross-questioned.

"The pilot tried to make me foul the boom. That's how . . ." he growled ". . . deliberately went the wrong side of the buoy. I stopped engines at once and we slid over all right. If I hadn't, we'd have had the jack-stay round our screws and been stuck there all night for sure."

It certainly sounded strange that the pilot should have made a mistake over such an obvious seamark; but why should the enemy wish to delay *Akhtari* if they had a U-boat waiting for her? John, however, insisted that they had tried, by this method, to force him to make a daylight passage. He would then have offered the easiest target to a submerged U-boat, who would herself have been invisible to the sentries along the Turkish coast.

Soon we left the subject of *Akhtari* and her possible betrayal. John was clearly obsessed with a suspicion of all "foreigners"; in any case, he was a badly shaken man and in no condition for reasonable discussion.

"What's the best thing for lumbago?" he asked suddenly, groaning as he shifted in his seat.

"Cut your throat . . . they say it eases the pain." Jesse was trying to cheer him up, but failed signally.

Shortly afterwards the Old Man adjourned the meeting. He looked very determined and in no way disconcerted by the turn of events. John and the Russians got up wearily and shuffled out. Montolieu followed, presumably in the hope of further information.

"Hilton's had a bad time," muttered the Old Man, as soon as the door closed. "Won't be much good for this game any more, I'm afraid."

Jesse and I said nothing and the Old Man dismissed the question of John with a final shrug.

"Now come on," he said vigorously. "Let's get down to the

details of this business. Hilton's convinced, as you've just heard, that the Turks at Ak Bashi split on him. I don't believe it myself, nor does our Vice-Consul at Chanak. The only thing the Turks are anxious about is to preserve strict neutrality. Their secret service is first class, and the idea of a German agent in one of their military zones is absurd." He paused and turned to look at me. "I believe it was *Olinda* they were waiting for."

I gaped at him; but he went on talking with complete equanimity.

"Furthermore," he said, "it's quite likely that they still think it was *Olinda* that they did torpedo. They had no reason to expect any other vessel than *Olinda*, so they naturally assumed that it was her they'd sunk. I'm certain they didn't even know of *Akhtari*'s existence."

We considered the possibility for a moment. Then the Old Man announced the next move.

"It's the 11th to-day," he said. I want *Olinda* to leave here to-morrow evening . . . that will have given things three clear days to settle down. . . . She's to pass Cape Helles at dawn on January 13th. If all goes well with *Olinda*, *Tarkhan* is to sail p.m. on January 16th. . . . The new moon's just about then; we'll look it up in a moment."

Jesse and I started noting down his instructions on slips of paper.

"Now, if *Olinda* gets into trouble during the first or second day, *Tarkhan* is to sail at once, the same evening. . . . Is that clear?"

Jesse nodded. Then the Old Man turned to me.

". . . If anything *should* happen to *Olinda*," he said, "I'm hoping that the Huns will be preoccupied for at least twenty-four hours. . . ."

"Hacking the pieces up small enough to eat?" suggested Jesse.

The Old Man permitted himself a faint smile before continuing. "Now get this quite clear, Matheson. I want *Tarkhan* to stand well out to sea, and to pass *west* of Mitylene, Khios and Samos. She can spend her first day at anchor in the Gulf of Mandelyah. . . . Have got?"

Again Jesse nodded his head. *Olinda*, I noticed, was once more to be the stalking-horse; but the plan was undoubtedly a sound one, with a good chance of success.

"Well, that's the lot, I think. Sure you've got it all quite straight?"

"Yes, sir. *Olinda* at dawn on the 13th and proceed by day only. *Tarkhan* p.m. on the 16th, or at once if *Olinda* gets into trouble. *Tarkhan* to proceed by night, passing west of the coastal islands."

"That's it." The Old Man rose and started to put away the charts. Jesse helped him. "Thanks for that signal, by the way, Matheson; the one about *Akhtari* being sunk."

"Oh, you got it O.K., sir, did you?"

"Yes, it reached me *via* Alexandria, nearly eight hours before the Turks came up with a report from their Army at Cape Baba." Jesse and I both showed some concern at this revelation about the time taken for Turkish information to reach Istanbul; but the Old Man dismissed it with . . . "Oh, there's no need to worry about anything like that this time. I've straightened the whole thing out with the Turks. They're going to have the tankers carefully watched all the way down the coast, and any mishap to *Olinda* will be reported direct to our Vice-Consul here at Chanak, as well as to me at Istanbul. . . . So you'll know what's going on as soon as I do, Matheson."

At midnight that night, *Evangelistria* sailed for Istanbul, and Jesse and I went back to *Tarkhan*.

Although it was so late, there were still several people in the saloon. At one end of the long table the second mate and the W/T operator were drinking tea. Round the other end sat a group of four—the second engineer and the electrician, playing draughts with the third mate and a buxom stewardess; the latter was dressed in a white wrapper, with a kerchief tied round her hair. They all greeted us in a friendly fashion, as we entered, and the W/T operator waved us to join them, while the stewardess went good-naturedly for more tea.

"Home comforts laid on in this ship," observed Jesse, winking at the stewardess as she set a cup of tea before him.

"Looks as if you're going to have an amusing trip," I agreed.

"Yea; but that one's nothing," he replied, with a sideways nod of his head at the retreating figure of the stewardess. "You ought to see the doctor."

"A woman doctor?"

"Sure, and what a woman! She may be a smart doctor as

well, but I ain't worryin'. She's a man-eating blonde with blue eyes and, oh boy, has she got personality?" Jesse rolled his own eyes, and made a gesture with both hands that seemed to have very little to do with the doctor's mental attributes.

18

NEXT morning I went back to *Olinda*. Jesse had been most impressed with her disguise, by the way; he had sworn that she was quite unrecognisable. She certainly looked a fairly normal cargo vessel, and I had felt considerably encouraged by her appearance from a little way off.

The Master and Mate were there to meet me as I climbed aboard, and so was the ferocious Malu, who had to be prevented, by main force, from flying at my throat. The Master swore at her and kicked her shrewdly in the belly; then he picked up a piece of wood and hurled it. She scuttled away with a yelp, and stationed herself on the poop, from which position she continued to offer vociferous threats and insults.

During the day I met the rest of the crew of *Olinda*; among them the two Chinese greasers, one of whom, called Mickey, was a lively little fellow with the heart of a lion and an unquenchable sense of humour. He had already been bombed out of Shanghai, bombed at sea and bombed into the anchorage at Suez; but seemed quite happy to risk a further dose. The other greaser was a tall, quiet individual, who did as he was bid at all times, though without any obvious pleasure.

The six Arab sailors were also quiet men, soft-eyed and friendly; but I noticed that they were going about their tasks with a certain sullenness. This seemed to portend a deputation from the forecastle—possibly at some awkward moment; so I told the Maltese storekeeper, who spoke Arabic, to ask the men whether they had any complaints.

After a long and vehement speech by the leader of the Arabs, the storekeeper turned to me.

"They say the Russians calling them 'Plotty Araps—Plotty Araps'—all the time."

"Tell them that 'Plotty' is the Russian for sweet-smelling."

He told the Arabs, and they retired in sorrowful resignation.

But a moment later there arose from the starboard alleyway the sound of a violent quarrel. It turned out that the senior Arab, whom I suspected of knowing more colloquial English than was good for him, had called the quieter of the two Chinese greasers a "Plotty yellow pansy." It began to look as though I would be faced with a most unmanageable mob in the event of a crisis. I thought with envy of the courageous, well-disciplined Russian crews of John's and Jesse's ships.

I was a little reassured, however, on meeting *Olinda*'s Bosun. He was a man who worked heavily, continuously, and with ferocity. When the Mate introduced us, the Bosun only paused for a moment to shake hands, then fell once more to his work of securing the dummy hatches. He looked the very best type of Russian—strong, reliable, willing, calm and clearly a prime seaman in any weather. I felt that, in emergency, the Bosun could be depended upon to keep his head. The only other man about whose courage and reliability I felt entirely confident was Ivan Oreshkin, the second engineer. Incommon with the Bosun, Ivan spoke only Russian, so we had not exchanged more than a nod and a smile since the day we first met; but I was taken with his energetic, intelligent face, his wiry frame—lithe and keen as a blade—and with his dashing, if somewhat insolent, bearing.

After tea, the Bosun and I walked round to test the staying of the jury mast, and to examine the lashings on the dummy hatches and derricks. When faced with the everyday problems of seamanship, I found that we understood each other perfectly; the language difficulty disappeared and, with it, any chance of future misunderstandings. I looked forward, therefore, with renewed confidence to the time of *Olinda*'s sailing, which had been fixed for five o'clock that evening.

The weather had been fine and clear all day, with a moderate easterly wind. Towards sunset the wind died, but the sky remained cloudless. It looked as though we were in for a spell of summery weather; forerunner of the spring which would begin in February.

I went to the monkey island, my little fortress at the summit of the ship's superstructure, and sat myself down in the deck-chair, with which I had been thoughtfully provided by the Master. I saw the Master now, pacing up and down the poop, his dog following humbly behind him. Whenever she got a little ahead of him, he gave her a kick that made her flinch away and then fall in again at his heels. No wonder Malu was bad-tempered, I reflected.

I found it difficult to decide upon the true character of this enormous man. His size and weight gave one an impression of great strength which did not necessarily imply steady nerves or abnormal powers of endurance. I watched him bend down to look in at the chicken-coop, where he kept a cockerel and a dozen hens. These chickens were under the Master's personal care. He took a special pride in them, for he was a vegetarian; the Old Man had mentioned this fact to me some weeks before; I remembered it now with surprise as I noted the Master's powerful frame and the fierce expression on his face.

For ten minutes or more, the Master squatted upon his haunches by the chicken-coop, apparently talking to the hens. He wore a cloth cap, which sat very flat upon his square, bald head, leaving a wrinkled brown nakedness from the collar of his shirt upwards.

The sun appeared to lean for a moment upon the shoulders of the hills to westward. The mountains of Gallipoli turned purple and then black against the orange light. Farther to the left stood a second group of crags, on the southern side of the Dardanelles. At the foot of these crags, I knew, were scattered the ruins of ancient Troy—the scene of a siege more memorable even than the allied attempt in 1915 upon the Gallipoli peninsular. And now they were surrounded again, these hard-bitten old Turks. I wondered whether there would soon be yet another savage struggle—to hold the Germans at the Dardanelles, the Russians on the Bosphorus or ourselves in the Taurus Passes.

The sun dipped and the light began to fade. Away forward a figure in blue overalls and a red woollen skull-cap climbed on to the forecastle head. The man looked about him, then I heard the thin, shrill sounds of the other Arabs, prattling softly together. Soon they all gathered upon the forecastle head to pray. Down they went, upon their knees on the deck, and for many minutes they prayed in unison; now bowing down to touch the iron plates with their foreheads, now sitting back upon their heels to face the east, where the first dark shoals of dusk were swimming upwards over Anatolia.

.   .   .   .   .

It was nearly dark when *Olinda* moved out of the bay.

As we passed *Tarkhan*, there was a friendly cheer from her ship's company and an answering cheer from ours. I saw Jesse leaning on the poop rail with, beside him, a young woman whose shining blonde head and mellow figure, set off by a bright blue sweater, called for closer inspection through binoculars. As soon as Jesse saw me raise my glasses, he began to semaphore. "HOW AM I DOING?" read Jesse's message. But before I could reply, his companion had turned and disappeared into the accommodation, with Jesse hurrying after her.

It might have afforded me some transient pleasure, had I known that throughout the ensuing voyage in *Tarkhan*, Jesse would never succeed in being alone with this gorgeous being . . . except, that is, on the three or four occasions when he was obliged to lie face downwards on his bunk, while she stabbed him dexterously in the bottom with a hypodermic syringe— the cure she had chosen for a painful and inconveniently situated crop of boils, to which Jesse unhappily fell victim. But there! I did not know it. . . . I only knew that Malu was barking furiously, that the Arabs were gazing sadly at the shore, and that the song of *Olinda*'s engines was growing louder, more urgent, like the beat of the war drums, sounding the tribes to battle. . . .

"Stop her." The musical throb of the engines slowed to silence. *Olinda* drove on, her bow wave stilled to gentle wavelets slapping against her sides. Then she settled into the calm water between black mountains, her stem pointing steadily at the green buoy flashing ahead.

The pilot came aboard and *Olinda* proceeded through the boom.

I spoke to the pilot for a moment before he left us. He was

a brown-skinned, fierce-eyed little Turk—polite but proudly neutral. He gave me a last note from the consul at Chanak:

> I have heard that Lieutenant Commander Hilton believes the pilots gave him away, when he passed this way in *Akhtari* [ran the letter]. I think he is mistaken. They are a trustworthy crowd, who hate and despise the Italians.
> If you get as far as the Gulf of Doris, please send me back a few combs of wild honey. I used to go there every year before the war to collect it. . . .

Olinda, with her engines turning once again at the revolutions for normal full speed, seemed nevertheless to do no more than creep across the glassy water. Off Chanak the gulf narrowed until there was scarcely a mile from shore to shore at the point where Leander must have swum the Hellespont. Then it broadened again, and eleven miles away to the westward we could see the two famous Capes of Helles and Kum Kale, nearly touching —Europe nearly touching Asia, but never quite. I stopped one engine, and rang down "*slow*" on the other, allowing *Olinda* to drift gently westward.

There had been no trouble of any sort at the boom, in spite of John's gloomy prophecies; so we now had three or four hours to kill before it was time to pass Cape Helles. I had not really expected any bother at Ak Bashi; but just to make quite certain that *Olinda*'s false identity could not be signalled or told to anyone, I had arranged, before sailing, for tarpaulins to be draped, with apparent negligence, over the bows and stern, so that the Turkish boom-pilots should not be able to see the actual name under which *Olinda* was to travel.

Whether the pilots had been in any way surprised at *Olinda*'s odd appearance I could not tell; but anyway we were clear at last . . . and, without any W/T, beyond recall! Beyond the reach of any distant and nebulous authorities who might, without even knowing very much about *Olinda* or the special problem confronting her, suddenly include her in a general order to all shipping in the Mediterranean. I had suffered from such signals before, and was to suffer from them many times again . . . no situation report attached to them, of course, nor any intelligence summary; no means by which the man on the spot might know how to modify his action so as to suit existing conditions and, at the same time, conform with his Commander-in-Chief's general intentions. Ah well, I thought, we're safe from all that now; and I suppose it's only natural for staff officers to be more concerned with the wide and immediate broadcasting of their golden commands—natural, but often disconcerting to the lonely suckling in "faerie seas forlorn."

At 3.30 a.m. we had less than four miles to go to Kum Kale. A waning chip of a moon was well up the sky, and there was the first hint of dawn above the hills astern. It was time to increase speed again. I spoke down the voice pipe and soon, with the engines rung on "full ahead together," *Olinda*'s bow-wave went sagging out again into the darkness on either hand, till she looked like a frolicsome old porpoise, balancing upon her nose in the bight of a phosphorescent tight-rope.

At 5.20 a.m. a small searchlight from Cape Helles suddenly split the twilight and the beam settled full upon us. We held upon our course, but I swore beneath my breath. I had hoped to slip out of the Dardanelles, unseen by any U-boat lurking off the entrance. None the less I was equally unwilling, perhaps illogically, to buy off this infuriating searchlight by lifting the tarpaulins and displaying, to anyone who might be watching, the false name *Orak* painted on *Olinda*'s bows. It was soon clear, however, that the ship's name was precisely what the Turks at Cape Helles were most anxious to discover, for the narrow beam of the searchlight settled upon her bow and remained there.

Hastily I grabbed an electric torch and started signalling. A light from the shore winked in answer; so, with my hand shading the torch from seaward, I made the name "OLINDA" in morse. This, however, did not satisfy them. The searchlight began to waggle peremptorily, to and fro, across our tarpaulin-covered bow. Then it jerked irritably to the bridge, where I was standing, and back again to the bow with a vicious flick. One could almost feel, in its movements, the exasperation of the Coast Defence Battery commander, and of the man who was handling the light.

But *Olinda* stood stubbornly on; albeit anxiously for, having heard the grim tale of John's misfortunes, we half expected one of the guns ashore to open fire at any moment.

10

Soon we were due south of Cape Helles, and it was time to turn. "Steer one nine seven degrees," I shouted down the voice-pipe in my best Russian. *Olinda* turned very slowly to port and, in so doing, presented a raggedly draped behind to the Turkish Army. The possibility of "violent exchanges" between our Embassy and the Turks, on account of this further insult, did not worry me unduly. I felt that our diplomatic boys at Ankara were paid to deal with such eventualities. The searchlight shone upon us for a few seconds longer; then gave one or two last infuriated waggles, and went out . . . leaving *Olinda*, like a little old man with his shirt tail hanging, to waddle ingloriously away into the Aegean.

IV

TROUBLED WATERS

19

LESS than an hour later we were abreast of the Rabbit Islands, and the sun was about to burst above the plain of Troy. The islands beside us were a favourite lurking-ground for our own and enemy submarines, when they were watching for ships leaving the Dardanelles. I did not doubt that the U-boat which had sunk John had waited for him among the Rabbit Islands and had then overtaken him, on the surface, at Cape Baba.

But I was not expecting to be attacked just yet. In the words of old Mathews, there was "no use getting in a panic just because we've lost one ship. *Olinda*'s disguise'll be much more effective if they aren't expecting her—if they think she's at the bottom of the sea." I kept a bright look-out for a periscope, but I was in the most carefree of moods and, when the sun rose over the land, I began to sing happily to myself and to pace about my little island kingdom. What had we to worry about in any case? The ship was bowling along with more than a knot of fair current to help her; the Master himself was at the wheel; the frosty haze upon a windless sea was already shot with morning sunlight, and melting before us; and, best of all, there came Ah Fong's great split pumpkin of a face, poking above the edge of the monkey island, followed by a huge plate of fried eggs, bacon and chips.

By the time I had finished my breakfast, we had Gadaro lighthouse close aboard to starboard, and course was altered ten degrees to port to bring the distant bluff of Cape Baba very fine upon the inshore bow.

The sky, by now, was clear as crystal, and the sea had freshened from grey, through silver, to peacock blue. . . . As the sun climbed higher, the blue of the sea also deepened and grew brighter; the slopes of the hills shone green—the green of downland in early spring, with here and there a dappling of pine forest, or a tuft of crags and boulders. Abeam of us now, to starboard, was the precipitous Turkish island of Tenedos, with its port facing east, and a small town swarming round it. Square houses of every hue clustered about the harbour; green, red, blue, white and yellow, gay and friendly in the sunlight, like a handful of marzipan cubes strewn among the rocks.

Another ten miles down the coast and we were skirting the shoals off Cape Eski Stambul. The sun was well up and shining on the ruins of Alexandria Troas. In the Acts, chapter xvi, St. Paul's friends had . . . *sailed away from Phillipi . . . and come unto them to Troas in five days.*

Far out upon the western horizon were two tiny specks of white, the sails of two *caiques*, hull down and heading eastwards like the followers of St. Paul. I raised my binoculars to inspect them. By the way the sails bellied and the masts leaned towards the south, there seemed to be more wind out there.

I looked again at the land. It was rising now in layer upon layer of pine-covered ridges, whose sides had grown more rugged and precipitous; at Cape Baba it would be over sixteen hundred feet high. What sturdy legs old Paul must have had; from Troas his friends had gone . . . *before to ship, and sailed unto Assos, there intending to take in Paul: for so had he appointed, minding himself to go afoot.* . . . The ruins of Assos were marked on the chart near Katagar Point, thirteen miles east of Cape Baba. At eight knots we would be off Assos before 11 o'clock. A *caique*, like the one in which St. Paul used to sail, would easily make seven knots in a decent breeze. I glanced again at the *caiques* on the western horizon, and saw that they were already much closer—standing down towards Cape Baba before a spanking nor'westerly breeze. They were, no doubt, traders from Lemnos; I remembered, with mild interest, that in the Island of Lemnos was the headquarters of the main German garrison of the northern Aegean; these *caiques*, then, would be sailing under German orders, carrying stores to the seaplane base at Mitylene or cargo for some Turkish port.

Between Troas and Cape Baba I started to make up a nursery rhyme to send to the children for Easter. . . .

> There once was a pussy cat wimbling round
> > the top of a garden wall.
> The wall was thick and of brutish brick
> > 'Gainst the jungly jiggers that crawl—and all,
> > 'Gainst the fungling jungle and all.

A tiger came roaring ravenously, through the darkth
 of the forest nearby.
He was longing to lunch, with a slushety crunch,
 off a pibly fat pussy so high—oh, my!
Could I springle and scloop her? I'll try.

At this point I took up my binoculars again and searched the
sea ahead, and all the way round . . . no tigers . . . no jungly
jiggers, as far as I could tell . . . only a couple of glinting
caique sails and calm blue sea, all the way to the horizon. *Olinda*
went wimbling along contentedly, and I tried another verse of
my poem. . . .

Ho! Ho! said the pussy cat, humping free,
 with a smile round the end of its nose. . . .

Out of the corner of my eye I thought I saw a winking flash
of light from the direction of the two *caiques*. I picked up my
glasses again, and inspected them closely, but there was no
sign now of any signalling between them.

At Cape Baba we closed the land to within a cable. The
chart showed the headland to be clear of any off-lying shoals.
On such a brilliant day, in any case, one could pick out shoal
water by its colour, in plenty of time to avoid it. This was an
excellent opportunity to make a close inspection of the coast
in case I ever had to use it at night; and, besides, I wanted to
make sure that there could be no misunderstanding about
whether or not *Olinda* was inside the limits of territorial waters.

At the very tip of the headland, upon a crag two hundred
feet high, stood a massive fort. Beside it I saw a small Turkish
ensign, flauntering from the top of a gaily painted staff. On our
seaward side, the two *caiques* had closed rapidly, and were easily
overtaking us. They were about three miles off, and standing
in to cross *Olinda*'s bows as she rounded the Cape. I saw now
that, above their blue-and-white Greek ensigns, they flew a
small pendant with red-and-white quarterings, and realised at
once that these were German store-carriers or patrol *caiques*.
They seemed to have a crew of ordinary islanders and, yes—
there were figures in field-grey uniform, German guards, in
the stern-sheets of the nearest *caique*; they would be armed with
a machine-gun or *schmeizers* and rifles. I could also see that

the *caiques* had powerful engines, for they were creaming along at a good nine knots.

Glancing up at the fort, now towering above us, I noticed a small crowd of Turkish soldiers, collected beside the flag-staff to watch us pass. One of them waved, and I heard a whistle blown shrilly once or twice. I looked again to starboard, and observed that the *caiques* were standing across towards us, as if to inspect us closely. This was a nuisance; it was doubtful whether our disguise would stand up to so careful a study at close quarters. There was shoal water jutting, just beyond the point—four fathoms or less by the colour; the chart showed three. *Olinda* was drawing eighteen feet (three fathoms) aft, so we turned her to port and she began to skirt the very fringe of the bank.

In turning, *Olinda* had put the *caiques* right astern for the moment; but they were coming up fast, with the obvious intention of passing down her starboard side. Suddenly there was another loud whistle from the fort, then three shots rang out. I swung round in time to see the splashes in the water, almost alongside the leading *caique*. With one accord the *caiques* went hard a-starboard, gybed in considerable disorder, and stood out to sea. Ten minutes later they had altered course again, and were heading for the Island of Mitylene.

Between Cape Baba and the ruins of Assos I set a tune to my nursery rhyme, singing loudly and happily with a hot sun full in my face.

From Katagar Point the mountains climbed gradually east-ward towards the black summit of Mount Ida, twenty-five miles away, at the head of the Gulf of Adramyti. All the after-noon I lay in my deck-chair, reflecting idly that, if this were war, I was content to let it drag on for some time. I read a few more chapters of the Acts, to see how St. Paul had fared on his *caique* trip down this coast.

> And when he met with us at Assos, we took him in and came to Mitylene.
> We sailed thence, and came next *day* over against Chios; and the next *day* we arrived at Samos, and tarried at Trogyllium; and the next *day* we came to Miletus.

That was the way to do it—no hurry, no fuss; I hoped

Olinda would come to Miletus, at the mouth of the Meander River, in the very same stages.

Throughout the afternoon we held on, down the northern coast of the Gulf of Adramyti. We were in no hurry to cross it until it became less than six miles wide, so that there could be no question of our leaving Turkish waters on the way over; for, once we left those waters, we could legally be stopped and examined by enemy patrol craft, and I was a little worried about the possibility of our having been "rumbled" by the patrol *caiques* off Cape Baba. So we kept close to the Turkish shore, as though we were bound for Edremit (or Adramyti) at the head of the Gulf; and when, at 2 p.m., we reached the anchorage abreast of that port, we gave our movements a touch of realism by anchoring, as though we had cargo to load or discharge. At 4 p.m. we weighed again and steered south-west towards Cape Kara Tepeh. On our journey westwards down the southern side of the gulf, we watched the haughty ranks of the Myssian mountains turn cold and darken against the sky. Light mist grew upon the sea beneath them, thickening as the night approached.

Suddenly, jet black against the distant hills, a tiny aircraft came spinning up the fjord. It was a monoplane on floats—a German Arado. Was it on routine reconnaissance, I wondered, or had it been sent to look for something? When it reached the head of the gulf, it banked steeply and flew away westwards again, towards Cape Baba, where it disappeared in the glare of sunset. A few minutes later we saw it reappear, much higher and travelling very fast from north to south, across Mitylene. Its engines stopped, and it began to glide; we lost sight of it finally behind the Mosko Islands.

We were not unduly disturbed by this incident; the aircraft had not taken the trouble to examine us closely, and our confidence in the effectiveness of *Olinda*'s disguise was, if anything, strengthened.

It was quite dark by the time we reached the northern side of Mosko Island, which we skirted closely, from point to point, keeping a background of black cliffs against the possibility of an E-boat lurking round the corner. One by one the islets to the south'ard came out clear of Pyrgo Island. A filmy strand of mist wreathed out of Ayvali Bay and spread, in drifts and

layers, over the Mitylene Channel, so that the tops of the
islets showed above it, like small rocks floating in the still night
air. Together they looked like a crowd of boats at first; so we
altered course to port, round the northern point of Pyrgo, and
crept down between the islands of Kalimo and Leiah. Then,
over the corner of Gymno Island, we raised the flashing red
light of Ali Burnu and anchored soon afterwards in sixteen
fathoms.

Next morning, an hour before dawn, the officers gathered
in the saloon for coffee. They were all there—the Master,
smiling quickly and awkwardly every now and then; Feodar
Pavlovitch, sitting grave and bright-eyed like an old heron; the
Mate, looking tired and a little more bent than before; Ivan
Oreshkin, his keen face wrinkling humorously. Ah Fong came
in beaming with the coffee and some hot cakes he had made
specially.

"Good morning. Fine day," pronounced Ah Fong, with a
giggle.

"Good job," said the Master. "You have coffee, mister?"
Ah Fong poured some out for me. The Mate offered me cakes
and then handed them round. Feodar Pavlovitch raised his
eyebrows, with an expression of rather odd fastidiousness, and
took one daintily between finger and thumb. Throughout the
meal Ivan Oreshkin sat apart—watching us all with darting
eyes that only sometimes smiled.

On the way to the bridge I passed the Maltese storekeeper,
Zamit, with his nephew, Johnny Caruana, smirking shyly
in the background. Zamit began at once to bombard me with
questions which he hastily answered himself; also comments
upon the weather, the voyage, the officers and crew. His
ardent stream of broken English continued without a pause
for nearly a minute.

"Us three, the only British on board," he proclaimed proudly,
at the end of it all, and I got the impression that he wished to
make it clear that he and his nephew were not seamen by
trade (which I had already decided), that their presence on
board was due only to a sudden urge of patriotism (which had
not occurred to me), and that we three ought to stick together
if there were any trouble.

I disengaged myself from the situation, which had become embarrassing; but I was touched none the less by Zamit's remarks. His blind right eye, which was jammed in the "hard a-port" position, gave him a permanent look of rather hideous ingratiation. Some of his remarks, however, had sounded quite genuine; he seemed pathetically eager for adventures in the cause of British glory—adventures which had never come his way during the forty years he had spent as the proprietor of a ship-chandlery business in Istanbul.

It appeared that Zamit and his nephew had both volunteered for the Navy in 1940, at the ages of 54 and 32 respectively. They had been bullying the British Consul at Istanbul about it ever since, and their presence on board Olinda was the ultimate result of this bullying. But Zamit was an inveterate chatterer, rather unhealthy and abominably thick-skinned, so I made up my mind to keep him at arm's length as long as I could.

At dawn Olinda weighed and headed for the narrow gap between Ali Burnu and the shore. The Bosun was at the wheel; the Master stood in the starboard wing of the bridge. The sun rose upon another cloudless day as we rounded Tuz Burnu and went chugging merrily eastward into Suna Bay.

A few miles farther on, there lay a patch of shoals round the end of a sandspit. Abreast of them, on the chart, was printed a cautionary note to warn mariners that these shoals had not recently been examined, and were reported to have extended considerably. One is inclined to treat such warnings lightly at times; but, being fairly hopeful that the ship had not so far aroused enemy suspicions, I felt it advisable to increase our distance from the shore before passing Suna Spit.

Near the foreshore there was a small hill, 440 feet high, which, if kept in transit with the 623-foot peak of Mosko Island, would lead us well clear of the shoals. So, just as the two peaks were coming together, the helm was put hard a-starboard, and, by the time Olinda had steadied on a course of 166°, the hills were in one, and dead astern. The sun had by now climbed well above Mount Sailejek; fine on the port bow were the black buttresses of Mount Karadagh, while Cape Mal-tepeh lay ahead. It was a sparkling bright morning, full of promise for a glorious day. On board Olinda there was the exhilarating smell of cooking breakfast and the sound of Ah Fong in his galley, singing a gay and barbarous chanty.

All at once we saw our friend the Arado seaplane, climbing over Mitylene's Mount Olympus to starboard. We watched him as he circled the island and then flew north, towards the Gulf of Adramyti. "Poor old Fritz," I thought to myself, smiling indulgently after him. "They get him out of bed early for these patrols." I saw the Arado turn and come back down the Mitylene Channel at about 3,000 feet and still climbing. Then another seaplane took off from Mitylene—a heavy old Dornier this time. It climbed south towards the Gulf of Izmir. Five minutes later both aircraft turned north again, and flew up the Channel together at about 5,000 feet.

Olinda was in the middle of Suna Bay, at her farthest (about two miles) from the Turkish shore, when the Arado suddenly banked and flew east across her stern; then banked again, and came diving down almost vertically upon her.

I watched him with little more than faint amusement as he grew rapidly in size. Soon I could hear the rising whine of his engine. This chap was bored, I thought, with endless patrolling, and in the mood to show us a few tricks, or to use us for dive-bombing practice. He held on till he was no more than a thousand feet above us and still diving straight for the bridge. A little prickle of alarm began to stir in me. "Come on. Pull out, you idiot," I heard myself mutter. Then suddenly I saw them—two yellow blobs, dropping clear beneath his wing. Next instant there was a shattering roar as the aircraft flattened out overhead. I ducked. There were two simultaneous explosions as a couple of grey and white columns of water leaped up close to *Olinda*'s port bow.

20

"HARD A-PORT!" "Stop port!"
A cascade of spray swept the foredeck.

"So that's that," I said to myself. "The Huns seem to have had us sized up after all." My first feeling was one of intense embarrassment. What fools we looked in our complicated disguise and our prim concern over remaining inside territorial waters. The ship's head was steadied on Aspira Point where we could see the red flag of a Turkish look-out post; then I went down to the Master's cabin to find another chart. I was promptly nipped in the calf by Malu, who no doubt wished to make sure that she was not forgotten in the general excitement. The Master came in and kicked her under the table, where she remained snarling furiously.

The Master's face was white and strangely pinched. I felt that mine was too; our complete defencelessness against attack was utterly discouraging. I felt, creeping over me, that dangerous forerunner of despair—that lassitude and inability to concentrate on immediate tasks. I goaded myself on in the knowledge that the feeling would ultimately pass. For the Master, however, this was the very first taste of war, and he felt both embarrassed and annoyed at finding himself so shaken. He felt he had to talk, make a joke, or try to appear unnaturally careless. I turned to the chart, striving to think clearly and to control the impulse to rush out on deck again, to resume the fruitless sky-gazing which instinct suggested.

The Master giggled on a high-pitched note that sounded very odd coming from so large a man. I glanced up at him quickly.

"I laugh now," he said, "when I think of my wife. She was all time in Odessa when the Germans was bombing." He started to giggle again.

"It doesn't sound very funny," I suggested.

"Ha ha ha! She live hundred metres from big ammunition factory."

I must have looked a bit puzzled; but I smiled at him, hoping that he would elucidate.

"It make me laugh now," he went on, his voice growing shrill and strained . . . "when I think of her in all that bombing. . . . She has weak heart!" . . . and he burst into fits of hysterical guffaws.

My immediate reaction to the situation in which we now found ourselves, was a determination not to be panicked into any hasty abandoning of the disguise under which *Olinda* had commenced this voyage. It seemed likely that the Germans might still be persuaded that they had been wrong about

Olinda's identity, provided that she continued to behave like a small Turkish ship which had been most unjustly attacked. For this reason we had turned towards the Turkish beach post on Aspira Point. I decided also to augment our appearance of injured innocence by going ashore in the boat, in full view of the enemy, as though bent upon lodging a formal complaint, or on calling upon the soldiers there to bear witness to this outrage upon an inoffensive Turkish vessel.

I took the chart up to the monkey island. As I passed through the wheelhouse, I felt a little thrill of grateful admiration over the impassive figure of the Bosun, standing like a rock behind the wheel. His cap was perched carelessly on the back of his head, a cigarette was drooping from one corner of his mouth, and he was gazing steadily at the compass without a thought, it appeared, for anything but his duty in keeping the ship upon her course.

When I reached the monkey island, I noticed that both aircraft were together again and patrolling in short sweeps up and down the Mitylene Channel. We were less than a mile from the beach now; so, without wasting any time, I told the Bosun to put the helm to starboard and *Olinda* grounded gently on the sandbanks off Aspira Point. Next I went down to find the old Mate. He looked sad but friendly, and agreed to lower the working-boat for me. The Arabs, who were standing in an anxiously jabbering group near the forecastle, came aft to swing out the boat. Johnny Caruana was detailed to pull me ashore.

Feodor Pavlovitch was in the engine-room, with Ivan Oreshkin beside him. As I entered, the latter darted a quizzical, half-smiling glance at me and turned away. I told Feodor Pavlovitch to start pumping at once so that the ship would be afloat by the time I returned; then I went into my cabin and put on my gaudy purple suit and my biscuit-coloured hat.

As soon as the boat was shoved clear of the ship's side and headed inshore, the Arado peeled off once again and came tearing in at sea-level towards us. Johnny Caruana looked uncertain about what to do, but I felt sure the Hun was bluffing, so I told Johnny to keep on pulling towards the beach. The Arado screamed over us at less than fifty feet; the rush of air and hot exhaust fumes swept the boat, forcing me to clutch at my precious hat; but his machine-guns remained silent, and we knew then that he would not attack us again in full view of the Turks—that he might, in fact, still be uncertain of our identity. The Arado circled round and came in once again. This time I heard two puny reports from the beach post, and saw a couple of Turkish soldiers, crouching in a trench, their rifles poking skywards in a gesture of futile defiance.

Our conversation with the Turkish soldiers was brief. There were only two of them, a corporal and a private, and they had already reported the whole incident by field telephone to their battalion headquarters. They also had orders for us. "He say Turkish Colonel order all people to come on shore because Germans will now destroy ship," interpreted Johnny Caruana.

Even if this prophecy had been correct, it was obviously out of the question for us to comply with such an order. As it was, I did not think it worth arguing about, so I turned away, signing to Johnny to follow me. But a Turkish soldier is well disciplined, even though he may often be a primitive mountain tribesman, without any powers of judgment. The moment we began to move off, the corporal made an angry remark and covered us with his rifle.

"He say we cannot return to ship," said Johnny, with an anxious look in his eye.

"How can we tell the rest to come ashore then? Ask him that," I returned impatiently. "He can come with us if he likes."

After a while Johnny managed to persuade the corporal to let us go, and we returned to the boat just as the Arado came in for a third run over us. As the aircraft approached, I saw the other soldier heave what looked like an ancient Bren gun on to the nearest parapet of the small trench. He sighted it at the aircraft, but did not fire, although the Hun roared past almost on top of the beach post.

"Why doesn't he open fire?" I asked. "They're here to enforce Turkish neutrality aren't they?"

But the corporal merely shrugged his shoulders as he replied to Johnny's translation of my remark:

"Gun no good," explained Johnny. "English gun. The corporal ask, can you fix?"

When they brought it to me, I saw at once that the magazine

The author (right) as an officer in the Royal Naval Reserve during World War Two

Olinda

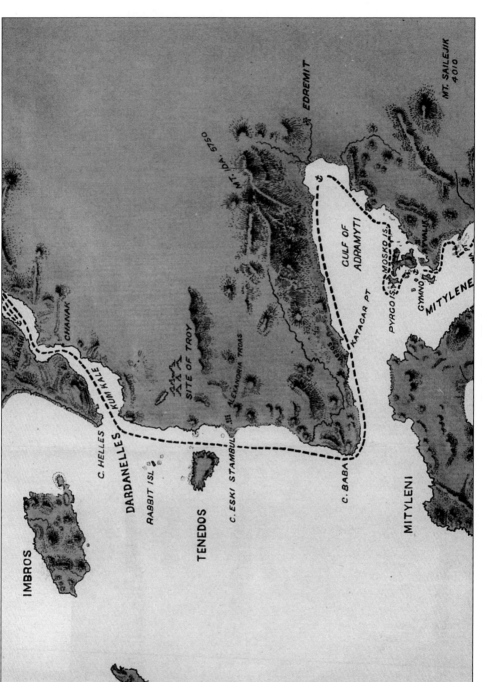

Dardanelles to Mitylene

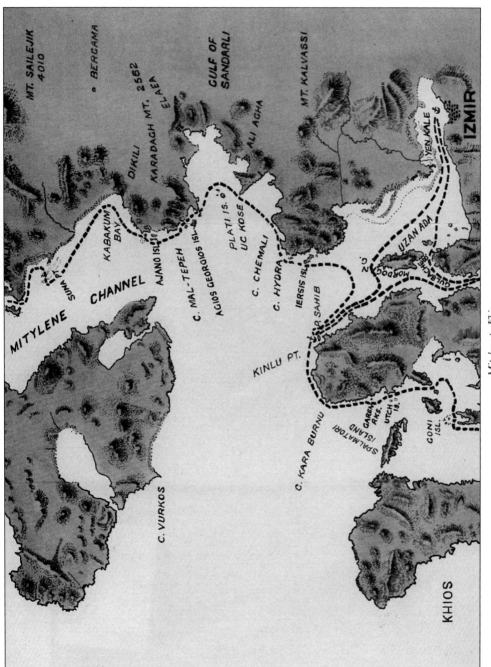

Mitylene to Khios

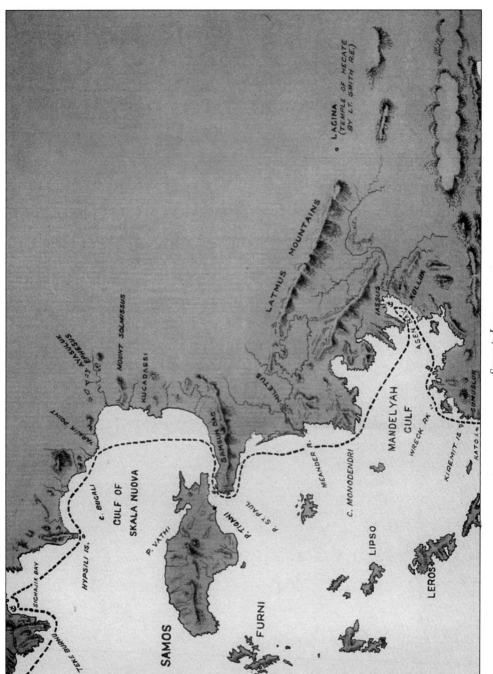

Samos to Leros

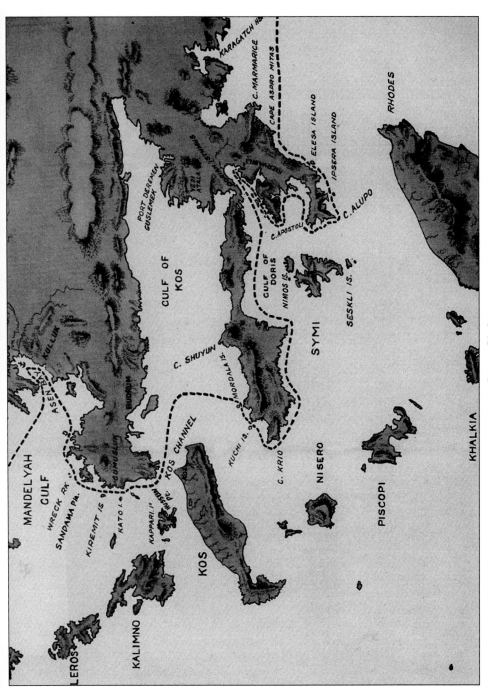

Leros to Rhodes

Fethieh to Adalia

Any further communication should
be addressed to—

The Director of Navy Accounts.
Northwick Park Hutments.
Watford Road. Harrow.

quoting Admiralty Reference " DNA No. 2. LV 6. 12. 41.
on the outside of the envelope as well as in
the text

Your Reference :

Admiralty.

2 February 1946

Sir,

Advance of Travelling Expenses.

It is understood that on 6th December 1941, you
received an advance of travelling expenses £T.50 (£6.17.5d)
from the Naval Attache, Ankara (through Consul, Adana).

Information regarding this advance did not reach
this department until November 1944, and on 9th November 1944
a request was sent to H.M.S. COTTESMORE for an account of
the expenditure of this advance.

In reply to this communication it was stated that
an account had been furnished to the Naval Attache, Ankara,
(through A.N.A. Istanbul) on December 9th or 10th 1941, and
that full details of all advances made to you at Ankara
between 6th December 1941 and 6th July 1942 were subsequently
forwarded to NILE for accounting action, which was then taken
by NILE.

It has not been possible, however, to trace this
accounting action, and the Supply Officer, NILE is unable to
state, at this late date, where recovery has been made.

I have therefore, to request that you will be good
enough to furnish as many details as can be remembered of the
journey in question, including period involved and route taken,
in order that the advance may be cleared in the books of this
Department.

I am, Sir,
Your obedient Servant,

Commander
Lieutenant A. C. Seligman, R.N.R.,
Salvage Department,
London.

DIRECTOR OF NAVY ACCOUNTS.

5th March 1946.

Sir,

With reference to your letter D.N.A. No. 2LV 6.12.41., since "as many details as can be remembered.....including period involved and route taken" are asked for, I am forwarding the full account of my journey which, by a strange coincidence, I have just completed in manuscript form.

2.   Although this manuscript may contain some pages not wholly relevant to the work of your department, it should nevertheless give you a good idea of the general circumstances of the journey.   The drawings of Konstance Pares, who knows Turkey well anddid in fact flit from time to time through the background of this operation and the maps of Commander A.T. Harrison, R.N.R. will, it is hoped, both brighten and clarify the narrative.

3.   In order not to embarrass or involve my friends in any way in this matter, I have peopled my story with a set of composite characters.   But the incidents recorded all actually happened to some of us at some time or other.

I am, Sir,
Your obedient servant,

A. C. Selig---

To The Director of Navy Accounts,
Northwick Park Hutments,
Watford Road,
Harrow.

was hopelessly distorted, and that the gun looked like a "drill purposes only" weapon. From the Arado's behaviour, it seemed as though the pilot knew that this was the case.

On the way back to the ship, I began to wonder about the unpredictable temper of *Olinda*'s crew. Most of them were badly rattled, and the fact that so few of them had any common language would make them difficult to control in the event of a general panic. I had no idea what their reactions would be if they heard that we had been ordered, there and then, to abandon ship; so, considering it wiser not to let them hear, I spoke earnestly to Johnny.

"Whatever happens," I said. "You are not to mention a word of our conversation with the Turks to anyone on board— not even to your uncle. D'you understand?" Johnny looked unhappy but promised that he would do as I told him, and I had to be content with his assurance.

It was now necessary to decide upon an immediate plan of action.

There were two courses open to us. . . .

(1) To stand on down the coast in the hope that the Germans were bluffing.

(2) To return to the port of Ayvalik, close by, and make a fresh attempt to slip down—*by night*.

The objection to the first plan was that the German aircraft had several times passed so close to the ship that they must have been able to read the name *Orak*, so boldly painted upon *Olinda*'s bow and stern. It would take their agents in Turkey less than twenty-four hours to find out the whereabouts of the true *Orak*. After that, *Olinda*'s doom would be sealed. She could either be attacked openly, farther down the coast, with our own Fleet Air Arm's regrettable attack on a Vichy French ship off Adalia as the pretext. Alternatively, a submerged U-boat could quietly pop a couple of torpedoes into us without showing herself at all.

For this reason, and possibly also because I had always preferred the idea of a night passage, I chose the second alternative. I was encouraged in this by the fact that the moon was nearly new, so the darkest nights were therefore at hand.

By the time we reached *Olinda*, the pumps had been going for close upon an hour, and she was already afloat; so she was

11

turned 'short round' to port, and course was immediately set
for Tuz Burnu. The Arabs looked exceedingly gloomy; but
they were not required to steer nor to work the engines, so
their nervousness did not matter a great deal, so long as they
remained calm. And calm they remained; for Johnny whispered no word about the Turkish orders; he stood rather
importantly on the lower bridge all the way back to Tuz
Burnu, and the sight of him awoke in me a new admiration
for his loyal Maltese spirit.

The aircraft remained in attendance until we finally turned
in towards the narrow pass leading into Ayvali Bay. When we
anchored at the mouth of the pass, they made one more close
inspection; then flew off in the direction of Mitylene.

My chief preoccupation, now that the ship was in safety,
was to get a full report away to Ankara. If we were to attempt
a night passage in a few days' time, it would be necessary for
our people at Ankara to inform the Turks as soon as possible.
Their troops all down the coast would have to be warned not
to fire on us.

I pulled ashore in *Olinda*'s boat to a point where there was
a Turkish flag flying on the beach of Mosko Island; but I
had not gone very far towards it, when I saw a car come
dashing along the coast road of the island and stop at the look-
out post. Two soldiers jumped out, and the next moment a
couple of shots and two splashes quite close to the boat warned
us that landing was prohibited at that point. This Turkish
habit of using rifles to control traffic as readily as a French
policeman uses his baton is alarming at first, but most effective,
and one gets used to it in time. We turned round at once, and
pulled back to the ship.

There was nothing to do now but to wait until the Turks saw
fit to send out a customs launch. This we did with some
impatience. I knew that I would only be able to telegraph to
Ankara, from Ayvalik, the bare news that we had been bombed;
my future intentions would have to go in cipher from our
Consulate at Izmir (called Smyrna before the Kemalists drove
out the Greeks in 1922), so it was essential for me to get
to Izmir as quickly as possible. I had visions of a difficult
trek through a strange and possibly suspicious countryside.

At last, about noon, a boat was seen approaching from

Ayvalik through the narrows. It wore a large Turkish ensign aft and, as it drew nearer, we could see in it the khaki uniforms of two or three soldiers and also several civilians. This would no doubt be the harbour-master's launch, bringing customs guards, a pilot, the port doctor and all the rest of the usual officials. The boat bumped alongside, and the customs officials came up the ladder first—an officer and two privates. Next came two civilians wearing the blue peaked caps of the Turkish Merchant Service; these were the harbour-master and the pilot. After them came two ordinary civilians. The first civilian was a pleasant-looking fellow, between thirty-five and forty, who introduced himself, surprisingly, as Peter. He was obviously a Turk or a Greek, but he none the less spoke good English. He told me at once that the news of the ship being bombed, and of an Englishman in charge of her, had reached Ayvalik about an hour before.

"I have been on the telephone to the British Consulate at Izmir," he said, "and they have asked me to arrange transport for you to get over there as quickly as possible. This is my friend, Suliman Bey."

I shook hands with the second civilian, who was a very jovial, plump fellow, always grinning and full of good fellowship.

"Good morning," he said beaming. "I am the manager of the —— Trading Company. I was in London for three years, before the war, and am delighted to be of assistance to an Englishman."

This sounded very encouraging; but I decided to ring up Izmir myself, before trusting to any transport that might have been arranged.

The boat trip in to Ayvalik took about thirty minutes, and was enlivened by the friendly chatter of Peter and Suliman Bey.

"No enemy agents in this place, I suppose?" My remark was made idly to Peter. Ayvalik was no more than a village, on a very remote part of the coast, and the unlikelihood of finding any foreigners there had considerably influenced my decision to seek the protection of its completely landlocked harbour. I was therefore somewhat disconcerted when Peter replied: "Yes, there *is* one," even though he went on to assure me that the Turkish police kept the fellow under close observation, so that he could hardly prove a direct menace to the safety

of *Olinda*, while she lay in Ayvalik harbour. No one knew this
agent very well. He was a German, it appeared, who had only
arrived in Ayvalik about a week before, to relieve an Italian
previously stationed there. He was a civilian, in charge of
buying provisions—mostly olives and eggs—for the Island of
Mitylene. These provisions were shipped, twice weekly, across
the five-mile stretch of water, in a *caique* from the Turkish
village of Dikili, down the coast.

During the next two hours I telephoned Izmir, sent a tele-
gram to Ankara and had an amusing lunch with Peter,
Suliman Bey and the Colonel of the local Turkish troops. The
latter accepted with good humour my apologies for having
disobeyed his orders a few hours before. The meal began with
a bottle of *raki*; then they brought us *dolmas* (rice and meat
wrapped in a vine leaf); then stuffed marrows; then more rice,
in the form of *pilav*; then *shish-kebab*, lumps of mutton grilled
on a skewer; and finally another bottle of *raki* and cups of
Turkish coffee. It was a very Eastern meal, and it went on for
nearly two hours, during which time we chattered and grew
cheery and forgot, for a moment, the war.

The "hotel" in which we lunched, was no more than a
large, bare café with marble-topped, iron-framed tables and
a charcoal cooking-stove in the centre of the room. Except for
the presence of so much cast-iron, this room could have
differed little from the eating-hall of an inn in Biblical times.
The charcoal cooking-stove would have stood in the same place;
the tables and benches, the cups, the plates, the knives and
spoons, could not have altered much. Even the people resembled, in face and character, the Roman legionaries and Myssian
peasants, who would have been sitting there two thousand
years before. There were Turks of many types—from army
officers, through clerks, to labourers and peasants. All of them
seemed to be submitting awkwardly to Mustapha Kemal's
twenty-year-old edict, compelling them to wear European
clothes. They still belonged in spirit to a more colourful age—
to the days when St. Paul had tried to convert them to Christianity and they had stoned him for his pains. One noticed it at
once when they began to eat; the way in which they put food
into their mouths was crudely practical, essentially old-world,
and common to all classes. It seemed a pity that they should

have rejected the teachings of St. Paul, only to fall victim, in the end, to Christianity's more hideous tumours—to become the slaves of the trilby, the bowler and the black umbrella.

It was the Colonel who brought us to earth by harking back once more to the events of the morning. His was a difficult position, he explained through Peter. His duty was to preserve strict neutrality at all times, whatever his personal sympathies; but the present strategic situation was particularly unfavourable for offering any offence to the Germans. They might be forced into following a well-known British precedent, by laying mines in Turkish territorial waters. I was obliged to agree with him over this. Any clash on the coast, between ourselves and the Germans, was bound to remind the Turks of the tragic fate of Norway in a similar situation.

After lunch I spent an amusing hour with Suliman Bey, on a tour of the local markets, where I bought eggs, fish, vegetables of all sorts and some meat, for *Olinda*. Suliman Bey seemed to have given up work for the day in order to devote himself entirely to me. We met Peter again in the harbourmaster's office, where we arranged for orders to be sent off to *Olinda*, telling her to enter Ayvalik Bay and anchor near the town.

By this time we were getting warm and rather dusty.

"High time we had another drink," announced Suliman Bey, starting off along the waterfront towards a group of large buildings.

"What about this German agent, by the way?" I asked presently. "What sort of a chap is he?" I had been thinking about this fellow for some time. If he had only arrived a week ago, he might even be one of the Istanbul Huns, sent down to Ayvalik to be handy in case *Olinda* should in fact turn up.

"You will probably see him in here," said Suliman Bey, as he led the way to a small club near the waterfront which, he informed me, was the social centre of Ayvalik, where all the business people collected in the middle of the day to meet each other and to drink *raki*.

As we entered the main lounge of the club, Peter tapped me on the shoulder and pointed to a figure sitting alone in the far corner of the room. He need not have bothered. I was already trying to control my amusement at the sight of the obvious embarrassment upon the pale countenance of Fritz Scheibel himself.

21

DEAR old Fritz. It was almost like meeting suddenly an old friend . . . someone whom you knew quite intimately before the period of your present worries and tribulations. I always connected Fritz in my mind with the gayest of our nights in Istanbul, with Nadia and music and our first exciting descent upon Anatolia through the snowy defiles of the Taurus. He had never been ill-humoured, in spite of Jesse's provocation and John's surly rudeness to him. He had always remained calm and studiously courteous, with a faintly humorous twist to his speech and an occasional twinkle of fun in his furtive little eyes. I felt I wanted to go up to him now, to clap him on the back and then sit down and pour out all my troubles; tell him of Malu the terrible, the dismal Arab sailors, my struggles to learn Russian and all the rest of the many trials that beset me.

All I did, however, was to stroll across the room and say, "Hello," in a cheerful voice . . . to the astonishment of Peter and Suliman Bey, and to the embarrassment of poor Fritz himself.

"Your job of tobacco merchant seems to take you all over the country, doesn't it?" I suggested, in the hope of starting him off. But Fritz only looked more embarrassed than ever. No doubt he was feeling acutely conscious of the several pairs of eyes that were watching us both from the bar.

"And yours of Port Inspector (if that is what you are) is not, it seems, without some excitements." His quick, nervous little smile flickered out. Then he got up and sauntered away, while I returned to Suliman Bey and poor old Peter, who were completely nonplussed by my behaviour. When I explained things they both became thoughtful.

"No wonder they sent this fellow to relieve the Italian," observed Peter, "if he knows you all by sight."

We finished our drinks; then Peter went off to see what had happened to my taxi, while Suliman Bey took me over to his office to wait. The taxi was to drive me as far as Bergama (the ancient Pergamus), whence I would travel by bus to Izmir.

We had not been sitting in the office very long before Suliman

Bey began once more to feel thirsty, and was constrained to send for another bottle of *raki*. Soon I was listening to a discourse on the relative merits of the Germans, the Turks and the British. After several *rakis*, it developed into quite a tirade. The Germans were brutes, explained Suliman Bey, but the British were far too soft. His jolly face and plump figure became alive with his eloquence. He dilated upon the supernatural courage of all Turks. Irrespective of class or profession, they were ready one and all, he said, to die fighting for their country. Their natural and implacable ferocity, he declared, was only curbed by the loftiest ideals and a determination to see fair play. These ideals alone prevented Turkey, at this very moment, from drawing her sword and quickly finishing the war. I was about to ask him on which side he thought Turkey would fight, but, before I could do so, he had rushed to his desk and wrenched open a drawer; from it he dragged an immense revolver.

"See," he cried, striking a warlike attitude. "Always the Turk has his arms at his side. He is born to fighting and trained to it from childhood. When the time comes, I tell you, it will be the Turks who will show the world how to fight. Tanks and airplanes are of no account against the spirit of the Turk in his mountains."

Suliman was by now perspiring heavily. He looked ridiculous, with his soft, plump body clothed in a dark business suit, brandishing a revolver almost too heavy for him to hold level. But I agreed politely with everything he said, and when the taxi arrived I was whisked away amid a shower of good wishes. As the taxi turned the corner, Suliman Bey came out into the roadway. My last sight of him was of a bellicose cherub, levelling his huge revolver at us with both hands.

The road to Bergama ran along the coast of Suna Bay; my taxi passed the look-out post at Aspira Point, where I had landed that very morning. A little farther on, at Dikili, the road turned away and began to skirt the mountains to the eastward. Later, in the bus from Bergama, we turned south again, and rattled on past the head of the Gulf of Sandarli; past the ruins of the Port of Elea, which now lie more than a mile inland, with sheep and cattle grazing in the elbow of an ancient mole. The bus was a tiny twelve-seater, little bigger than the modern station wagon; but into it had crowded at least twenty peasants of all ages, as well as the inevitable chickens, and one small sheep. The driver was in a hurry, and the road was rough and tortuous; but it was nearly sunset when we reached Ali Agha and, by this time, the strain of bracing myself against the lively motion of the vehicle had tired me out. I was also sick of the heavy smell of animals and primitive humanity.

At dusk we paused upon a hill-side south of Ali Agha. The bus engine had overheated, so the driver set about changing the water from a pond by the roadside. The passengers all got out to stretch their legs—all, that is, except the unfortunate chickens; even the sheep was taken for a stroll by its owner, a boy of twelve or so.

I sat down upon a rock and lit a cigarette. At my back were the slopes of Mount Kalvassi; before me they fell away towards the Aegean, which lay dark, "wine dark" and placid, over towards the crags and headlands of Mitylene.

It was just a week since *Olinda* had left Istanbul; two weeks since Jesse's quarrel with Nadia. I thought of Jesse now . . . bold, impatient, dashing; but brutal and rather selfish as well. I had resigned myself to the nasty little scene in the Casino at Istanbul. I now believed that Jesse had quarrelled with Nadia on purpose, in order to make a clean break between them— Montolieu's disapproval having at last become too insistent. I still felt, however, that Jesse could have found a more graceful way out—could have spared us such a stark unpleasantness. I gazed at the darkening mountains of Mitylene. Jesse would be approaching them from the other side, I thought; then standing out to sea. He would have heard by now of the attack upon *Olinda*, so *Tarkhan* would have sailed from the Dardanelles at dusk. It was a perfect night for him; no moon, but clear enough to pick up his landfalls on Khios and Samos. I wondered whether Jesse had nerves like the rest of us; whether he would spend an anxious night alone on the bridge of *Tarkhan*, or whether he would steam straight down, bold and careless, wisecracking as usual and succeeding as always.

A flash of light from the Mitylene Channel caught my eye and made me glance a little to the right of the island. That significant strip of pale water lay unruffled between Mitylene and the Turkish coast. Woefully narrow it looked, and yet so short. Once through it, *Olinda* might have a chance; not a chance like Jesse's, with his good ten knots of speed and a first-class diversion, in the shape of the cornered *Olinda*, to help him; but a good sporting chance none the less. There it came again; a blue-white flash, followed this time by the sudden brilliant pencil of a searchlight. I gazed at it more intently; the light itself seemed to come from the water somewhere out

in the channel. Then I noticed that there was a little necklace of smaller, yellower lights, stretching on either side of the searchlight; all at once another beam snapped into life from the end of the necklace—almost from the middle of the channel.

The line of yellow lights might well have marked the mast-heads of a small fishing fleet—probably did; but the search-lights could mean only one thing: that the Germans were determined to close the channel, to prevent any ship from sneaking through unseen. What a break for Jesse. The Huns certainly appeared "preoccupied!" Just Jesse's luck, I reflected ironically, but I had to admit to myself that Jesse's dashing brilliance deserved the luck—he expected it and got it. In three days from now, I felt sure, he would have steamed, with-out a check, past Kos and Castelorizzo, whilst I was still trying to juggle my awkward burden through the shoals and islets round Mitylene or Khios.

I could not restrain a wry smile at the thought of all the effort and ingenuity we had put into *Olinda*'s disguise; of all the trouble I had taken to board her unseen; of our bouts of spy fever and the complicated strategies resulting from them. The Germans had, after all, taken the simplest and most obvious course; the moment *Olinda* left Istanbul, they had closed the Mitylene Channel, and had sent Fritz Scheibel down to watch the Turkish side of it. How, I wondered, were we going to prevent Fritz from seeing and reporting *Olinda*'s departure from Ayvalik? And how was *Olinda* to get past these searchlights, and run the gauntlet of the E-boats carrying them? I had no idea; but I decided, for the time being, to shelve all such problems and to think of other things.

Over in the south-west I could see the glare of Izmir looming yellow. There was a bloom of mist upon the trees of a nearer forest, which made me think of our day on the island of Heybeli, when we had gathered fir cones with Nadia on a Sunday forenoon—a forenoon which seemed very distant now, and tender with distance was the memory of it. I thought of Nadia, of her pale face, cocked sideways like a robin's, and of those large dark eyes gazing at you with a whimsical seriousness. I fell to wondering again what her true history might be. Was she working for us, or for the Germans, or for the Russians, or for none of them? It was difficult to fit Nadia into any conventional background; she was, I felt certain, too full of whims and childish fancies; too impatient to be compassed and disciplined by the rules of either side. Since the final quarrel between her and Jesse, we had neither seen nor heard of her again. For all we knew she might have gone straight to the Germans after that—full of spite and a keen desire to be revenged for Jesse's insult. I could not believe, somehow, that she would have reacted in such a commonplace way; but who could blame her if she had?

The dusk was over; already the night was closing in. The musical note of a sheep bell nearby made me look round. The passengers were drifting back towards the bus, so I got up and joined them. I took one last look to seaward before climbing in. My imagination showed me Jesse, standing boldly out to sea—direct and dashing. . . . And here was I, a week out from Istanbul . . . climbing humbly into the back of a crowded country bus.

On my arrival at Izmir, I went straight to the British

Consulate, where I was told the true identity of Peter; also that Suliman Bey was "reliable." I made the necessary signals to the Naval Attaché and to the Old Man; after that, there was an interview with a massive American—an engineer in charge of some road building in southern Turkey. He promised to provide me next day with a thousand sandbags and a ton of sand. As an afterthought he offered me a couple of pounds of blasting charges, some detonators carefully packed in a cotton-wool lined box, and a few yards of safety fuse—"in case they might come in handy."

Later there was a meeting with a man whose name and nationality cannot even be hinted at. He was small and dark and strikingly handsome; he reminded me a little of Ivan Oreshkin except that, in place of Ivan's slightly insolent air, he had, behind his eyes, a look of deep suffering and patient hatred. I felt that, somewhere in Europe, his friends and family had died hideously or were still, perhaps, in the last horrid throes of starvation, disease or death by torture. He had been brought into our discussion of plans by the problem of how to deal with Fritz Scheibel.

After a moment's thought he went to a locked drawer from which he took a phial of tiny yellow tablets. "One of these," he said casually, "will put a man out for three or four hours. Two will cure his insomnia for several days"—he paused, and looked at me very intently; I could feel the hatred twisting inside him, biting into him—"three, in a glass of *vodka*," he went on quietly, "might save a great deal of trouble afterwards. . . ."

I felt embarrassed; then I wanted to laugh, but could not, for fear of hurting his feelings. It was not that I was concerned about dirty dealing where fat Fritz was concerned; it was clear that his comfort was a relatively unimportant consideration against the absolute necessity of getting *Olinda* to sea unreported . . . but, after all, I was only a General Service naval officer, and doping was well outside my terms of reference. I would be certain to make a hash of it; I could even see myself, in my agitation, complicating an already embarrassing situation by getting the glasses mixed; and thereafter suffering the crowning indignity of being bundled on board *Olinda*, in a heavy stupor . . . possibly even by a triumphantly solicitous Fritz himself.

But no amount of diffidence on my part could alter the fact that Fritz must be dealt with somehow. The only alternative to doping seemed to be kidnapping, followed by a request to the bellicose Suliman Bey to shoot the good Fritz deftly in the stomach. This procedure seemed equally fantastic. At any rate in the end, I put the tablets in my pocket; then I went off to dinner at a nearby "Restaurant-Night-club."

I had finished my dinner and was sitting back at a corner table, waiting for the cabaret show to begin, when I first saw her. Three young women in dancing frocks had collected in a hovering group by the door leading into the kitchen, *and one of them was Nadia*!

To say that I was surprised to see Nadia in Izmir would be an understatement; I was astounded. First Fritz; then Nadia. All the people we had ever met in Turkey seemed to be flocking to the Aegean coast, on various pretexts, to watch our efforts. It was as though we had been taking part in a gigantic University bumping race, with a crowd of supporters following us along the bank of the river.

Nadia was dressed, like the two girls, in a short skirt and bodice, with dancing shoes upon her feet. All three were heavily rouged and powdered and wearing silver wigs with diminutive, disc-shaped hats perched upon the sides of their heads. A more incongruous get-up for Nadia could scarcely have been invented. I would certainly not have recognised her but for the childish movements of her hands and an occasional upwards glance towards the band leader, which reminded me of the evening she and Jesse had walked up the hill from Galata ferry landing. None of the girls wore any stockings. How slim and neat were Nadia's legs; how easily she moved. Beside the other two, who were buxom, rather florid and obviously sisters, Nadia flittered like an eager sprite. Then the music began, and the three girls tripped on to the floor together, clasping each others' waists; nodding their heads and smiling to the audience.

The dance was neither polished nor very original; but soon they danced away from each other—Nadia and the younger sister moving to the sides of the floor, leaving the elder sister in the middle. Thereafter Nadia began to give to her own movements that gipsy charm which was so much a part of her. She reminded me of an infant at a dancing display—uncontrollable and personally excited by her own rendering of a particular theme, a theme which the mistress, in the middle of the room, is pounding out with a woodenly insistent precision. After a few moments the elder of the two plump sisters began to sing, and Nadia drew back with the other one to the orchestra platform. She stood there, gazing idly about her and, a moment later, our eyes met. Soon afterwards the girls made their exit but later they all reappeared through another door. While the remaining acts of the cabaret were in progress, they sat down among the guests.

Nadia came across to my table. She was now wearing a somewhat pretentious evening gown and, over it, a black velvet cloak, that ruffled up round her throat and behind her head. Her hair was waved, and shone with a new light; her fingernails, which had formerly been short and unadorned, were now varnished a lively pink; her eyes were as lustrous as ever. The make-up on her face gave her an appearance of rather comical sophistication without changing or spoiling the childlike shape of it. The contrast between her personality, as I knew it, and her present appearance made her look, if anything, younger than before, like a girl at her first party. But there was a slow drag in her step, as though she were tired or depressed, and she did not smile until she reached my table, and was standing before me.

"Well?" she said, cocking her head on one side as of old and brightening a little. "Did you like my dance?"

I got to my feet and pulled another chair over beside mine. "It's wonderful to see you again, Nadia, dear, and I think you dance beautifully—far better than the others." I was delighted to find that she seemed to have forgiven me for being a witness of that unpleasant scene in Taxim Casino two weeks before.

Nadia accepted the chair with a smile. At that moment a waiter approached and remained hovering. I asked Nadia what she would like to drink; but she shook her head impatiently, then said: "Oh, anything. It doesn't make much difference what I order; they usually bring us syrup and water, anyway."

"Well, don't have anything then."

"Oh, I've got to I suppose. *Consommation* is in my contract."

I ordered a bottle of white wine, and turned to her again.

"What made you come to Izmir?" I asked. "Surely your parents live in Istanbul?"

She frowned, and I saw that my question had been an unfortunate one.

"The police," she replied shortly, looking away.

I raised my eyebrows, but remained silent; presently she turned to look at me again.

"I got nothing but unhappiness out of meeting you people," she said. "I suppose it was my own fault, really, for letting myself have any human feelings." She paused again and then went on: "The day after I last saw you, the police sent for me and told me that if I continued to mix with agents from the fighting countries, I would be arrested. They advised me to leave Istanbul; so I came here . . . I shall probably get into more trouble for sitting at your table now," she added despondently, then flared up. "But they can all go to hell! I'm only doing my job, and I shall speak to anyone I like, till they stop me!"

Something in Nadia's manner and tone convinced me that she was speaking the truth. She stayed at my table for the rest of the evening and, when the restaurant closed, we walked away together.

It was a still, fine night and fairly warm; only the faintest breath of air was stirring down the mountain-sides, into the bowl of Izmir harbour, bringing with it the sweet heavy tang of damp heather and grass. We dawdled along the two-mile promenade which runs down one side of the harbour, and sat, for a while, upon a seat facing out over the bay. Yellow streamers of light darted and wavered across the still, black surface of the water from the street lamps of the city. In the pale, soft glow around us, Nadia's face had lost a good deal of its recently assumed air of sophistication. Wisps of hair, straying from beneath her kerchief, gave to her the more youthful charm of a Peter Pan's Wendy. But she still seemed very despondent, and not very anxious to talk. Suddenly she flung round with a gesture of frustration and an expression very near to despair in her eyes.

"Oh, how I wish I could get out of this awful country!" she exclaimed. "Can't you take me in your ship?"

"What ship?" I asked guardedly.

"They say that a ship was bombed this morning, and is now at Ayvalik. There was an Englishman on board. I suppose that was you?"

"Oh, she's a Turkish ship," I lied. "I was only a passenger in her—bound for Izmir."

Nadia sank back again into her corner of the seat, regarding me gravely for several minutes, but saying nothing. I wondered how much she really knew about us, and how much she only guessed. My thoughts turned from Nadia to Fritz Scheibel; suddenly an idea occurred to me.

"Would you like to come with me to Ayvalik to-morrow?" Then, hastily I invented a reason for my return to the place: "There are some stores and baggage I have to fetch from the ship."

A slow smile began to light up Nadia's face as she sat watching me. Then she leaned forward and looked at me oddly. "Would you really like me to come?" she whispered, "or are you just being kind?"

Her expression was half appealing, half challenging, as though uncertain of my sincerity. A wave of shame swept over me. Surely Nadia had been treated unkindly enough already. What right had I, whoever she was, to drag her any farther into our conspiracies?

But there would be no need to involve her directly; she could meet Fritz Scheibel almost as though by accident. Once they had met, his attention would quite naturally be occupied with Nadia for just those few vital hours which would give me, in *Olinda,* the necessary lead.

"Of course, I want you to come, Nadia, dear," I assured her, and realised, as I said it, that my words were indeed more sincere than I had thought. I began to picture the drive to Ayvalik and the fun of seeing Nadia's eyes sparkling again. I thought of a picnic by the edge of the Ayvalik lagoon, and an evening in the guest-house café which I had seen standing there.

"Then I will," said Nadia eagerly. "It sounds lovely. I don't have to be back here till eight o'clock. How will we go?"

"I expect we can get a lift in a truck," I replied, knowing that my sand and explosives were being sent by road next day. We sat talking for an hour or more. It was after 3 a.m. when we finally strolled away.

Nadia was happy again, and unaffectedly thrilled at the idea of to-morrow's outing. She took my arm, her hand resting lightly, almost caressingly, upon my wrist.

"How wonderful to get away from this place for a day," she murmured, as we wandered along. "I can hardly wait to see the countryside again. . . . I was brought up in the country, you know."

Her happiness was infectious. "I'm looking forward to it too," I confessed. "What a pity you can't stay longer than a day. There's a guest-house where you could live—amongst the trees beside the lagoon."

Nadia smiled at me enchantingly. "Aren't you getting a little romantic, darling? Don't forget I'm only a bar girl," and the bright red tip of her tongue poked out at me provokingly.

"You're the most unsuccessful 'bar girl' I've ever met," I retorted emphatically. "I don't believe you'd ever seen a bar before the war."

Nadia laughed quietly to herself. Presently we turned down a side street and arrived at some steps leading up to a dingy-looking door. We climbed the steps together, arm in arm; then Nadia drew away from me on to the top step. With the door ajar, she paused a moment and looked down.

"Where shall I meet you to-morrow?" she whispered.

"I'll call for you here. Can you be ready by half-past eight in the morning?"

She gave a low murmur of a laugh. "I'll be ready," she whispered back . . ." then: "You have made me feel happy again."

"You must still be happy when I come for you to-morrow. . . . I do wish you could stay at Ayvalik a little longer."

Her brow puckered lightly; a half serious, half smiling and wholly bewitching look of uncertainty crossed her face. She gazed at me for a moment then, very lightly, as though without knowing it, she swayed a little towards me. I felt the glow of enchantment spreading through me—overwhelming, dangerous. My head was no longer clear. There was a sudden swift flutter of a white hand upon my arm as Nadia leaned quickly down. "I might," she whispered, and I felt her warm breath for a moment, softly against my cheek. Then, in a flash, she was gone.

I walked away through the silent streets of Izmir feeling more than bewildered. A nightwatchman's whistle shrilled suddenly and was answered from a distance. As I came out beside the water, I glanced across the bay and the hills and over to the mountains beyond. First light was rising beyond them towards the moon—a slender wisp of a moon that told of the darkest nights at hand. It was as well; for this whole affair was becoming a great deal too involved. On the second night from now, at latest, *Olinda* and I must be gone.

22

"I SEE that you return from Izmir well equipped for a long voyage. . . ."

Suliman Bey had come out of his office, disturbed by the clatter of our three-ton truck over the ruts and cobbles of his side street. He now stood beaming at us in a jovial way, with Peter at his side. They were both staring with frank admiration at the slender figure of Nadia who, clad in grey flannel trousers and a dark red jersey, had just scrambled up from a pile of sacks in the back of the truck, and was in the act of climbing out.

". . . very well equipped indeed," repeated Suliman Bey, while Peter nodded his head and smiled.

Nadia was wearing her black beret on the side of her bobbed head, and she carried her mackintosh over one arm. Ignoring Suliman Bey's fussy efforts at assistance, she jumped lightly down on to the cobbles. There she stood for a moment, gazing at him calmly, but with a hint of wonder in her large brown eyes—wonder, perhaps, at the comical figure he presented. For Suliman Bey held his great revolver in one podgy fist and a strip of oily rag in the other. We had obviously interrupted a gun-cleaning session. It seemed as though the visit of *Olinda* to Ayvalik had struck a resounding chord in the warrior breast

of this plump Turk. When I remembered my last sight of
Suliman, as I turned out of this same street in my taxi twenty-
four hours before, I even wondered whether his revolver had
ever left his hand from that moment to this.

Our drive back to Ayvalik from Izmir had been pleasant,
though uneventful. The ton of sand and about seven hundred
bags had not taken up much room in the truck. Nadia, clutching a small suitcase, had sprawled comfortably throughout the
journey upon a pile of bags in the back. I sat beside her upon
more bags that covered the small wooden case containing our
precious explosives. Nadia had been excited over the outing
and ready to laugh at anything—at the jolting of the truck,
at the peasants in horse-carts we sometimes passed, at our
cheerful young driver and, above all, at me in my purple suit.
Nor was it long now before she was laughing openly and
provokingly at Suliman Bey, who looked far from offended at
what he took to be Nadia's appreciation of his great wit.
(And Suliman could be very witty—especially when standing
upon his dignity or other people's toes.) He now swept Nadia
into his office, and started bawling immediately for coffee and
raki and plates of cakes.

Peter and I left them chattering gaily to each other, and
drove off again in the truck. At Peter's direction, we twisted
and turned among the side streets and lanes of the poor
quarter, remote from the banks and offices near the main town
quay. As we drove along, Peter mentioned the searchlights
and the line of small craft in the Mitylene Channel the night
before. He and Suliman Bey had seen them also, he said, from
the hills near Ayvalik. I told him that I had obtained a good
view of them myself and that they seemed to extend no farther
than the middle of the channel. It had appeared to me that
the searchlights were fairly small ones, unlikely to show up
a black ship at more than a mile or so, and I was hoping
that *Olinda* would be able to creep past them, keeping close
to the Turkish shore.

"You'll need to be very careful of the shoal water off Suna
Spit," he warned. "It runs out quite a long way."

"I know," I said. "There's a note about it on the charts;
but we'll have to take some risks, otherwise there's no hope of
getting through."

"Have you discussed the problem with the Master of *Olinda*?" asked Peter.

"No," I replied shortly, "and please don't make any mention of it to him. The people in *Olinda* are quite worried enough already without suggesting new dangers to them."

Peter nodded and changed the subject.

At last we rumbled down a steep alley to the water's edge. The alley ended in a stone ramp running out into the harbour; against the side of this ramp lay a motor boat and a large pulling-boat, both belonging to Peter. More than a mile away, at the end of a tongue of houses which jutted into the harbour, we could see the large white building that contained the club. As it was after twelve o'clock, Fritz was no doubt sitting in the club at this very moment; or he might still be in his room at the "hotel," scanning the harbour, and inspecting *Olinda* through binoculars. In any case he was not likely to see anything suspicious in a boatload of stores going out to a ship at anchor; but, all the same, we took the precaution of bringing the boats round to that side of the ramp which was hidden from the club. As soon as we got them there, we placed the box of explosives on the floor-boards of the pulling-boat; then, taking two shovels from the back of the truck, we began to shovel the sand in on top of the box. The bags were next spread over the sand; then Peter started up the motor boat and, with the heavily laden pulling-boat in tow, we went chugging out across the harbour towards *Olinda*.

She looked a self-conscious lump, poor thing, sitting awkwardly upon the smooth face of the lagoon as, hunched in bewildered trepidation, she waited upon the uncertain future. No dashing destroyer she, nor mighty cruiser, about to sharpen her fighting teeth in readiness to engage the King's enemies . . . just a homely old body, tossed from one piratical faction to the next, as helpless as a 'black market' goose at Christmas. Poor *Olinda* . . . the British had snatched her from her Persian owner, the Germans were determined to sink her, and the Turks were ready to arrest her the moment she got into any more trouble. It all seemed very unfair upon a respectable old lady, born to the peaceful pursuit of carrying oil across the more sheltered stretches of the Aegean and the Black Sea.

The only aggressive note, as we came alongside, was sounded by the vociferous Malu, who was ready, as usual, to fly at us the moment we reached the top of the jumping-ladder. The remainder of the crew looked very unwarlike. The Arabs were busy on the foredeck, washing their clothes in wooden buckets; the smaller of the Chinese greasers was asleep on the tank-tops, while the Master rose from a deck-chair on the poop and came shuffling forward in carpet slippers, to greet us and to deal with Malu. The Master seemed surprised to see us; so did the Mate, who poked his head out of the door leading into the accommodation; so did the Arab sailors, who paused in their washing, then started to drift aft in pairs and singly. Soon we were surrounded by most of the crew, some of whom glanced dubiously over the side into our boats. The Master made the general feelings clear in his first remark.

"Not thinkin' you comin' back," he said calmly, "I bin goin' to send crew for holiday."

After a certain amount of jocular back-chat (covering a certain irritation at this bland assumption), I succeeded in arranging for the Arabs to commence their holiday by collecting spades and buckets and digging the sand out of the pulling-boat, which we had secured on *Olinda*'s seaward side. They began the task with some ill-grace; but this gave way, in the end, to mournful resignation; and, in less than one hour, the sand was all piled on deck against the bulwarks, while the task of filling the bags had already begun. We hoped with these sandbags to turn the wheel-house into a citadel that would be reasonably safe against bullets and splinters.

The sandbags were first of all to be piled round the wheel, and the space behind it where the helmsman stood. Then they were to be built up round the standard compass upon the monkey island above, so as to make of it a solid protective pillar round which I would be able to dodge if necessary. It was a little uncertain, as a matter of fact, whether the first bullets to come inboard would be Turkish or German; for we could not be sure, in spite of my signals to Ankara, that the Turkish coastal troops would be warned in time to prevent them from firing upon us. There was other work to be done besides the filling of the sandbags, however. All the white superstructure had to be painted brown and grey, in order to make

the ship less visible against the cliffs or at the end of a searchlight beam; but this could not be begun until after dark. Nor
could the sandbagging of the standard compass, although our
friend the Colonel had placed on board two armed sentries,
who were more than ready to fire their rifles at any inquisitive
boats.

While the sandbags were being filled, Peter and I took the
explosives up to the monkey island. Ivan Oreshkin joined us,
bringing with him a dozen or so empty cigarette tins, a bag of
old nails and a box of assorted nuts and bolts. With these
accessories we all sat down to manufacture a few home-made
hand grenades. We made them by placing in each tin three
sticks of gelignite lashed together, then packing round them
as many assorted nails, nuts and bolts as the tin would hold.
Next we cut off seven centimetres of safety fuse, which is
supposed to burn at the rate of one centimetre per second; this
we inserted in a detonator, and stuck the detonator into the
gelignite. The seven centimetres of fuse now poked up out of
the middle of the tin, so we made a hole in the lid for the fuse
to protrude; then bound the whole thing firmly together with
engineers' tape. The method of firing the grenade was crude
but reasonably safe. You struck an extra large safety match,
specially made for the purpose, and held it to the end of the
fuse till the latter started to splutter; then you got rid of the
bomb as quickly as possible.

We made a dozen bombs in all, and put them in a sandbag
beside the standard compass. They were intended for hurling
from the monkey island into any craft which might attempt
to board us at sea. Just to make sure that the bombs would
work, Ivan Oreshkin made an extra one for demonstration
purposes. To prevent this bomb from arousing the neighbourhood, he stuck into it a fifteen-centimetre fuse, then dropped
the bomb straight into the water as soon as the fuse was lit.

The bomb disappeared and, for what seemed like an age,
we waited for something to happen—Ivan with an expression
of eager anticipation, Peter looking only mildly interested, and
myself somewhat dubiously. Suddenly there was a loud metallic
explosion, just as though someone had struck *Olinda*'s bottom
plates with a gigantic hammer. The old Master sprang out
of his deck-chair on the poop, and Feodor Pavlovitch peered

bright-eyed and inquiring from the wheelhouse door beneath
us. A few seconds later a swirl of muddy water welled up
beside the ship, a few tiny fish wriggling feebly around its
fringes. We waited longer—several minutes; then there was a
glance of silver amongst the clouds of brown water, and next
moment a plump bream came flapping spasmodically to the
surface. In a flash Ah Fong was half over the side with a large
waste-paper basket, into which he scooped the bream. The
Arab sailors, who had gathered round, were wildly enthusiastic
and wished to make more bombs at once; but happily we had
already used all the gelignite, so they turned again reluctantly
to their task of filling the sandbags.

By 2 p.m. all the sandbags were ready for stacking. They
looked as though, against ordinary, low velocity rifle bullets,
they would make a fairly solid breastwork for the Master, the
helmsman and myself. The rest of the ship's company would
be able to keep under cover below. A chance torpedo was, of
course, a danger against which no protection could be hastily
improvised. We therefore did the next best thing by deciding
that we were unlikely to encounter one.

It was now necessary to work out in detail a plan for the
night. Peter, the Master and I held a conference lasting nearly
an hour, as a result of which it was decided that the ship must
be ready for sea by 7 p.m.; and the Master also promised to
send a boat inshore for me at 7.15. At 8 o'clock *Olinda* would
sail. We hoped, if all went well, to be able to slip through the
Mitylene Channel and Khios Strait in one night, reaching
Egrilar, on the southern side of the Chesme peninsular, before
dawn. On the following night, January 18th, we would attempt
the Samos Strait. The day of January 19th we would spend
somewhere in Mandelyah Gulf.

After all these arrangements had been made, Peter and I
returned ashore. My confidence was somewhat restored by the
day's achievements; *Olinda* still looked like a grubby old barn-
yard fowl, and in no respect more warlike than before; but one
could imagine the old dear cocking a wily old eye at the
enemy island opposite, ruffling up her feathers, and settling
herself upon the water, as though she had at last thought of
a way out of a most embarrassing predicament.

23

WE drove out of town in Peter's own car, a Ford V8 saloon, towards the southern side of Ayvalik harbour, where we had arranged to meet Suliman and Nadia at the guest-house by the water's edge.

On the way out we went over all our plans once again, and discussed *Olinda*'s chance of getting through unseen. I was pleased, in one way, that the ship's company had been so surprised at my return. If, in fact, they had come to the conclusion that no further attempt could be made to complete the voyage, there seemed to be a good chance that Fritz and his masters would have reasoned likewise. To achieve surprise, therefore, it would only be necessary to prevent Fritz from noticing, until next morning, that *Olinda* and I had left Ayvalik. If this could be done, we would gain those two or three vital hours which might give us a chance . . . a chance of slipping past the enemy patrol line in the Mitylene Channel before their E-boats could be warned that *Olinda* was already at sea.

I was confident that, with Nadia's innocent assistance, it would be fairly easy to get Fritz away from the harbour for a few hours; and strangely enough Peter, whom I was prepared to find sceptical about Nadia's innocence, agreed with me. He was dubious, however, of such a complicated scheme for what he considered a relatively simple business. He did not actually suggest kidnapping Fritz, just: "Leave it to Suliman and me. We'll soon get him out of the way!"

This sounded too much like "rough stuff," so I refused to leave it to Peter . . . certainly not to Suliman anyway, with his revolver and his "lofty ideals." I felt sure that, if I did, we should soon all find ourselves in gaol, and *Olinda* arrested as well.

After a drive of less than ten minutes we reached the guest-house, which was really a small hotel, catering normally for summer visitors only; owing, however, to the war-time influx of a large number of merchants, it had been kept open throughout the winter. It was situated among pine trees beside the southern arm of the lagoon; on the other side of this arm, or backwater, was a low ridge; beyond this lay the open sea. In the middle of the ridge stood the 440-foot hill that *Olinda* had used as a turning-mark the day before.

We found Nadia and Suliman having an early tea on the veranda. They appeared to have become the best of friends, and Suliman was full of a possessive importance which he now expanded to embrace us all.

"Come along, my friends," he cried, as soon as we had all finished tea. "Let us walk over the hills, and take a look at the perilous waters of the Mitylene Channel." I hoped he was not going to become too indiscreet in the presence of Nadia; but, luckily, she excused herself at once on the pretext of having to unpack or change or something, so the three of us went off without her.

I expected Peter, as soon as we were alone, to warn Suliman that he must be careful what he said in front of Nadia; but for some reason or other he did not; so: "Nadia is not in the know about me and *Olinda*," I ventured after a while. "In fact she might even be an enemy agent. We must be careful what we say in front of her."

"My dear fellow, I am always careful what I say in front of charming young women like that," replied Suliman Bey reproachfully, ". . . careful not to bore them."

I smiled. "But she mustn't on any account suspect that I am leaving," I insisted.

"Let me assure you . . ." Suliman Bey began to puff a little as we climbed the lower slopes of the ridge. "Let me assure—*puff*—you most earnestly—*puff, puff*—that you and your—extraordinary movements are—the last subject—I should dream of—mentioning—to the charming Nadia. . . ." Here he slowed down and glanced up at me sternly while he recovered his breath. "In fact it is my ambition," he went on more evenly, "soon to command Nadia's whole interest and attention. . . . She will, I hope, no longer care whether you are alive or dead," and he gave me a friendly little pat on the shoulder.

Peter grinned to himself over this; but I thought it best to explain to Suliman my plan for arranging a meeting between Fritz Scheibel and Nadia.

Suliman Bey showed great indignation at my proposals. He

stopped and glared at us both; but, for the moment, he had no breath to speak, for we had nearly reached the top of the ridge.

"It is a crime," he burst out at last, "to allow so enchanting a young woman to become embroiled in the vulgar processes of war. And can you, without feeling ashamed, try to force her to associate with so fat and unromantic figure as this German?"

I grinned to myself at such a remark from the portly Suliman. In the end, however, he was persuaded; but not without dire vows, on his part, about what he would do to Fritz, if the latter tried to take advantage of the great Suliman's temporary withdrawal from the lists. By the time Peter and I had extracted from Suliman a promise to leave his revolver at home that evening, we had crossed the ridge of hills between the lagoon and the sea, and had arrived upon the foreshore between Aspira Point and Tuz Burnu.

Before us stretched the sheet of water upon which I had gazed from the mountain south of Ali Agha. It now lay bright and lifeless throughout its length and breadth. The sun had just dipped behind Mitylene Island, and we ourselves were in shadow; but rays of yellow light still fell slanting upon the cliffs of Cape Maltepeh, away to the southward, which seemed very close in the clear atmosphere of evening. Just beside these cliffs lay a small group of islands; the distance from us to the islands looked no more than two or three miles, over which *Olinda* might take but a few minutes to swim into the security of the Gulf of Sandarli beyond. We knew, however, that Port Ajano, lying behind the nearest island, was in reality over fifteen miles away. *Olinda* must steam at full speed for at least two hours to reach it.

Yes, the Mitylene Channel lay bright and lifeless; there was no sign of any fishing craft, nor any *caiques*, nor E-boats, nor any hint of movement upon the enemy coast. But we continued to watch the Channel as the daylight began to fade, and in the end we saw what we had waited for. A tiny black speck appeared upon the glassy white surface of the water, just clear of the reflection from the Mitylene mountains. The gap between this speck and the mountains began to widen; then three more specks appeared behind it, in orderly line—much too orderly for fishermen.

It was nearly dark, so I could not afford to spend any more

time in watching a performance that we had all observed closely
the night before—that might in fact have been put on for our
special benefit. So we hurried away, but no sooner had we
recrossed the ridge, on our way back to the guest-house, than
the first searchlights flared out, and a brilliant white halo of
light silhouetted the hills behind us, waxing and waning as the
beams were swung steadily, rhythmically, backwards and
and forwards over the sea.

By the time we got back, it was half-past five in the evening.
Nadia was ready for us. She was dressed in a pleated blue
skirt and white blouse, open at the neck, which suited her
admirably and emphasised her youthful appearance. She was
in very high spirits, eager for a party; she wanted to "dine and
dance" as splendidly as though she were in Istanbul, but with
more deference paid to her position as the only woman present.
She was disposed to act in a queenly manner. Her attempts to
do so, though genuine enough, were not impressive; they
tended, if anything, to make her appear more of a child
than ever.

Unfortunately there was nowhere in Ayvalik where one
could "dine," in the accepted sense, and the only cafés in
which there was dancing were not of the sort to which anyone
would care to take his friends. In the end we drove off to the
"hotel," the one at which we had lunched the day before with
the Turkish colonel. It was the only hotel in Ayvalik (apart
from the guest-house) in which one could actually live, and we
knew that Fritz Scheibel had a room there. We expected to
find him having his evening *raki* in the restaurant.

As we came in through the street door, we saw him sitting
at a table by himself. He looked more than usually pudding-
like with his soft, white hands, flabby body and a rather sour
expression on his otherwise featureless countenance. He
showed no surprise, however, at our entry, though he must
have been a little astonished to see Nadia with us. I myself
was more puzzled by Nadia's reaction to Fritz. She gave a
perceptible start at the sight of him, and I saw her dart a quick
glance at Peter before going forward with the gladdest of smiles
upon her face. Fritz's face also brightened as she advanced
towards him; he looked pleased at being noticed by her, and

made no objection to our joining him at his table. It occurred
to me, as we sat down, that Fritz must find Ayvalik a miserable
place in which to be marooned without any friends: there
were no amusements or gaiety of any sort to be had. Suliman
shepherded Nadia to a chair which was on the opposite side
of the table to the one occupied by Fritz; then he sat down
beside her. Nadia made no objection, but went on exchanging
greetings and banter with Fritz across the table.

It looked as though Fritz were going to be easier to deal with
than I had thought. He made no attempt to be in any way
mysterious. "I do wish you would give up all this stupidity,"
he said to me plaintively. "Surely you must realise by now
that it is impossible to steal a ship in these days and to escape
with her; our navy will on no account let you pass."

"They certainly have made me look rather foolish," I
admitted.

"Then you will take *Olinda* back to Istanbul?" he suggested
eagerly.

"I dare say. I'm waiting for orders."

"Ah!" His voice took on a tone of rather heavy patronage,
which made me smile. "Then we shall all be able to go home
again."

"Or to Izmir," suggested Nadia. "Why don't you come
there for a little, Fritz? I find it just as dull all by myself there
as you do here." She seemed quite uninterested in what Fritz
and I had been talking about, but only determined to get into
the conversation.

Raki and *cognac* were brought, and nuts and numerous dishes
of beans, eggs, cucumber and so forth, known as *mézés*. After
a few drinks poor old Fritz began to cheer up. Soon he became
heavily jocular. I was relieved, for it was all too evident that
he was pathetically anxious for a party, especially with Nadia.
There would be no need for me to resort to those stupid little
yellow tablets which were at the moment burning a hole in
my pocket.

By six-thirty there was quite an atmosphere of carousal about
our table. Peter and Nadia seemed reasonably sober, though
very gay; I myself was endeavouring to appear realistically tipsy
without actually drinking very much; but Suliman and Fritz

were downing drink for drink—Suliman with an ill-concealed ferocity, and both of them with such enthusiastic abandon, that it was difficult to forecast the order in which they would ultimately fall under the table.

Suddenly I remembered a mysterious occurrence of which I had always longed for an explanation from Fritz. "I say, was it you or Alphonse who locked my friend in the washplace just before our train got to Ankara that day?"

But Fritz would not commit himself. "It is an old trick of the English to get themselves locked in lavatories," he observed dryly. "They also enjoy being stoned by the Indians . . . and having their trousers removed. They believe this exposes their fundamental majesty, and makes them look such good fellows. . . . There is indeed a certain majestic insouciance," he conceded grudgingly, "about the sacrificial ox in his shirt tails. . . ."

I thought a song might help matters to mature, and tried to start one without relaxing my efforts to appear slightly drunk.

"Do you have to make a face like that when you sing?" inquired Nadia, unkindly. "You look half-witted."

As soon as the party reached the stage at which my presence was no longer of the slightest importance to anyone (except, possibly, to Peter), I got up from the table, hoping to slip quietly away. But I was prevented from doing this by Fritz, who began to sing a Turkish song with Suliman Bey, in opposition to mine. Before they had got very far with it, Fritz suddenly stopped singing, went first white, then a greyish green, then sprang to his feet and darted out of the restaurant. A few moments later he returned—*apparently quite sober*. This time he sat down next to Nadia, who seemed pleased to have him there, and immediately took his arm.

I was now in some doubt as to what was the best thing to do. Fritz, after this, would most certainly be careful not to drink too much again. It was nearly seven o'clock. By eight o'clock at latest, *Olinda* must leave Ayvalik Bay if she was to reach Egrilar before the following dawn. To make matters worse, Nadia suddenly decided that it was time to eat a proper supper. She summoned a waiter and began to order food. With the deepest misgivings, I started to plan for an opportunity to use the dope.

I was assisted by the fact that the waiter was now busy with
Nadia's order for supper, so that he was not available to get
us the next round of *cognacs* and *raki*. "What will you have to
drink?" I asked Nadia. "I'll go and get it from the bar
myself."

"Nothing, thank you," replied Nadia coolly. "I'll wait till
after supper."

"What about you, Fritz?"

"I have already drunk enough for the present." Fritz gave
me a sickly smile, and turned to stroke Nadia's hand in a
maddeningly affectionate manner. Peter and Suliman, however, both asked for *raki*.

I strolled off towards the bar, which was on the other side
of the central stove, and hidden from the table at which we
sat. When I reached the bar, I paused undecided for a moment.
How exactly was I going to set about doping Fritz? About his
passing out, when he had taken the dope, I was not in the least
worried. Everyone in the restaurant had seen him rush out to
get rid of his first overdose of *raki*; they would not consider it
in the least odd if he suddenly fell under the table after a further
indulgence in the stuff. But how on earth, I wondered, was
I going to force another drink on Fritz without arousing his
suspicions, and how was I going to make sure that he took the
doped glass? In the end I decided to get five drinks instead of
three, on the pretext that this would save us trouble later on.
I would then put their drinks beside Fritz and Nadia with the
suggestion that they drink them later. Fritz, I felt sure, would
soon be at his glass none the less and, as for Nadia . . . Yes,
what about Nadia? Once more I found it difficult to come to
a decision.

The barman had just served two Turks who had arrived
before me; now he looked at me with inquiring eyes. I still
hesitated, however; I wanted time to think . . . to ask myself
a question I had repeatedly shelved. The barman turned to
attend to some other customers who had just strolled up.

Was I going to dope Nadia too? The idea of being obliged
to do such a thing had certainly never occurred to me when
I had first thought of asking her to come to Ayvalik. But then,
nor had I ever seriously considered doping Fritz; and now that
I was forced to deal with Fritz, what of Nadia? If the girl

happened, after all, to be an enemy agent, she was just as much a danger to us without the preoccupation of Fritz as *he* would have been without *her*. But what if she were no more than she had always appeared (to me at least)? There was something about Nadia—her odd way of looking at you, her quick brain, her easy mocking laughter—that I found irresistibly charming and convincing. Then I remembered a mocking smile upon the face of Peter when first I had told him of my plan to use Nadia as a bait for Fritz. My vanity, I am ashamed to say, was touched—no, I decided; in spite of any personal feelings of mine, Nadia must take her chance with Fritz.

As I approached the bar once more, I felt unhappy . . . miserable. I began almost to regret ever having entered Ayvalik Bay . . . to wish that I had stood straight on, after being bombed. *Olinda* would then have been neatly torpedoed somewhere in the region of Leros and the whole business would have been over and done with.

I ordered my five drinks and placed them on a tray. There was no difficulty whatever about slipping one tablet each into two of the glasses before I reached the stove in the middle of the room; nor was there anything unusual in my excuses to Nadia and Fritz, nor in my putting Fritz's drink down beside him . . . at least no one would have thought so; but, when I moved round to put Nadia's drink beside her, she suddenly flew into a passion.

"I thought I told you I didn't want one," she said, between her teeth, with a cold fury in her eyes.

I repeated my explanation. Whereupon Nadia sprang to her feet and faced me.

"What sort of manners are these?" she stormed. "Am I once more to be treated as the common bar girl; to have unwanted drinks forced down my throat; to have them thrown at me whenever and however it may suit my so-called host?" Fritz encouraged her from the background with a muttered remark about the barbarous English, but I took no notice, hoping that Nadia would calm down. My silence seemed only to enrage her further, however; "Take your filthy drinks away and yourself too for all I care," she shouted and pushed, the tray violently from her. Over went the glass of *raki*; and the tray, slipping

out of my hands, went crashing to the floor. There was a
sudden hush in the restaurant as I stood irresolute.

Then suddenly I saw that it was done—neatly and cleanly.
I could go now, and I went. A few minutes later I was out
upon the dark waters of the bay. Then we were clear of the
glare from the lights on the town jetty. The two Arab sailors
pulled strongly towards the dark shadow of *Olinda* upon the
water and chanted together as they pulled.

V

THE DITCH OF DESPAIR

24

WORKING up slowly to her full eight knots, *Olinda* moved sluggishly down the narrow pass leading out of the lagoon. The sand dunes to port gleamed faintly white against the darker hills behind. On the other side, dense olive groves covered the slopes of Mosko Island, which towered black and massive out of the haze. Between the island and the sand dunes lay a short avenue of flashing buoys—red, green and white, in pairs. *Olinda* threaded her ponderous way between them. As soon as she was clear of the narrows, her head was steadied upon the northern end of Gymno Island, whose rocky outline stood clear cut against the searchlights' glare.

For ten minutes *Olinda* remained upon this course. I thought of old Feodor Pavlovitch, with his thin, cultured face and his musical French accent. How did it feel to be an engineer in a ship like this? The Master would no doubt have told him that we were to hug the coast as close as possible—that there were poorly charted shoals off Suna Spit; and everyone on board would have seen the searchlights blazing across the Mitylene Channel these past two nights. How did it feel to be carried, at the whim of a young foreigner, into what must seem to Feodor a most foolhardy, almost an unseamanlike adventure? Yet all depended upon Feodor Pavlovitch. Suppose he took it into his canny old head to stop the engines—to be a little careless about the oiling; to find suddenly that a bearing was running hot, or to discover a choked pipe in the cooling system? Any such breakdown was enough to bring about the failure of our attempt—to prevent *Olinda* from ever poking her nose beyond the shelter of the islands. By craning out over the back of the monkey island, I was just able to see down the engine-room skylight, which was still open. There was Feodor, standing with his cap on the back of his head, staring moodily at the throttle and reversing wheel. He was slouched a bit, with his hands in his pockets, and there was a look of half-humorous resignation upon his face.

I turned to stare for a moment into the night ahead; on the port bow the flashing red light of Ali Burnu popped up over the end of Rowley Point, so I started my stop-watch and glanced at the standard compass. *Olinda* was dead upon her course. The Mate was steering, I reflected. In seven and a half minutes exactly it would be time to turn south.

Then I swung round again to look down into the engine-room. That skylight would have to be closed and the ship completely darkened before we reached open water. One of the Chinese boys, Mickey, the jolly one, flashed into view, scrambling over the top of an engine and greasing busily as he went; and there was Ivan Oreshkin, by the electric lighting plant. Even from this distance, one could observe the keen, tense poise of Ivan's body, and imagine those sharp, black eyes snapping fiercely. Everyone down there seemed oblivious to life outside the engine-room—interested only in the little whirring kingdom that was all their own.

I returned to the standard compass, and settled myself behind it; then bent my knees to squint across the top of it at the red light to port . . . 208 degrees . . . I glanced at the stop-watch . . . three minutes to go. The hill on Mosko Island lay well out upon the quarter now. To port, the sand dunes fell away and lost themselves against the high ground farther off. "Steer 187" . . . slowly *Olinda*'s head crept round until it was pointing directly at the flashing red light.

The Master climbed on to the monkey island beside me. The white loom of the searchlights had grown much brighter in the hazy air; it shone pallidly upon the Master's face—a gnarled and expressionless face, above a massive body. All around us was very dark and still; no breath of air stirred in a heavy, misty atmosphere. A wavering black line of ripple stretched out and back from *Olinda*'s bow as she crept along. There was an occasional spot or two of rain.

The Master put his hand in his trousers pocket and pulled out a large watch, which he held sideways towards the glare ahead.

"Eight o'clock," he grunted, and put his watch away. Then we both stood in silence for several minutes. My mind wandered back over the day's events. Idly I wondered what it was that Nadia had ordered for supper. She would be just finishing it now, unless the waiter had been slower than usual . . . and Fritz, was he enjoying his food too? All the more perhaps, on

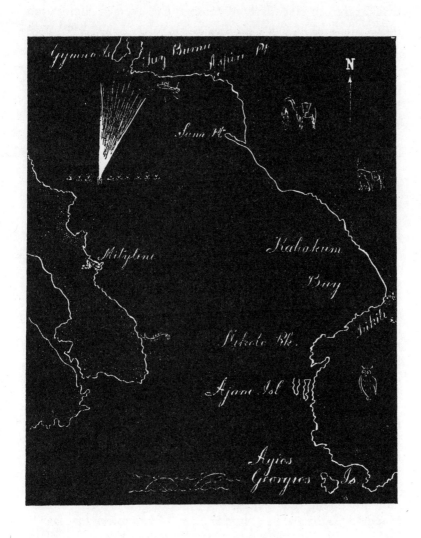

account of a certain triumph at my abrupt dismissal. I thought
again of the way in which Nadia had deliberately upset her
drink. Her sudden flash of temper had seemed almost too
unprovoked to be genuine, and yet you never could tell with
a girl like Nadia. Had she allowed Fritz to drink his? Would
she have cared or not if she had known that Fritz's drink was
doped? Anyway, Peter would be watching the situation carefully. He would no doubt be having some difficulty in restrain-
ing the bellicose Suliman; but if, between them, they could
keep things going for only another hour, *Olinda* would either be
past the enemy patrols or . . . Ali Burnu blazed out red and
close aboard to the starboard. In the same instant *Olinda*
passed through the last shreds of mist which lay among the
islands, and the whole expanse of open sea burst out clear
before us. I heard the Master draw in his breath sharply at
what he saw. Then he grunted, shrugged his shoulders, and
turned towards the ladder which led down to the wing of the
bridge.

From where *Olinda* now was, the line of enemy lights seemed
to stretch right across to the Turkish shore. A distant memory
of Southend pier flashed through my mind, making me
smile; the Huns must have collected every fishing boat in the
neighbourhood to have achieved such a gala display, completed by the two searchlights flaring from near the middle of
the line. And the sight was, if anything, encouraging. If they
had hoped to sink *Olinda*, the Germans would obviously have
placed no lights in these craft. They would have waited for the
ship to blunder unsuspecting into the line of darkened boats;
then a few flashes from the one nearest to her would have told
them her exact position. No, they obviously hoped, at present,
merely to scare *Olinda* back to port. We altered course slowly
to a little south of east, keeping as close as possible to Tuz Burnu.

Both searchlights were motionless and slightly elevated. But
suddenly one of them jerked down and began to sweep slowly
round across the water. "Stop engines . . . half astern together."
We had beside us the mottled background of the cliffs of Tuz
Burnu. If only there was no movement to catch the eye as the
beam swept over us, the ship might not be noticed. Gradually
Olinda lost way. "Stop both," and the engines fell silent, while
the ship continued to creep very gently ahead—just fast enough

to make steering possible for a little longer. The searchlight beam came sheering, like the sword of Gabriel, across the sea. For a moment it hovered upon the gap through which *Olinda* had just passed, between Gymno Island and Tuz Burnu; then, very slowly, inexorably, it came on . . . the centre shaft of white in a sheath of hazier luminosity—bulbing out at the end against the mist, and blazing. I became fascinated with the deadly thing . . . with the bright patch it sent chasing along the cliff side on our inshore quarter . . . stumbling among the rocks and leaping the gulleys, like a herd of white horses— ghost horses—steeds of the Valkyrie stampeding—galloping after us along the shore.

"You remain long time stopped?" It was the Mate's quiet voice passing along to me a complaint received through the engine-room voice-pipe. "Engineers worrying about leaky air-bottle."

I tore my eyes from the searchlight. It was beginning to blind me anyway.

"I don't know yet. Better start the compressor, though." I imagined them down there in the engine-room—oblivious to all but the practical needs of their machinery—with a friendly contempt for the ignorant people on the bridge.

Down on the foredeck I could see the Arabs and the two Maltese, staring to seaward in silence—crouching a little, like rabbits mesmerised in the headlights of a car. In the starboard wing of the bridge stood the Master, with Malu beside him; her forepaws were up on the rail, and the Master had her muzzle gripped in one massive hand to prevent her barking. Upon the poop stood Ah Fong; I could see the bright buttons of his eyes gleaming black out of the bland half-smiling expanse of his yellow face.

Once more I glanced at the beam astern . . . closer now and larger . . . a moving wall of incandescence that seemed to be creeping after us with a sinister deliberation. All at once there appeared a faint swelling far down near the heel of the shaft; it spread into a fuzzy inflamation that came running swiftly up the moving beam . . . now it was expanding into a luminous cloud . . . into a filmy swathe of mist, hardly dense enough to be seen until the searchlight shone through it; but dense enough, just, to blur *Olinda*'s outline against the cliffs—to make her

invisible to the eyes behind the light, and possibly even to save
her in the moment of discovery. With a "swish" that one
could almost hear, the searchlight beam swept over us, and the
galloping herd of light flashed past along the cliffs, and beyond,
and away into the hills. Suddenly the beam glowed orange
and died. A faint streak persisted for a while; then the darkness
returned and stood before us like a wall.

"The ship no longer steers." The old Mate's voice was calm
and sadly patient. I glanced at the compass. *Olinda* having
ceased to move, her rudder no longer functioned, and her head
was falling off slowly towards the land. I slipped down the
bridge ladder and into the chart-room to check our position.
"Slow ahead port. . . . Hard a-starboard," and, a little
later, "Full ahead together." Then a rough bearing of Tuz
Burnu, which was still visible on the port quarter in the
general glare. Once more the stop-watch was set and the ship's
head steadied on a course of 105 degrees.

We soon realised that it would be impossible to use our
former marks for turning on to the next course. The blaze of
light to seaward made the northern sky pitch black by contrast,
while the mist among the islands and over the lagoon had
blotted out all signs of Mosko Island. Even if we were able
to pick out the nearer 440-foot hill, there would be nothing
farther off upon which to line it up. *Olinda* would have
to stand south upon a compass course. We must hope that
no currents would set her to the eastward—towards the
shoals, since there would be no visible landmarks upon which
to check the line of her advance.

In less than a minute we were abreast of the first small headland after Tuz Burnu, and course was altered to due east, so as to pass as close as possible to our 440-foot hill. But just as *Olinda* reached the vicinity of this hill, the searchlight came sweeping over us once again. We were much farther away by now, so there was no longer any chance of our being seen; but the light blinded us, and we were obliged to alter course by stop-watch, since not even the 440 hill could be seen. For the second time in thirty-six hours, *Olinda* was laid upon a course of 166 degrees, and so far she had not been challenged. With high hopes we stood away from the land and out across Suna Bay.

We could now see that the eastern end of the lighted patrol line finished nearly three miles out from the Turkish coast. Unless the Germans had a few unlighted boats farther to the eastward, *Olinda* seemed to have an excellent chance of getting through—especially as she had not been picked up by the searchlight. For the next twenty minutes we all stared into the darkness ahead, looking for any suspicious black smudge that might be a patrol craft lying in wait, or for the white plume of an E-boat's bow wave. Nothing appeared, and our spirits began to soar. Soon we had the enemy patrol line right abreast and end on to us. The nearest boat looked at least a mile away. There was more room than we had thought. *Olinda* would get through easily.

The Master went to relieve the Mate at the wheel. The old Mate looked up, smiling a little, as he left the bridge to go down to his cabin. I began to hum softly to myself, and to think of all the amusing moments during our stay in Turkey— of one or two parties; of spoiling the Germans' dinner at the Tokatlian Hotel in Istanbul; of John struggling with the carriage window in the train at Kayseri; and then once more of Nadia. Would we ever see her again? Would we ever see Fritz or Suliman Bey in peace-time? What a gay adventure it had all been, and how dull to go back to a regular naval life—to a frigate, perhaps or to a corvette.

The nearest light was now well abaft the beam—had been for nearly half an hour; it must be very far away, for its bearing seemed hardly to have changed with the minutes. How silently and smoothly *Olinda* crept along; scarcely a ripple upon the

202 NO STARS TO GUIDE

dull, black sea to mark her passing. Fine upon the port bow, the mountainous headland of Mal Tepeh looked clearer and more massive, but still a long way off. Distances at night were so deceptive. In the hazy darkness to port, it was not possible to pick out the thin tongue of sand which would be Suna Spit, but we ought to have passed it by now; it must nearly be time for the course to be altered again—for *Olinda* to close the land and skirt the beaches of Kabakum Bay. Once more the search-light beam came tearing the darkness, slicing it through, then extinguishing suddenly to let the night come swarming back upon us, more blinding than before.

All at once I found that I was no longer alone in the darkness. Feodor Pavlovitch was beside me; I could see his pointed grey beard and dimly, in the dull glow from the standard compass bowl, those two twinkling eyes and a few lines of faint inquiry about his mouth. Beneath us mumbled the steady rhythm of the engines, beating musically throughout the ship. Feodor glanced at the compass, then looked away into the darkness.

"Your engines have not let us down anyway," I observed, in halting French, trying to show appreciation of his efforts.

"*Non. Elles marchent toujours*," he replied non-committally.

Strange fellow Feodor. I wondered whether he came from a family of impoverished nobility, dispossessed during the revolution. His face, upon which the weak light shone upwards, wore an expression of kindly patronage, the usual expression of an engineer upon the bridge; not arrogant, nor critical; just detached, and full of a friendly interest—interest in the strange uses to which his precious horse-power is being put. No doubt the heat of the engine-room had sent him up for a breath of fresh air. I asked if it was hot down there:

"*Il fait chaud auprés des machines?*"

"*Non: il fait froid.*"

"Oh."

What should I say next? I wanted to be friendly; but neither of us spoke French very well. I wondered how long he had been on deck: "*Vous êtes sur le pont depuis long temps?*"

"*Oui. Une demi heure.*"

He moved to the side of the monkey island, and stood gazing down into the water for a moment. "*Venez voir,*" he said, after a while, and beckoned to me to come and look. "*Pourquoi nous marchons pas?*"

Why weren't we moving? What did he mean? I joined him at the rail and looked down.

On the water alongside there was not a single ripple—not a streak of any bow wave. It was almost too dark to have seen one anyway; but I could make out the bubbles and phosphorescence from the main cooling-water discharge pipe, shooting out from the ship's side with every beat of the port engine—shooting straight out from the ship's side into dead, still water!

"*Tres drôle, n'est ce pas?*" observed Feodor.

Very comical? I should think it was. *Olinda* was plum stationary. She was hard aground.

Feodor Pavlovitch strolled to the ladder and started down it unhurriedly. He paused for a moment, with his head just above the edge of the coaming, and attempted a remark in English:

"Half-hour not moving," he announced pleasantly. "*Si vous permettez*, I start now the pumps." Then he cocked his old head on one side and, smiling brightly, disappeared.

The engines were set full astern and, for an hour or more there was nothing to do but to watch the main discharge and wait. What a miserable end to all our hopes and plans! But there was no need to be too downhearted. True, we could never hope now to make Egrilar before dawn; there was still Port Sahib, however, at the mouth of the Gulf of Izmir, or even Ali Agha, less than thirty miles ahead of us. Provided we managed to get her off within an hour or two, *Olinda* would still be able to shelter in one of these. Suddenly, as I watched, I saw the faint phosphorescent plume of discharge water bend like a comet's tail; the bubbles, like green sparks, started drifting forward. She was off!

The helm was kept amidships; *Olinda* gathered stern-way, and was soon travelling swiftly back along the path by which she had entered the shoals. We held our breath, waiting until we felt she must be well clear, then, "Full ahead port," and hard a-starboard with the helm. *Olinda* turned upon her heel and started moving ahead, due west, straight out into the channel.

Triumph and relief surged through us. But our exaltation was short-lived. *Olinda* had moved no more than a few hundred yards before her bows suddenly lifted, and she stopped dead—hard aground upon another bank.

The time was getting on. It was already after midnight. Unless *Olinda* was able to get clear within the next two hours, she would have no chance of reaching shelter before dawn, so whatever action was now taken must be decisive. A third of her ballast had been pumped out in order to float her off the first bank. The removal of the remaining two-thirds might lighten her sufficiently to get her clear of this one; but if she grounded again after that, we were done.

The pumps were once more started and, while we were waiting, the working-boat was lowered and manned by the bosun and two Arabs. For an hour and a half the bosun sounded with a lead line in various directions. It was difficult for him to tell the depth accurately, since, in the darkness, he was obliged to feel with his hands for the markings on the line; but, when he returned at last, he reported that for nearly half a mile ahead of the ship, there was no depth greater than seventeen feet; astern of her there was deeper water for a few hundred yards, then another bank with less than sixteen feet of water upon it.

By this time the slight movement of the ship, with sometimes a gentle bump, told us that she was nearly afloat, so we had to decide at once whether to attempt to work her off astern into the narrow gulley of deeper water, or whether to try to force her right over the bank ahead and into the open sea beyond. The first course would have involved the risk of being unable to stop or turn *Olinda* before she grounded again aft; if she did that, her screws would certainly be damaged; besides which, she would still be sandwiched between two shoals, and we had no time left in which to sound out a deep-water channel through them. We decided, therefore, to keep the ship pointing in the same direction, west, and to set both engines full ahead. If the bosun's soundings had been accurate, she would then be likely to force her way fairly easily over the bank, since she would soon be drawing less than seventeen feet of water instead of her normal eighteen. This plan had another advantage; apart from the fact that it involved no risk of damage to

Olinda's screws, the screws themselves were naturally designed to be at least fifty per cent more efficient when turning ahead than when pulling astern. The bow of a ship, furthermore, is obviously better shaped than the stern for forcing a passage through any form of resistance.

Ivan Oreshkin came up with a message from the chief. Only one more tank remained to be pumped out; should they continue pumping? Yes, we must make certain of it this time; it was our only hope; we must stake everything on giving the ship her best chance of struggling clear.

In the pitch darkness we waited. Men stood about in groups in various parts of the ship. One could hear the low mutter of conversation from time to time, and occasionally a short snatch of a tune whistled softly between the teeth. The two search-lights went out, but the line of lighted boats remained in its former position—between *Olinda* and Ayvalik. I climbed down to look at the chart-room clock; it showed twenty minutes to four. Good heavens, we could never make the Gulf of Sandarli by dawn! We would have to try for Port Ajano, which lay only ten miles away. There seemed to be a little more movement in the ship now; it felt as though she were about to float. The Master rang "stand by" on the engine-room telegraphs and I returned to the monkey island.

For another ten minutes I stood there waiting, controlling with a great effort, the impulse to keep on asking for reports from the engine-room. At last the sound of pumping ceased. "Full astern together!" The two engines burst into life. Immediately, with an almost sobbing relief, we saw that the ship was moving. I let her go a full ship's length astern, just to give her a short run at the bank, then, "Full ahead together!" She trembled a little; then started to forge ahead.

Olinda gathered way . . . two knots . . . three knots . . . she must be right over the bank again now. For a moment or two she seemed to be dragging; her engines laboured mightily; we held our breath. Then she surged ahead again . . . faster now, and still steering due west . . . she was away, she was clear! In spite of the need for silence, a ragged cheer went up from all the ship's company as the conviction swept through them that the worst was over. And while the last high notes of the cheering were still echoing round the ship, *Olinda* heeled over to starboard and came to a final shuddering standstill.

For a full minute we all stood motionless and dumb. A flood of dark despair came rolling after us and poured like an avalanche upon us. We all stood bowed and listless beneath the weight of bitterest defeat.

After a period of desperate churning, ahead and astern, with the helm put this way and that, the engines were finally stopped, for there was no moving her. *Olinda* was stuck fast. Helpless and glum we stood and stared towards the open sea, which now we could never reach—towards that futile line of lights, which we had circumvented so easily and, beyond them, at the threatening coast of Mitylene from which we must, at dawn, be plainly visible . . . from which, as and when they pleased, the aircraft would come to finish us. In the overwhelming darkness and silence of that winter's night, fear—hopeless whimpering fear stole over the ship. No one looked anywhere but towards the west, whence our inevitable doom must come. Then, suddenly, clearly, smashing the silence, and with a maddening insolence, the cockerel in the hen coop aft began to crow.

At the gruesome unreality of so homely a sound, stark unreasoning terror gripped us. Instinctively we turned to look eastwards and there, sure enough, we saw the first dull streaks of dawn above the mountains. With an oath, the Master went clattering down on to the poop; next minute a furious fluttering and clucking told of a misbegotten bird who had made the last tactless mistake of his life. So violently did the frantic man wring the cockerel's neck, that its head came clean off, and the blood gushed and spurted. Then the Master returned to the bridge, his hands red and dripping, wiping them upon his trousers, and together we stood beside the standard compass to watch a grim dawn breaking slowly.

25

THERE would be no sense in denying that panic, at this moment—common, crippling panic—was on the point of claiming us all. With the ship stuck fast among banks, whose shape and size it was impossible to guess, and without a single weapon to use in her defence, there seemed little excuse for remaining in her. All were convinced that the bombers would soon be over; that within an hour or so, they would be carefully and deliberately smashing *Olinda* into small pieces. The growing light showed us the outline of Suna Spit, less than two miles away to the eastward; instinctively people drifted aft on to the poop and began to gather near the boats.

But there was still an hour to go to sunrise. It was unlikely, I felt, that any attack would be made upon us until well after dawn—probably not for another three hours. The enemy, when they saw us, would guess at once, by the direction in which *Olinda* was pointing, and by the way in which she listed to starboard, that she was aground. They would be in no hurry to deal with her, for she was clearly unable to escape so long as daylight lasted. Meanwhile a panic must somehow be prevented; something must be found for the hands to do, some essential task to occupy their minds, no matter how unavailing their efforts. What further attempt could we make to get the ship afloat? Of course!—the anchors: we must clear away some anchors, ready for carrying out in the boats.

In which direction should we lay out our anchors? They must be dropped in deep water so that, when we hauled upon them, *Olinda*, if she moved at all, would come clear of all the banks, and be able to manœuvre. But we had no inkling as to the size, shape or number of these banks; nor could we discover this until we had made careful soundings over a wide area round the ship, or until the sun was high enough to show the difference in colour between deep and shoal water. The anchors could, however, be cleared away; the two lifeboats and the working-boat lowered in readiness.

It took a great deal of bullying and persuasion to get the crew started upon these tasks; and, even when they began, they went listlessly about the business. The bosun found it exceedingly difficult to make the men concentrate upon their work; they all had one eye upon Mitylene and upon the sky above it. Whenever the bosun grew impatient and charged in among them to do the work himself, the Arabs would stand back and gaze out to sea with lifeless, hopeless expressions of dread upon their faces. Under the violence of the bosun's threats they would return unwillingly to fumble and jerk at the lashings, but their efforts were puny, so it took nearly an hour to get the anchors cleared and into the water.

As soon as it was light enough to take accurate bearings of the headlands and islands, I was able to fix the ship's position within a few hundred yards. When this position was laid off on the chart, it showed the ship to be lying nearly one mile to seaward of the shoals. But the chart's cautionary note about these shoals, spoke of other shallows "considerably farther west." We had found these other shallows all right, but we had no means of telling how far, nor in which direction, they extended.

At sunrise the Mate informed us that the work on the anchors was finished. A sling of stout wire had been passed through the ring of the starboard bower anchor to secure it while the heavy chain cable was unshackled. The anchor had then been lowered by means of the sling, until the whole of it was out of sight below the surface of the water. In this position it had been left until the lifeboat could be brought up alongside it, when it would be transferred to the boat. While this was going on, all three boats had been lowered. Then a second anchor, this time a "stream" anchor, lighter than the first, was also lowered into the sea.

By now we could see the outlines of individual craft in the Mitylene Channel. They had extinguished their lanterns, and were already moving away in a ragged line towards the opposite shore. Most of them, as we had expected, were ordinary island *caiques* and fishing boats manned, no doubt, by local Greeks. There was possibly a German soldier in each as well; but this we were unable to see. Among the *caiques*, though, was a group of three naval-looking craft—small motor launches by their appearance.

All these boats now withdrew, except one—a medium-sized sailing *caique*. She looked like one of the *caiques* that had inspected us three days before off Cape Baba; but now she was under sail only, beating slowly up and down the Channel upon a light easterly breeze, that sprang up with the dawn. She remained on patrol after the others had disappeared. The Mate picked up the binoculars and stood looking at her for some time, then he turned and said something in Russian to the Master. The Master turned to me.

"He say airplanes coming soon. What you goin' to do?"

"As soon as it's properly light we must start sounding. Then we must lay out some anchors."

The Master passed this information on to the Mate, who nodded gloomily, but made no move. Presently, the Mate spoke again.

"People not wanting to stay in ship." He stated this with gloomy finality.

I had expected as much, but had hoped that matters would not come to a head so soon. However, it was no use getting angry. Half these men had little or no stake in the war; they had been landed in their present plight by myself, and through no fault of their own. They were still willing to work for their keep as seamen, but they saw no future in just sitting on board, unable to do anything to protect themselves or the ship—calmly waiting to be butchered.

How much use were they in any case? If the ship were attacked they would undoubtedly stampede; they would simply jump over the side and either swim ashore or be drowned. Besides which, all the heavy work with the anchors had now been done; the work of running them out with the boats could all be accomplished by four or five good men. It would be far more sensible to keep on board, for this work, one or two volunteers who could be trusted; the remainder might as well be sent ashore. The Turks, I knew, would not allow them to disperse inland, so it would be easy enough to get them back later—if we succeeded in refloating *Olinda* before dark.

"I want four volunteers," I told the Master. "One engineer, one greaser, one upper deck officer and one seaman . . . the rest had better take a lifeboat and go ashore on to the sand spit there."

A wave of excitement passed through the ship's company when the news of these instructions reached them. It took the hands a surprisingly short time to get into the boat, and I was

14

interested to observe that most of them had already bundled up all their belongings and stowed them in the handiest places for abandoning ship. By the time the boat was ready to leave, it was loaded down to its gunwales with a great pile of bags, carpets, shoes, boots, pots and pans, blankets, pictures and several musical instruments, as well as two canaries in a large wire bird cage, and also a couple of cats.

In the stern-sheets of the boat sat Feodor Pavlovitch, the Mate and Ah Fong—all looking calm and a little bit bored, but obviously relieved at the prospect of getting clear of the ill-fated *Olinda*. The remainder of the hands were laughing and chattering like a bunch of happy schoolchildren—all except the tall Chinese greaser, who had dressed himself in a neat lounge suit and wore a black felt hat upon his head. He sat self-consciously upon the pile of assorted gear in the middle of the boat, and clutched the canary cage upon his knees. His face wore an expression of philosophical melancholy. In his incongruously smart get-up he had the comical appearance of a high-ranking diplomat, who had inadvertently become involved in some public demonstration—a fact that was causing him acute embarrassment.

The Master locked Malu in his cabin; then returned to the monkey island.

"Did you find the volunteers?" I asked him.

"Yes, you got five. Second engineer and Bosun stopping, and one greaser and two sailors."

This sounded an excellent team. I could not have chosen two better men than Ivan Oreshkin and the Bosun. I knew also that I had Mickey, the smaller and livelier of the two Chinese greasers; but who were the sailors, I wondered.

"What you like me to do?" asked the Master.

I thought a moment before replying. The Master was by no means a young man, and he certainly had no personal interest in the war. Furthermore, he was not in active command of the ship, and it hardly seemed fair to keep him on board as a sort of staff officer.

"You'd better go ashore," I said, "and try to telephone the British Embassy at Istanbul. . . . If the Turks are helpful, they'll probably escort you up to Dikili village; you may be able to get through from there. . . . If you can't speak to

Commander Mathews, try to get Captain Dick Rees, the salvage officer."

The sun was just beginning to peep over the mountains as the lifeboat drew away from the ship's side. The boat was so overcrowded that they had some difficulty in shipping the oars

but in the end they got going, and I watched them through binoculars as they shaped up for the tip of Suna Spit. As they approached the land, two Turkish soldiers appeared at the inshore end of the sand spit; they did not open fire, however, but merely sat down on guard, with their rifles ready across their knees. The boat reached the shore without mishap, and soon all its occupants were camped on the sand beside it, with the colourful litter of their belongings spread around them.

I lowered the glasses, and was about to turn once more to look in the direction of Mitylene, when a voice at my elbow startled me: "You like bully beef and eggs?" And there was

Zamit. His face wore its normal hideous grin as he offered me a magnificent plate of food and a mug of tea.

I was astounded to see him. I had forgotten all about him during the past two days. "What on earth are you doing here?" I asked, wondering whether by some unlucky chance he had not heard of the instructions for all except the volunteers to leave the ship.

"Me and Johnny the only British sailors on board," proclaimed Zamit stoutly. "We stop."

"But do you know anything about seamen's work?"

"Johnny is good sailor," asserted Zamit. "Me good cook. Ah Fong he goin' ashore. I stop for cooking." He giggled happily, and my own spirits rose at the very sight of him. At his time of life, Zamit was no longer a very active man and definitely not inspiring in appearance, but he seemed at the moment to be quite undaunted by our predicament, and to radiate good humour and confidence. "Me British," he repeated. "Me not frightened of bloody Germans," and he slapped his chest defiantly and spat over the side in the direction of Mitylene.

"Excellent, Zamit. Then I can send for you to hold my hand if they come. I'm terrified of them."

Zamit grinned and clambered down the ladder. I looked over the fore edge of the monkey island, and saw the rest of them sitting on the tank-tops eating their breakfast. They seemed quite unconcerned. The little Chinese Mickey was laughing happily at something or other, and the bosun had a sober smile upon his face. The Bosun had taken off his cap; I noticed that his hair was very thin on top; it gave him a homely and human appearance. Ivan Oreshkin and Johnny Caruana were talking together nearby, but I could not hear what they were saying.

The sun was well up by now and the sky was clear. A few wraiths of morning mist still lay among the islands and between the shoulders of the hills; but out across the sea the air was clear and fresh—it was a sparkling morning, with a bright day ahead. If it had not been for the gnawing anxiety and the frightful sense of failure inside me, I would have been thrilled at such beautiful surroundings—at the splendid mountain scene, at the placid blue water and at the brilliant greens and browns upon the Island of Mitylene. For one brief moment I started to offer a bargain to God. I found myself actually saying the words—making certain promises in return for our salvation. But suddenly, and with equal gravity, I formally withdrew my offer; and I could not help smiling at the ludicrous solemnity of my words, and particularly at the grave and businesslike manner in which I had formally cancelled my quotation to the Almighty.

The breeze, which was still very light, had veered to south-east; the *caique* patrolling in the Channel was standing across towards us upon the starboard tack. I looked at her through the glasses, but I could not make out the appearance of any of her crew. They were probably inspecting us just as busily. Well, let them look; my spirits had risen to such an extent at the sight of Zamit, that I had begun to feel instinctively that we were far from lost—that we might still succeed in extricating *Olinda* and ourselves from this mess.

Suddenly I realised that I was intensely hungry; I sat down on some sandbags and fell upon my breakfast with a good heart.

26

AFTER breakfast we had a short conference, using Zamit as interpreter. Our first concern must be to find out the depth of water in the immediate vicinity of the ship. The sun was not yet high enough to show up the colour of the water; but it seemed likely that the deepest patches would be found to the north of where *Olinda* lay—in the direction of Ayvalik.

Since there was nothing for Zamit or the engineers to do, I did not feel inclined to leave them on board while the rest of us were away from the ship; so we divided ourselves between the working-boat and the second lifeboat, to form two sounding parties. The Bosun, Johnny Caruana and Mickey went away in the lifeboat; I went off in the working-boat with Ivan and Zamit—the latter sitting plump and jolly on the transom seat, chattering irrepressibly as he steered.

For an hour we pulled backwards and forwards to a distance of several hundred yards all round the ship. We were careful not to let the patrolling *caique* see what we were at; we just pulled about, with apparent aimlessness, lowering our sounding lines gently into the water every few yards, just as though we were fishing. We hoped that the occupants of the *caique* would come to precisely this conclusion. By eight-thirty, as there had been no sign of enemy aircraft in the sky, we began to feel reasonably sure that the Germans had decided not to attack us, in such an obvious way, while we were lying in Turkish waters. At nine o'clock we returned to the ship to compare notes.

Both the bosun and I had carried with us in the boats a rough diagram of the ship and the compass bearing upon which she was lying. Upon these diagrams we had marked the depth of water found in various spots. When we transferred these soundings on to a large plan, they produced a picture something like this:

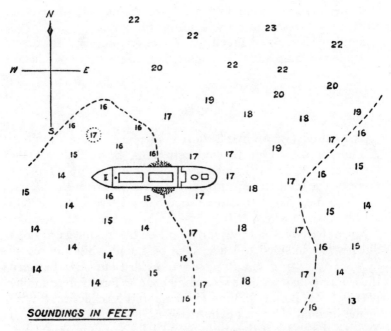

SOUNDINGS IN FEET

The situation looked very hopeful. *Olinda*'s draught, without any ballast, was about 16 feet 6 inches; it seemed therefore that her after end was in water deep enough to float her. Unfortunately, however, there were two mounds of sand on either side of her. They had been piled there, when we had first tried to get her off, by the wash from her screws going astern. Now they formed a sort of cradle in which she lay snugly.

The sun being by this time well up in the sky, the bosun and I went up to the monkey island and immediately saw the whole situation at a glance. To the north of us lay deep blue water in every direction. *Olinda* had stranded on the very tail of a bank: one ship's length farther north, in fact, and she would have passed clear.

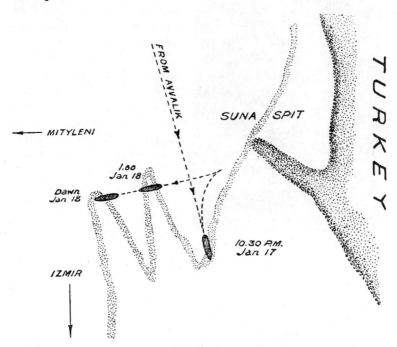

We decided to lay out our anchors at once—one right astern, and one on the starboard quarter. The bosun, with Johnny Caruana and Mickey, brought the lifeboat round under the starboard bow of the ship. The two-ton anchor was now slung beneath the boat on a short length of manila rope, and the end of a long mooring wire was shackled into the ring of it. Away went the lifeboat on another fishing expedition, watching my signals, which directed her to the deepest water on *Olinda*'s starboard quarter. When she had proceeded to the full extent of the mooring wire, plus another wire which we had meanwhile shackled into the end of the first, the Bosun cut the rope strop holding the anchor beneath the boat, so that the anchor fell to the sea bed, and lay there ready for us to start hauling from the ship. We repeated this performance with the lighter stream anchor, which was laid out directly astern of the ship on the end of two more mooring wires.

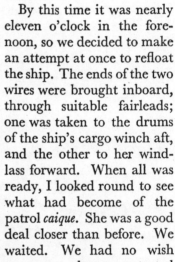

By this time it was nearly eleven o'clock in the forenoon, so we decided to make an attempt at once to refloat the ship. The ends of the two wires were brought inboard, through suitable fairleads; one was taken to the drums of the ship's cargo winch aft, and the other to her windlass forward. When all was ready, I looked round to see what had become of the patrol *caique*. She was a good deal closer than before. We waited. We had no wish for her to see the wash from our screws when we started the main engines, nor the wires rising taut out of the sea as we hove upon them. For we did not doubt that, if the Germans realised that there was a chance of *Olinda*'s being refloated, they would take immediate and decisive steps to see that she was not.

In a little while, however, the *caique* turned into the wind, which was now blowing more freshly from south, and stood away upon the port tack. We gave her twenty minutes to get well over on to the other side of the Channel, then Ivan Oreshkin went below; a few minutes later both *Olinda*'s engines started up and were set at "full astern."

For half an hour we hove and struggled with the anchors— first on one, then the other, then on both of them together, hoping to shake the ship free of the sand; but at the end of that time she had not shifted an inch. All we had succeeded in doing was to drag both anchors through the sand and home to the ship. We left them there, hanging in the water as before; for by this time the patrol *caique* had tacked again, and was once more approaching us.

During another short conference it occurred to us that if we were to pump *Olinda*'s ballast tanks full, at the same time working the engines alternately ahead and astern, the extra weight of water inside her might cause her to settle a little, thereby deepening the cradle she had made for herself in the sand. If she succeeded in doing this, we had only to pump all the water out again and possibly then the ship would float. So Ivan went below and opened the flooding valves. Then we all collected in the saloon to see what Zamit had produced for dinner.

Upon the saloon table was a magnificent roast chicken; behind it stood Zamit, proudly flourishing a carving-knife and fork.

"Double rations and no tips," he cried, and added happily, "for maybe we all goin't get minced up to-day or to-morrow"; whereupon he hacked a large slice out of the bird's breast and slapped it on a plate. I realised that the bird we were about to eat must be our loud-mouthed and luckless cockerel. I remembered the fussiness of that stalwart vegetarian, the Master, over his poultry; no one else on board was allowed to eat chicken. I wondered what would happen when he returned to find that the plumpest, albeit the most exasperating of his precious brood had suffered this final indignity. In the meantime, however, we all enjoyed a veritable banquet . . . Zamit had made us a whole pile of roast and boiled potatoes and also, no doubt as evidence of his British sympathies, a large basin of bread sauce. He had even hunted up two bottles of Turkish red wine which we drank to the dregs.

As soon as the meal was over I took the smaller of the boats and, leaving the bosun and Ivan Oreshkin to carry on with the business of working *Olinda* into her bed, I pulled ashore alone towards the end of the sand spit, where the rest of the crew were still lying.

As I drew nearer to the beach I noticed that the Master was standing apart from the rest of them; he came down alone to

the water's edge to meet me. As a matter of fact I had seen
through my glasses, nearly two hours before, that the Master
had returned from his telephoning expedition, and I had
wondered then why he did not come back to the ship in the
second lifeboat; I now found out the reason.

"Crew saying they not coming back on board . . . never,"
said the Master.

"Do they all say that?"

"Yes, all."

This was something of a puzzle. I was by now convinced
that we would ultimately succeed in refloating *Olinda*, so we
would need the rest of the crew for watch-keeping duties later;
it would have been wellnigh impossible for only seven of us
to work *Olinda* all the way to Syria. In any case the Turks
would make trouble at once if we attempted to leave half the
crew behind, without papers and without authority. And, but
for the continued benevolence of the Turks, it would be an
utter impossibility to force *Olinda* through the Straits of Khios,
Samos and Kos.

I clambered ashore and followed the Master across the sand
to where the crew were lying. I went up to the Mate first.
"Come on," I said encouragingly, "time to get back to the
ship." He smiled weakly and shook his head.

I approached Feodor Pavlovitch.

"*Il faut retourner abord,*" I tried, but he merely turned his
quizzical gaze upon me for a moment, then looked away
again.

"*Nous avons le temps d'attendre la nuit,*" he remarked evenly.
"The sun is warm here—all same Monte Carlo."

I smiled at the picture of old Feodor basking indolently on
the beaches of a millionaire's paradise. The part of a dilettante,
a Russian *émigré* in Monaco, would have suited him admirably.

The rest of the crew were all determined to follow the example
of Feodor and the Mate by refusing to return on board, at any
rate before nightfall. It was clearly absurd for me to start
shooting at them with my revolver; besides being very bad
manners, it would have resulted in our immediate arrest by the
Turks. In the end the Master and I left them where they were,
and pulled back to the ship in the working-boat.

The Master had eaten nothing all day, having refused the

bully beef and biscuits which the crew had taken ashore. As a result he was ravenously hungry, so the first thing he did, when we reached *Olinda*, was to hurry on to the poop to fetch his precious cockerel. In the scene which followed the Master's discovery of his loss, old Zamit only just succeeded in escaping hideous bodily damage. He rushed on to the poop in answer to the Master's bellowing summons, armed with two limp, wet fishes which he had been enterprising enough to catch. As he came scuttling up the ladder with these measly offerings held out before him, he looked so like a distracted savage, bent on appeasing the mighty god of battle, that we all burst out laughing.

About two o'clock in the afternoon we started again to lay out the anchors. *Olinda*'s ballast tanks were now full, and Ivan Oreshkin had already begun to pump them out again. At five o'clock they were empty, so the time had come for another attempt to heave the ship off.

There was still no sign of any impending attack by the enemy, but we were delayed for another ten minutes by the patrol *caique*. While we were waiting for her to move away, it struck me that we must be careful, should we manage to refloat the ship, to prevent the enemy from noticing our success. We would of course be obliged to drop *Olinda*'s port anchor immediately, so as to prevent her from drifting; and, unless we could think of some way of checking her, the southerly wind would cause her to ride with her head pointing south, instead of west as it did at present . . . a fact which must at once be remarked upon by the crew of the patrol *caique*.

At last the coast was reasonably clear so, with both engines racing full astern, we began to heave upon our anchors once again. This time, at the first heave, *Olinda* drew sweetly astern and went plunging off the bank into deep water!

Immediately we let go the port anchor forward, and by holding on to one of the other anchors as well, we managed to check the ship and eventually to hold her, pointing in the same direction as she had been lying before. Then we opened some flooding valves once again, and began to fill a few of the starboard tanks only. In this way we soon put a marked list to starboard on the ship and, by the time the patrol *caique* had once more reached the Turkish side of the Channel, *Olinda* was lying in her original posture—looking as though she were still aground; but actually afloat in deep water, some two hundred yards north-east of her previous position.

We felt relieved and excited, but not yet jubilant. We must still escape from Suna Bay, and this had to be done in the face of an enemy who had once already discovered us in the act of evading his patrols. I wondered what measures he would take to deal with us to-night. There was also the matter of our own crew, still lying sprawled upon the sand spit; it looked as though even they had not noticed that *Olinda* was now afloat.

About half an hour before sunset the Master and I made yet another expedition to the beach; but this time we pulled to the inshore end of the sand spit, opposite the spot where the two Turkish soldiers were patiently sitting. I knew how dearly the Turkish soldier loves to fire his rifle (they are reputed to use yachts and coasters for target practice, even in peace-time); so I had made a plan which was based on this habit of the Turks, and I outlined it carefully to the Master on the way ashore. He was to explain the position to the Turks and then ask for their co-operation . . . if they should see us pulling away from the shore alone, after once more parleying with the crew, they were to fire a few rounds over the heads of the men in order to frighten them into the lifeboat and back to the ship.

The Master went ashore and stood arguing with the soldiers for more than five minutes. From what subsequently occurred, I had reason to believe that either his command of Turkish was somewhat sketchy or that the soldiers came to the conclusion that the wretched fellow must be a fifth columnist. When he returned to the boat, however, we pulled along the beach to where our crew were sitting . . . watching us with mild amusement.

Hardly had the Master started addressing his men when two loud reports rang out, and next moment a couple of bullets whined over the boat. Two more shots kicked up the sand right in amongst the shore party, and set them scrambling wildly to their feet. After that a steady fusillade was maintained, with bullets landing all round us. No one was hurt, and I am prepared to concede that this *may* have been due to the superlative markmanship of the Turks. But all I can really remember of those thrilling few minutes, is a feeling of sheer terror and some astonishment at the speed with which the men piled themselves into the boats. I was also surprised at the determination with which the sailors clung, even in their panic, to every one of their personal possessions.

We were more than half-way back to the ship before the bullets finally ceased from plopping into the water around us. When at last we arrived alongside, there was an ugly scramble for the privilege of being first man to reach *Olinda*'s deck.

At six-fifteen the sun went down, and the shadows of the peaks of Mitylene came spreading out across the Channel towards us. When the flare in the western sky began to lessen, I climbed to the bridge and once more took up my binoculars. The cavalcade of small craft was already well out in the middle of the Channel; but there were not so many of them this evening, and they did not appear to be moving to the same stations as on the previous night. No, they were coming over towards the spot where *Olinda* lay; it looked as though they intended to line the limits of territorial waters abreast of her. There were half a dozen fishing boats; but behind them came the three motor launches. Before it grew quite dark we saw them still creeping towards us—the fishing boats showing their lights, while the motor launches remained darkened.

It seemed quite possible that the enemy intended to attempt a boarding. The fishing boats, we thought, would no doubt remain where they were, fully lighted, as a deterrent to *Olinda* and as a distraction for the Turks, while the unlit motor launches sneaked inshore in the darkness. They would probably wait until midnight or later, however; for as far as they could tell, *Olinda* was still aground and helpless, so their chief concern would be to avoid being caught red-handed by the Turks in so flagrant a violation of neutrality.

"We'll wait until ten o'clock," I told the Master. "Then we'll slip our anchors, and have a go at it. If the mist comes down before that, we'll sail at once."

Everyone looked dubious. But we were clearly no safer in our present position than we would be under way, so we kept a keen watch upon the enemy craft and waited as patiently as we might. Meanwhile, however, our home-made grenades

were served out. The Master, the Bosun and Ivan Oreshkin
took two apiece; the remaining six were kept ready for use on
the monkey island.

Gradually the time passed. Occasionally a shred or two of
mist would drift down off the land, or form for a few minutes
upon the sea; but always, just as we were about to slip, the
mist faded or blew away, and the lights of the watching boats
shone out brightly once more, right across the path that
Olinda would have to take. I noted the compass bearing of the
village of Dikili—134 degrees. Then I went down to the
Master's cabin and laid it off on the chart. From this I could
see that in order to clear the outermost shoals which had been
clearly visible to us in daylight, *Olinda* would have to continue
on a westerly course, towards the enemy boats, until Dikili
bore 131 degrees or less. I returned to the monkey island,
determined not to turn a moment before this bearing was
observed.

At last it was ten o'clock, and our departure could be delayed
no longer. The wind was still light south-westerly, so the
sound of our windlass and the beat of *Olinda*'s main engines
would not be heard by the enemy at any great distance.
"Weigh and slip." The windlass began to clatter, but it was
kept turning slowly so as to reduce the noise of it to a minimum.
As soon as the port anchor lifted from the bottom, *Olinda*'s head
began to pay off towards the nor'rard. Immediately the
mooring wires were slipped from the after bitts. They ran out,
and fell with a splash into the sea. "Slow ahead together."
Olinda was under way.

Creeping along as quietly as she was able, *Olinda* stole out
from the land towards that group of yellow lights. When she
had proper steerage-way upon her, the port engine was
stopped in order to reduce her speed still further. Then I
glanced again, over the top of the compass, at Dikili . . . 133
degrees . . . still a long way to go.

For every ship's length that *Olinda* moved forward, the
lights ahead of her seemed to grow brighter and more menacing.
They were no stronger than ordinary ship's masthead lanterns;
but they were actually beginning to light us up faintly, while
the bearing of Dikili still remained obstinately at 132½ degrees.
Surely those people would see us, or even hear us against the

wind. My imagination began to play tricks—I thought I
heard a hail, but it was not repeated; then I thought I heard a
high-speed engine, but it was only one of *Olinda*'s shrouds
humming gently in the wind. From every part of the ship,
eyes were staring rigidly into the darkness; I could see all
hands collected forward, leaning over the rails on either side,
and glaring, tense and motionless, across the water. . . . Dikili
bore 131½ degrees.

Then, all at once, when I looked again at the bearing of
Dikili, it was 130½ degrees. "Hard a-port. Steer 130 degrees."
Round came *Olinda*'s head—quicker than usual, because the
port engine was stopped. "Slow ahead together." The port
engine joined the other, and the ship increased her speed.

For ten minutes more the Master and I stood watching the
lights as they faded astern; then, "Full ahead together" and,
with a huge sigh of relief, we went down to the chart-room to
consider the next move.

At midnight *Olinda* was deep into Kabakum Bay, and course
was altered to 224 degrees to clear Ovrea Kastro Point. When
we reached it, there was still no sign of any opposition, but in
order to make quite certain of not being spotted by some
prowler to seaward, *Olinda* was steered so as to pass inside
Nikolo Rocks, then out again to skirt close round the western
cliffs of Ajano Island. It was 1.20 a.m. when we reached
Agios Georgios Island. *Olinda* slipped through between this
island and the mainland, and entered Sandarli Bay.

27

IN the Gulf of Sandarli, we were safe at last. A strong
reaction from the past excitement began to make me drowsy,
for I had been on my feet for nearly forty-eight hours. To keep
myself awake, I strode vigorously about the monkey island.
When I tripped over a couple of our hand grenades, I smiled
happily at the memory of the plans we had made for using
them. I was thankful that we had been spared the necessity.
There was no knowing how violent an explosion would have
been caused by the detonation of three sticks of gelignite; and

to tell the truth, the idea of using these infernal contraptions had frightened me almost more than the idea of an enemy boarding party.

At two o'clock in the morning we passed inside Plati Island, and turned to steer as close as possible to Üc Köse Burnu. The gentle motion of the ship was irresistibly lulling. I paused to lean against the compass binnacle. Once or twice I nodded off, to wake with a start as I began to topple over.

Then suddenly I was broad awake. From immediately above us on the black-hillside of Üc Köse, a shot had rung out sharply. Then there were two or three more, in a ragged volley, followed at once by the whine of a ricochet off the water and the clang and rattle of a bullet coming inboard somewhere forward. There was no need to shout a warning to the hands; they were gone from the deck like rabbits. I crouched down behind the binnacle and waited. We were not kept long in suspense. A few loud, high-pitched calls echoed down to us from the hills, then there followed another group of shots.

It was clear from this reception, that Olinda was entering a military area. But our people at Ankara had been told nearly three days before of our intentions: surely, by now, the Turks could have warned their coastal defences! I suppose it was due to lack of sleep that I lost my temper over this final vexation— no more than a vexation at the moment, because we were well protected by sandbags from rifle fire; in the darkness, more-over, the range was being grossly underestimated, and only from time to time did a few spent bullets come inboard. Even so I began to curse and to swear hysterically (and unreasonably) both at the Turks and at our own "half-baked diplomats."

Five minutes later, when Olinda had passed beyond Üc Köse, and was forging across the bay towards Chemali, the true reason for all this uproar occurred to me. The Turks must at least have warned their coastal heavy batteries of Olinda's intentions, or else we should by now have had starshell bursting round us and a heavy plunging fire over the hill-tops. But the infantry defending the foreshores had not been included in the warning; it had no doubt been thought unlikely that Olinda would pass close enough to the shore to disturb them; for security reasons, therefore, they had not been told of Olinda's plans. And now it was too late; this firing from Üc Köse must

have alarmed the whole coast; we could, therefore, expect
further ruderies from all the remaining outposts. I also wondered whether those German motor launches or E-boats had
by now discovered our escape from Suna Bay, and whether
they were at this moment searching for us along the route to
Izmir. If they were, then all this shindy would undoubtedly
attract their attention.

In the hope of avoiding further Turkish reaction, I altered
course about 10 degrees to seaward, intending to pass well
clear of Chemali. This manœuvre was of no avail. Long
before *Olinda* was within range, the riflemen on Yildirim Kaya
opened up on her, and were at once supported by a Bren gun,
sited upon the hill-side above.

For ten minutes or more a steady fire was maintained. The
sporting blood of the Turks was clearly roused. No doubt they
had been sitting upon this bleak headland for many weeks
without a chance of discharging their pieces at anything more
substantial than one or two unwary sea-birds. Now they were
bent upon making the most of their opportunities. Once more,
though, only a few spent bullets actually struck the ship, and
I was beginning to grow accustomed to the racket, when a new
and more disturbing sound began to rise above the din. . . .

15

Whether they were attracted by the firing, or whether it was part of their general search plan which brought the E-boats so close to the Turkish coast, I cannot tell; but all at once I heard the typical falsetto hum of high-speed engines and, glancing to seaward, I made out three tiny white jags of spray . . . far off and moving in swiftly from the north-east. They were more than a mile farther out to sea than *Olinda*, so without a moment's hesitation we turned the ship straight towards the land, towards the jet-black background of the cliffs and mountains.

The effect of this tactic upon the Turks can easily be imagined. At the sight of their target steering straight towards them, with the apparent intention of effecting a landing in Canakia Bay, the entire garrison of that part of the coast woke to life. The rate and volume of both rifle and machine-gun fire rose to a frenzied crescendo, and soon *Olinda* came well within range of most of it. The sky began to rain bullets from several different angles, which seriously reduced the protection afforded by my single pillar of sand bags. Most of the bullets still fell into the sea nearby, but many came singing and rattling aboard, where they ricochetted in all directions.

The Turks, by now, must also have heard the E-boats. They may even have seen them, and begun to imagine poor old *Olinda* as the spearhead of a landing-in-force—a veritable invasion. If he had not actually sighted the E-boats, the simple soldier had no doubt decided that he was facing some new and secret weapon—a sort of lethal pantomime horse, consisting of several E-boats speeding along beneath a large protective shell disguised as a tanker.

Within two or three cables of the rocks, *Olinda* turned to resume her previous course; it was then that the general confusion reached its peak. In the face of so hot a fire, which they must have believed to be directed at themselves (and without, I am certain, catching sight of *Olinda*) the E-boats turned away. *Olinda* continued to cringe among the rocks and headlands, determined to hide herself against a dark background, and also to make use of this impromptu barrage as a protection against more dangerous torpedoes. But the Turks, convinced that D-Day had arrived at last, now supplemented their attack on *Olinda* with a lively cross-fire upon their own beaches. We rounded C. Hydra less than two cables off, with the bullets whistling and splattering through the rigging. I could only hope that one or two unlucky shots would not cut the stays which supported the jury mast, and send that crazy edifice crashing into the sea.

Between the bursts of fire, we still heard the Turks shouting at us from the hills. Suddenly, remembering the Turkish word for steamer, I poked up my head and screamed back at the top of my voice: "*American vapuri! American vapuri!*" The only reply, however, was a fresh burst of firing, so I ducked down hastily and remained there, crouching behind my sandbags. I felt uncomfortably like an old gentleman in a new silk hat driving down a street full of schoolboys armed with snowballs. Then I thought of Adolf Hitler driving through Prague, beneath a shower of bouquets, some of which landed painfully on his head, and wondered whether he had felt the mingled anxiety and embarrassment which assailed me at this moment.

At last we rounded Iersis Island, and entered the Gulf of Izmir. Thankfully I steadied *Olinda* upon a course which would take her out into the middle of the Gulf. I even felt relieved when a searchlight from Uzan Ada blazed out and caught us in its beam. It continued to hold us for several minutes; then, satisfied about our identity, it left us and went out.

At 4.30 a.m. the dawn was once more at hand. Port Saip, where we had decided to spend the day, was only five miles distant; so *Olinda*'s speed was reduced to "slow," and she ambled gently towards the mountains of the Kara Burnu peninsular. In order to make our approach look reasonably inoffensive, we intended waiting until daybreak before entering harbour.

Once more an overwhelming sense of reaction claimed me. Stamping violently to keep myself awake, I tramped backwards and forwards across the monkey island. But it was no good; three times, in as many minutes, I fell over, asleep in the middle of my stride. Such an experience had never befallen me; it defeated me utterly. Fortunately the Master was still fairly wakeful, so I handed over to him and flopped down upon the sandbags as if poleaxed.

It seemed that only a second or two had elapsed when a violent and prolonged shaking aroused me. In reality it was nearly six o'clock, and *Olinda* was already sliding in behind the Island of Buyuk Saip. She anchored in twelve fathoms, just

within the arms of the first small bay she reached. The usual
boatload of soldiers came off to her at once, and were met by
the Master and Mate at the head of the jumping-ladder. Zamit
was there too, but I kept in the background. Soon, however,
seeing that a fierce argument had begun, I strolled up to the
outskirts of the group and asked Zamit for the general gist of
the conversation.

"Turkish officer say he gettin' orders from Izmir Area
Commander that *Olinda* arrested. . . . Not can leave without
more permission."

28

FOR the moment this appeared to be the end of it all.
Presumably the Turks had decided that they were playing
with fire where *Olinda* was concerned; in any case there was
no choice for us but to do as we were told. Any idea of kidnapping our guards and continuing down the coast was, of
course, ridiculous; for, with both the Turks and the Germans
our enemies, it would have been utterly impossible to wriggle
out of the Aegean. I went to my cabin, determined at any rate
to get a few hours' sleep before the next problem presented
itself. Meanwhile three or four Turkish soldiers were posted
on board as sentries.

At noon, still under guard, *Olinda* left Port Saip and began
to steam up the Gulf towards Izmir. We had been told that
the waters inside Uzun Ada were prohibited to merchant
ships; but, chiefly because it looked a more interesting channel
and also, no doubt, from irritation at the sight of the Turkish
soldiers standing insolently about *Olinda*'s decks, I decided to
pretend ignorance and to steer for Mordogan Gulf. As we
approached it, the Turks on Ardic Burnu opened fire on us—
a surprisingly accurate fire. *Olinda* turned away at once; but
the Turks continued to pot at her as long as she was within
range.

From the protection of my sandbags I was now able to take
pleasure in the behaviour of our own Turkish sentries. They
could not at first make up their minds whether they should
remain calmly on guard, scuttle below for shelter with *Olinda*'s

crew, or return the fire of their compatriots. In the end they
gallantly remained where they were; but it was amusing to
watch their faces as the bullets came hissing across the ship
and clattering about the decks. They rightly suspected me of
having deliberately aimed at embarrassing them.

At four o'clock we passed through the narrows guarded by
the ancient fortress of Yene Kale and, forty minutes later,
Olinda anchored abreast of Izmir town.

"You've certainly done it this time," observed old Mathews
grimly. I was not exactly surprised to see him amongst the
party of minor officials and guards who boarded *Olinda* at
nine o'clock next morning; but I was a little disconcerted by his
calm and colourless manner. It was unlike the Old Man to
be politely resigned to a difficult situation. I noticed that he
behaved almost meekly towards the Turks; that he waited for
them all to get on board, for instance, before clambering up
the ladder himself. When he reached the deck, he did not at
once rush forward to take charge of the situation, but remained
in the background until all the formalities had been completed.

The first of these formalities was a thorough search of the
ship by a team of Turkish customs guards. They were presumably looking for explosives, and I was on tenterhooks, throughout the search, lest they should discover the hand grenades and
my revolver, which had been hidden in various sandbags.
When the searchers reached the bridge, however, they appeared
more interested in the red-painted canvas which covered the
deck of the monkey island, and in the large white Turkish
crescent that we had described upon this red field so that
Olinda's pretended nationality should be clearly visible from
the air. This crescent and all the other Turkish markings on
the ship were noted and carefully measured. Every part of the
ship, including the main tanks, was explored by the soldiery;
but they found nothing more incriminating than the stinking
dregs of *Olinda*'s last cargo of fuel oil, most of which they
removed on various parts of their uniforms.

"When did you get here, sir?" I asked the Old Man, as soon
as the customs officials had finished with me.

"I left Istanbul the day before yesterday, when I received the
message that you were aground. Dick Rees got a salvage vessel

away to you as well; but we turned her back at Chanak when
the news came through this morning that you had reached
Port Saip. . . . Why on earth didn't you wait for a salvage
vessel? They're all Turkish-manned ships. With one of them
alongside, the Huns would never have dared attack you."

"I'd no idea whether you'd be able to send a salvage vessel;
there might not have been one available, and meanwhile I
was expecting to be boarded at any moment." I told the
Old Man about the German patrols and about everything
that had happened to *Olinda* during the past three days. He
heard me in silence, nodding from time to time to show that
he understood.

"H'm," he grunted, when I had finished. "Well, we're in
a complete mess with *Olinda* now. The Germans in Istanbul
and Ankara are raising hell in the Court of Appeal . . . look at
this. . . ." He handed me a cutting from a newspaper printed
in French. There was about half a column of it, with striking
headlines:

IMPUDENT PIRACY ATTEMPTED

Ship Stolen by Englishman from Istanbul
British Embassy Implicated?

During the night of January 9th, a young man, reported
to be an Englishman, went on board the tanker *Olinda*,
which was lying at anchor in the Bosphorus; he either
threatened the Captain or persuaded him, by means of
forged orders, to sail.

Olinda had recently been the subject of an action
brought by U.S.A. Authorities in the Istanbul Courts.
The Americans had hoped to gain possession of *Olinda*
on the grounds that, being a ship registered under the
Panamanian flag, she was subject to American requisitioning laws. *Olinda*'s owners were on the point of filing
an appeal against the decision of the Court when the
crime referred to was committed.

It has been suggested that, fearing the outcome of the
owners' appeal, the British Authorities decided to arrange
for the vessel to be stolen. Inquiries at the British Embassy in Ankara, however, have resulted in a refusal to
comment on this suggestion.

Fortunately for Turkey the ever-watchful German Navy
intercepted *Olinda* soon after she left the Dardanelles, and

prevented her escaping on to the high seas. She was subsequently escorted to Izmir, where she was handed over to the Military Authorities.

Turkish Colours Compromised

A most serious view is taken of the fact that this *flagrant act of piracy was committed under Turkish colours*, which had been impudently painted upon the ship. We owe a deep debt of gratitude to the Germans for their promptness in barring *Olinda*'s escape and thereby safeguarding Turkish honour and Turkish interests.

It is understood that the young blackguard responsible for this outrage will immediately be brought to justice; but our correspondent, who endeavoured to obtain the views of the Public Prosecutor upon the incident, was unfortunately not able to see him. An official at the door of the Law Courts, however, gave the following opinion: "The Turkish Law will know how to deal with this impertinence."

It is to be hoped that Justice will move swiftly, and that the sentence imposed will be sufficiently heavy to deter such irresponsible elements from ever again abusing our hospitality in this outrageous manner.

"Well, the wretched reporter seems to have been flung out of the Law Courts. . . . No wonder he feels a bit testy about the whole affair. . . . I should like to have heard what the door-keeper really said to him? Whose impertinence was he referring to, d'you think, sir—the reporter's or mine?" I was still smiling to myself as I handed the cutting back to old Mathews. But my grin faded at his next remark, delivered in casual tones, and with an air of fatherly tolerance.

"I'm afraid you'll have to be thrown to the wolves, my lad," announced the Old Man cheerfully.

"How's that, sir? Surely our right to requisition *Olinda* is fairly clear?"

"That's our opinion," replied the Old Man airily. "But, of course, it may not be the opinion of the Izmir Courts. . . ."

"I thought all that was settled in Istanbul before we sailed." The Old Man's manner worried me. He was still wearing his smart black hat—the hat in which he had recently developed such a childish pride. Had he then abandoned altogether the character of a forthright old sea-dog, and begun to cultivate the wily and ruthless outlook of the diplomat? Was I to be deliberately sacrificed?

"The trouble is that, according to Turkish Law, the Izmir Courts are in no way bound by the rulings of the Courts of Istanbul . . . they are an entirely separate legal body, and there's a certain amount of healthy rivalry between the two. Anyway, the charge of stealing *Olinda* has not yet been preferred against you; the owners, with the help of the Huns, are still busy preparing that one. . . . Meanwhile, they're hoping to hold you here on another charge."

The cheery indifference of his tone had by now reduced me to fatalistic silence. I waited for him to continue.

"Our Consulate here has been served with a summons for you to appear in court to-morrow morning . . . to answer a charge of 'illegally using the protection of Turkish colours'."

"What's the maximum penalty?" I asked in quick alarm.

"About ten years, I believe," was the cool reply. "But they'll probably accept a fine," added the Old Man in a more encouraging tone.

"And who pays the fine? The Director of Navy Accounts, I suppose . . . 'recoverable from officer on Form 359x/p, in monthly payments for the rest of his life; thereafter a charge upon his heirs and assigns.'"

"Oh, it won't be as bad as that. Anyway we've got hold of the best lawyer in town to defend you. You may get off."

"*May* get off?" I echoed, now thoroughly scared.

At lunch-time that day I noticed that there was a party of Germans at a nearby table, and I recognised one of them, a small, blond fellow, quite young and very good-looking in a blue-eyed, Nordic way. He was reported to be a disabled Luftwaffe pilot; he had been one of the Germans staying in the Park Hotel at Istanbul. There was no sign of Fritz; I wondered whether he was still at Ayvalik, and whether Nadia was there too.

The remainder of that day I spent in friendly surroundings . . . in one of the villages near Izmir, where the European community have built their homes amongst ancient trees and gay, enchanted gardens. To these people hospitality was more of a pleasant pastime than an obligation; but they had never yet been called upon to include a common thief amongst their guests, and a few showed concern at this new problem in sociology. Most of them, however, were amused; in any case I was made whole-heartedly welcome.

In the evening I went alone to the place where Nadia had formerly been working. I could not help a certain anxiety on her account. I knew that I ought never to have asked her to leave Izmir and so defy the orders of her own police. When the cabaret began, my anxiety increased, for Nadia did not appear; the two sisters came on alone to do their dance and to sing. Later I was able to speak to the elder sister.

"Where is Nadia?" I asked.

"Is she not still with you?" returned the girl coldly. "She left here with you three nights ago. Since then she has not been seen." I said nothing, but my heart was very heavy. "The police were here to-day . . . questioning the manager," added the girl and, turning her back on me, she moved away to a table occupied by a party of Greeks.

There was nothing I could do. I strolled back to the Izmir Palace Hotel, where old Mathews and I were staying. "Whatever happens," I told myself, "I'll be careful never to see Nadia again." I realised as I said it, however, that this resolution might well have come too late; Nadia might already be arrested, or the Germans might have got hold of her . . . unless she and Fritz . . . No! I just could not believe that fat Fritz could have any attraction for our Nadia. What did it matter anyway? The point was that I must avoid her at all costs myself. And the thought of never seeing Nadia again made me sad as I wandered along; she had become so much a part of this adventure, so much a part of our lives.

Next morning I was escorted by our Turkish lawyer to the Courts of Justice. These were in a large, bare building resembling a military barracks. We climbed some stairs and joined a nondescript crowd of litigants and malefactors. They were of all sorts, from beggars to business men, and they sat upon the floor or stood against the walls of a long gallery, awaiting the hearing of their cases with varying degrees of impatience. A policeman strolled up and down to keep an eye upon this throng. Every now and then, one of the waiting figures would rush up to gesticulate before him wildly, but the policeman remained impassive or made some curt reply before strolling on. For more than an hour we stood about the gallery. At last the clerk of one of the courts came out and called a list of names. My lawyer gave me a shove and together we entered a small, square room which I recognised, from memories of certain American films, as a court-room.

Behind a large desk set upon a raised dais sat the judge, looking very stern and rather ill-humoured. We took our places upon the lowest of a tier of benches; I wondered, as I sat down, whether anyone in the small crowd behind us had been sent to watch the case for the Germans. But when I turned to whisper a question to my lawyer, I was immediately "shushed" by the clerk of the court, who began to read rapidly from a document—presumably the charge.

I folded my arms, crossed my legs and tried to assume an expression of grave attention to what was being read, though I was unable, of course, to understand a word of it. But, all at once, I noticed that the judge had lost interest in the clerk and his reading, and was glaring at me with an expression of bitter malevolence. I decided straight away that no less than three years of my life were about to be spent in a Turkish prison. "Uncross your legs," hissed the lawyer in my ear. "It is a gross insult to the judge to cross one's legs." Hastily, but with some surprise, I did as I was told. How could I have known that it was insulting to cross one's legs? I began to feel worried at my ignorance of Turkish Law Court manners and the behaviour required of a defendant . . . or was I technically a prisoner already? The clerk of the court, who had also paused to frown at me, now continued his reading.

When he had finished, the case proceeded on formal lines. Prosecuting counsel addressed the court; then my friend beside me had his say. At one point there was an interruption from the benches behind. ("The lawyer from the German Embassy," whispered my friend.) The judge, who had not so far spoken, replied with what sounded like a sharp rebuke. I never heard what objection the Huns had endeavoured to raise; I was quite satisfied with the knowledge that it had been overruled.

Next there came two minutes of complete silence during

which the judge stared icily in front of him, and everyone in the court watched him expectantly. Then his face began to harden, and his eyes to bulge a little. I wondered what was coming next. Just as the tension was becoming unbearable, I felt a sharp blow upon my left knee; some court official had come up beside me and had struck it with his baton; to my horror and alarm I found that my legs had once more become crossed.

With even greater dispatch than before I uncrossed them and gaped at the judge; then I tried to smile hopefully, but this only resulted in a sickly grin which the judge seemed to find more than ever repulsive. I believe he shuddered slightly as he turned to say something to the clerk. Presently he turned again to survey me with an even more marked expression of distaste upon his stern judicial countenance.

"Stand up!" hissed my lawyer in a hoarse whisper. The verdict was about to be given or sentence passed upon me; I could not tell which for there was no jury. Without any change in the look of deep loathing upon his face, the judge began to speak. When he had finished, my lawyer grabbed my right hand and shook it violently. "Wh-what did he say?" I stammered.

"He says that according to Turkish law it is permissible for a ship to masquerade under the Turkish colours whenever it can be proved that this is done in order to save her from attack by a superior enemy force." He made this declaration with some pride and a legal disregard for punctuation.

"Good Lord! Who on earth dug that one up?" My astonishment and admiration were difficult to conceal.

The lawyer patted himself upon the chest.

"*Is* that the law?" I asked, frankly amazed. The lawyer looked offended; so did the clerk of the court, who by ill-chance understood English. "What I mean is, can I do it again?"

There followed a commotion which confounded all my preconceived ideas of legal procedure, and I never obtained any reply to my question. . . . I was lucky to get out of the court at all.

VI

PAUSE WITHOUT LAUGHTER

29

LISTLESSLY the days passed by in Izmir. *Olinda*, still under arrest, was sent out to the military anchorage in Gulbache Bay, but I was not on board her: I remained at the Izmir Palace with the Old Man, who became daily more morose. John, he told me, had already left Turkey; for the Russians, now counter-attacking strongly all along the eastern front, needed every one of their ships to supply their armies, and had decided to send no more tankers to the Dardanelles.

On the second day after my episode in the Turkish courts, the laconic phrasing of a routine "movements" report from Cyprus gave us news of Jesse, which cleared the air for a few hours. The signal—passed to Ankara for information—read as follows:

From N.O.I.C. Famagusta
Tuesday, January 23rd.

Arrivals: *Empire Flounder, Maple Branch, Samson J. Irving*
from Haifa.
Tarkhan from Istanbul.
Departures: *Tarkhan* to Beirut.

For a few hours, as I said, the Old Man became cheerful again, but by lunch-time he was, if anything, more surly than ever. Now, however, his ill-humour was due more to impatience than to depression. He had begun, all at once, to chafe at the whole atmosphere of delicate diplomacy which surrounded our operations. It was probably not an intentional gesture; but one could not help noticing that, from the moment he received the news of Jesse's safe arrival in Allied waters, he took to going out without his hat, the cherished black hat. He seemed suddenly to have grown tired or ashamed of it, and to prefer instead to flaunt his atrocious red wig, like the fiery emblem of a belated crusade, in the face of Smyrna.

Almost every day now there appeared in those papers which were under German influence, some smug little reference to the way in which our "futile machinations" had been curbed. "And until the owners' appeal against the decision of the

Istanbul courts has been heard, the Turks'll hold *Olinda*,"
growled the Old Man. "We're probably stuck here for
months, and the Huns crowing their bloody heads off about
the whole business."

"Surely the owners haven't any real grounds for appealing,"
I suggested.

"Maybe not," replied the Old Man, "but that won't stop
them; and the Turks can't openly direct the courts to refuse
them a hearing, even though the Turkish Government is
really quite keen on *Olinda* getting down to Syria. We've
promised to use her for bringing oil up from Haifa to Turkey
. . . the Germans only want her for supplying Rumanian oil
to their own armies in Russia. But the Turks are determined
not to have any more rumpuses in territorial waters; they're
scared stiff of the Germans making an excuse to invade them."

"Will they hold her here indefinitely then . . . even if the
appeal fails?"

"They will, unless we can think up a scheme for getting her
clear away without being seen."

It looked, however, as though the Germans, with customary
thoroughness, were not prepared to take the risk of our hitting
upon any such scheme, for they now started a daily air patrol
to watch *Olinda* where she lay in Gulbache Bay. The Turkish
anti-aircraft batteries put up a few formal bursts at them from
time to time; but the guns were not equipped with modern
instruments, so there was little danger of the aircraft being
hit, and neither side took the trouble to complain of these
incidents. Meanwhile, the Old Man and I racked our brains
for a plan; but after two days we were no nearer to discovering
one.

The difficulty lay in *Olinda*'s speed. At eight knots, she would
only just be able to get through Khios and Samos Straits in
one night; but, having done so, she would still be obliged to
spend the whole of the following forenoon at sea, for there were
no fjords or other hiding-places for her south of Samos until she
reached those in the Gulf of Mendelyah, a good thirty miles
farther on. And, as soon as the enemy reconnaissance over
Gulbache Bay reported (shortly after daylight) that *Olinda* was
no longer there, it would be a simple matter for aircraft to find
and attack her off the mouth of the Meander River . . . as

simple as it had been in Suna Bay, for, off the Meander, too, there were extensive shoals which would force *Olinda* well out to sea down the whole of that part of the coast.

No, it was out of the question to attempt both Khios and Samos Straits in one night; but how were we to obtain *two* nights' grace? Immediately the German aircraft spotted that *Olinda* had left her present anchorage, the enemy would also close the Samos Strait. This they could easily do, since it was no more than a steep-sided gorge, three-quarters of a mile wide, with an islet in the middle, which reduced the Channel on the Turkish side to less than 440 yards. Some plan must therefore be found by which *Olinda* could leave the Gulf of Izmir without being missed by the Germans for at least forty-eight hours. Unless some method of doing this could be discovered, the Turks would hold her in Gulbache Bay indefinitely.

Then one day, at lunch-time, the Old Man came back from the Consulate like a veritable ball of fire. His face was full of eager excitement, and he could hardly wait to pay his taxi before bounding into the hotel to find me. I was in the lounge, and had watched his tumultuous arrival through the window.

"Look here," he boomed, "I want you to come out at once. I've got something to talk to you about."

"Will you have lunch first, sir? I've had mine."

"To hell with lunch . . . this is urgent! Come on, we'll go for a walk."

As soon as we were out on the promenade which skirted Izmir Harbour, he broke the news that "owing to a legal hitch" the Izmir Courts had, in fact, refused to hear the appeal of *Olinda*'s owners!

This in itself was better news than we had ever dared to hope for, but this was not the only piece of intelligence which had made the Old Man so jubilant.

"You remember *Orak*, don't you?" he rattled on, ". . . the ship you've been trying to impersonate in *Olinda*? Well, she's loading in Mersin now and coming north in a week's time, bound for Istanbul."

Old Mathews chuckled to himself at the thought. I remembered that *Orak*'s owners were reported to be pro-British, so I was not surprised when the Old Man went on to inform me

16

that they were already being approached by our agents in Istanbul, with a view to obtaining their co-operation in a new plan for getting *Olinda* away.

The Old Man's plan was very simple. *Orak*, coming north along the coast upon her ordinary occasions, would be asked to anchor one evening in Port Saip. As soon as it was dark she would proceed to Gulbache Bay and anchor in the place which *Olinda* now occupied. *Olinda*, meanwhile, would have left the anchorage and be on her way round the coast to the Khios Strait. Next day, when the German reconnaissance aircraft came over, it would see a ship *that looked like Olinda*, still sitting peacefully in Gulbache Bay. *Orak* would remain at anchor for another forty-eight hours, by which time *Olinda* would be safely hidden, well beyond the Khios and Symi Channels.

"The first thing is to get the Turks to agree to the plan and to give permission for *Orak* to enter Gulbache Bay," said the Old Man.

"If possible, without being fired on," I observed feelingly. "Or she may turn away before she gets to the anchorage."

"Yes, and the next thing is for both of us to disappear. I can go back to Istanbul, but you must disappear completely. . . . We must make it look as though we have abandoned all attempts to get *Olinda* down. They must think you've left the country. . . . I'll arrange with Ankara for the news to be spread about that we have sold the ship to the Turks at last. That ought to be easy enough."

"How are you going to get instructions down to *Orak*, sir? They'll have to be very clear and definite won't they?"

"Yes, I'll send a letter down to the Vice-Consul at Adana. He'll know how to fix everything. You'd better take the letter down to him. Adana's on the main line out of Turkey. . . . You must be seen catching the Taurus Express from Ankara, and we'll leave it to Vice-Consul Ensor at Adana to arrange for you to be smuggled back later, when we're ready for you."

.   .   .   .   .

The train whistled, and a moment later, started to move. I gave the Old Man a final wave from the corridor window, then closed it and entered my compartment.

I did not start at once on unpacking and stowing away my gear. I wanted to think—to get the Old Man's intentions clear in my mind.

"Spend the day in Ankara," he had said, "and report to the N.A.; then go on by Taurus Express to Adana, where Ensor is expecting you. Make sure you're seen on the Taurus."

This sounded simple enough, but the second half of his instructions had been more interesting: "From the moment you reach Adana, I don't want to hear another word either from you or about you for a week. Is that quite clear?"

I had told him that it was, and he gave me a final order: "At 19.00 on Tuesday, February 6th, you are to walk out of Ayasuluk on the road to the coast. I'll pick you up soon after you're clear of the town." Ayasuluk, near Scala Nuova?— Scala Nuova and the ruins of Ephesus! "Meet me in Ephesus," the Old Man might have said, and memories of St. Paul's journeys returned to my mind at the thought. The Old Man's fiery presence would have suited a prophet of God. Yes, at 19.00 on February 6th I would walk *into Ephesus* on the road to the coast. What would happen after the Old Man met me there I did not know; but I was not worrying just then about the future. My orders were: first to be seen on my way out of the country, and then to disappear among the hills of Anatolia or Cilicia. Cilicia . . . St. Paul's own country?—yes, indeed, for he had said to the chief captain of the band: "I am a man, which am a Jew of Tarsus, a city of Cilicia, a citizen of *no mean* city." And Tarsus, I knew, was only twenty miles from Adana on the road to the Port of Mersin.

At Ankara the Naval Attaché saw me for a moment; but he was in a hurry to get away to some meeting, and for the rest of the day I was left to my own devices. I managed to find in the Embassy Library a book about St. Paul's journeys through Turkey, which I spent most of the forenoon in reading. In the afternoon I went for a walk.

As far as I could tell I was not being followed, and the immediate sense of freedom and release from the atmosphere of war was exhilarating. None the less the situation was full of irony; for at this stage of my journey it was my duty to be seen, if possible, by the enemy . . . it was part of the plan in which the Old Man was to endeavour to obtain Turkish co-operation. The Germans were to see me on my way to the frontier and to assume, from this, that I had left Turkey or joined the Boom Defence party at Iskenderun. I sauntered down the broad avenue running through the centre of Ankara's modern garden suburb, built by Kemal Ataturk as a residential area for Government officials and foreign missions; but there was definitely no one behind me as I strolled along—past the Czech Embassy, past the British Counsellor's house and on towards the town.

In the end I decided to take a few hours off from the "affairs of state." I turned up a side street, which ought to have been called Acacia Avenue or possibly Mostyn Road, so closely did it resemble a street in some London suburb. Soon I was clear of the houses and looking down upon the exact counterpart of a large area of Leigh-on-Sea, Essex. This "desirable locality" was laid out upon the side of a hill, which was also dotted with Embassies. They stood out above the trees and bushes like hen-houses upon the sloping paddock of some up-to-date chicken farm. Above each hen-house flew the flag of a different country, as though the teams of hens inside had been competing in an international egg-laying contest. I amused myself for a moment with the picture of several hundred secretaries, attachés and typists—some broodily amassing a pile of documents in a basket marked "pending" and sitting upon them stubbornly; some laying little secretarial eggs into their "out" baskets, and all of them clucking, squawking or crowing in a variety of chickenly emotions. I wondered whether "diplomatic action" was already in progress among them over my proposed attempt to smuggle *Olinda* away.

An hour before midnight I caught the southbound Taurus at Ankara station.

A sleeper had been booked for me as far as Aleppo in Syria. The wagon-lit attendant came round to collect our tickets and also the passports of those travelling out of Turkey. I gave him mine, and was pleased to see a tall, nondescript-looking fellow, lounging in the corridor by my compartment door, trying to read the name of my passport over the attendant's shoulder. In case he had been unable to read it, I put down my suitcase for a moment as I entered the compartment. A few seconds later I came to the door again in time to see the tall fellow straighten up quickly. With a frown I yanked my bag inside and shut the door.

Next morning I stayed in my bunk until nearly ten o'clock, when a glimpse of Mount Erdjias in the distance brought me out into the corridor to watch our approach to Kayseri.

The snow was even thicker on the ground than it had been in early December. Mount Erdjias towered above the plains in isolated splendour, as grand as Matterhorn. Its summit, I had been told, was twelve thousand feet high; a full nine thousand feet above the town of Kayseri.

From Kayseri the train wandered away southwards and began to climb in curves and S's till, by the early afternoon, we were high among the Taurus peaks. Soon we began to nose our way down through the gorges and cuttings to Cilicia. The gorges became a canyon, whose floor fell away on our left until we were a thousand feet or more above it. By tunnels and steep embankments the railway was carried across the face of the canyon's southern wall. In between the tunnels, one caught occasional glimpses of a swollen mountain torrent, winding backwards and forwards among the drifts and boulders below, through fields of shale and ancient glacier debris, round islands of stunted trees, choked with sticks and branches from the floods. The floor of the canyon sank lower yet; the opposite wall drew nearer and stood up steeper and blacker against us; the snow peaks peeped above its edge. On our own side, the tunnels became more frequent and occasionally one saw, beside the railway line, the scars in the earth and a disorderly scatter of rocks and stones from a recent landslide.

Suddenly we came out of a tunnel to find the valley had broadened into a final bowl. The main ridge of the Taurus was now behind us; but below, on our left, the river seemed to flow straight into a hill-side which closed the end of the valley. A few minutes later we curved round the shoulder of a spur and saw that the valley really ended in a narrow cutting—a gorge several hundred feet high and less than a hundred yards across. Into the gorge the torrent disappeared, with a rough road running beside it.

These were the famous Cilician gates through which Alexander had marched his armies, and through which ran the only road from Anatolia into Syria and the lands beyond. Cyrus and his host had passed through them more than four hundred years before St. Paul, who had come that way on his journeys to Iconium and Ephesus.

The afternoon sun was slanting across above us to shine on the narrow black cleft into which the road and river jostled each other for room. I wondered whether German tanks would soon be rumbling through this defile and R.A.F. Wellingtons battering its cliffs into the river bed. In these days, when parachutes and precision bombing had destroyed the importance of such puny natural obstacles, it seemed more likely that the Cilician gates would remain only as a memorial to the Crusaders and all the conquerors before them. The train seemed to think so too; with a disdainful hoot it turned its back upon antiquity and swept into a tunnel, to emerge a few minutes later above the wide plain of Adana.

"*Reculer pour mieux sauter*," suggested Vice-Consul Ensor, as we entered the Adana "hotel" for an early supper. "Your boss certainly gets some funny ideas. Why come all the way to Adana and back? More likely to make the Huns suspicious than puzzle them."

I explained that the idea was for me to disappear in circumstances which would suggest that I had left the country. Ensor sighed and nodded in resigned acceptance of the obligation to help me; then he sat in frowning silence, considering the pros and cons, while Williams, his assistant, ordered food.

"The Adana airfield is carefully watched by the Huns," said Ensor presently. "But I might be able to spread the tale that you'd gone to Mersin to join an allied merchant ship. You'd better not actually go there. You don't want to be seen hanging about *Orak* just at present. . . . I'll deal with her."

"You won't forget to tell them to paint over all their white paint with grey and brown like we have in *Olinda*, will you?"

"No, I won't forget. . . . Now let me see, you'd better get straight on to a slow train for Konya and Afyon. You could catch it at the junction down the line, where the Taurus railway turns north. . . . It's just a tiny wayside station. I don't suppose anyone would notice you."

"How would I get there?" I asked. "By car?"

Ensor pondered a moment before replying. "The trouble is," he explained, "that my own car is too well known in these parts, and a hired car would be too insecure. We're watched all the time, you know."

"I suppose you are, but do they actually follow you about? Is there anyone watching you now for instance?"

Ensor turned with an ironical smile to Williams, who grinned back and then lifted his head a little to stare over my shoulder at a distant corner of the room. I shifted my position and followed the direction of his eyes. At once I recognised the man sitting at a table by himself; it was the tall, nondescript fellow, who had been so interested in my passport the day before.

"That chap came from Ankara by to-day's Taurus," I said, turning back to Ensor.

"Yes," he agreed, "and he'll go on by the next one to the Syrian frontier and back to Ankara. He's a Hungarian who's lived all his life in Turkey. He and two Austrians work the Taurus in turns."

"What about the slow trains into Anatolia?" I asked.

"Oh, they don't watch those as far as I know. Not the third class anyway. But you'd be spotted at Adana station, and they might follow you."

"I suppose the answer is to go as far as this junction of yours on foot, then. How far is it?"

"About fifteen miles, I think."

As we discussed this plan my enthusiasm for it grew. (Prolonged sessions in a Turkish eating-house were inclined to breed enthusiasm, if only on account of the great quantities of *raki* one drank between dishes.) I would change into old clothes, I decided, and leave the town an hour or two before dawn, like St. Paul when he fled from Iconium. I would take the road to Tarsus. My suitcase could be sent on to await me at Ayasuluk station.

To-day was January 29th, I would be free for eight days to go about, by devious ways, through St. Paul's Galatia and Phrygia to Mysia, and possibly on to Bythinia, where "the Spirit suffered them not," before I returned to meet old

Mathews at Ephesus—yes, at Ephesus—on February 6th of this year of 1942.

Bloated and reeking of *raki*, but in the best of spirits, we left the hotel at last. On the way back I bought myself a gaily coloured woollen scarf and a stick. When we reached the Consulate, Ensor gave instructions about calling me in the morning to the old night-watchman who let us in.

"Good night and good-bye," he said then. "You'll be gone before we're awake in the morning. Don't get into any trouble, for heaven's sake. It might take me days to get you out of jail, and I'm up to my eyes in work as it is."

"I'll be careful," I assured him.

"I can fix the Turkish police for you, provided you keep to the main road; but they'll insist on that." He started upstairs to bed. "I still can't think why your Old Man has to cook up such complicated schemes," he said plaintively, as we parted on the landing at the top. "Whenever a consul gets into trouble there always seems to be an Irishman in the background somewhere."

He sighed and, with a final "Good night," he left me.

30

WHEN the night-watchman shook me it was still quite dark. I dressed with difficulty by candlelight, and packed away my famous purple suit. Instead of it I wore a pair of old trousers, a sweater and a woollen balaclava helmet, turned up into the shape of a rough cap. Next I wound round my neck the scarf I had bought the night before; then I struggled into my ragged old greatcoat. This had been recently patched, with a truly Oriental eye for colour that had worried me when I first fetched it from the tailor; but now, its realistically Turkish appearance pleased me enormously. When I was ready I looked almost too Kurdish to be true—even my tattered desert boots fitted into the picture quite naturally. My disguise would hardly have deceived a trained agent, but it gave me a sense of adventure, and helped to recreate for me the atmosphere of Pauline wanderings in which I was setting forth.

The old night-watchman brought me a tray upon which he

had set a large cup of black coffee, some slices of country bread, a pat of goat's milk butter, a dish of rose-petal jam, two fried eggs and a spoon. He padded about in mournful silence while I ate. No one else in the house stirred.

When I had finished, the old man beckoned to me and left the room. I heard his dilapidated old pumps slapping gently down the passage to the street door, so I took my stick and a small parcel of food, wrapped in a cloth, and followed him. I gave him a smile and a few Turkish *liras* as he let me out. For a moment a look of downright friendliness kindled upon his tired old face; then the door closed and I went down three steps into the roadway.

It was a heavy, calm night and deathly still in the streets of Adana. My crêpe-soled boots made no sound upon the cobbles, and I kept to the middle of the road for fear of coming, with alarming suddenness, upon anyone else who might chance to be abroad. Arriving at some cross-roads, I turned to the left, away from the first faint hardening of the roof-tops against the sky.

A cockerel shouted from close at hand. I jumped, and then pressed on, while the silence seemed to bear upon me more heavily than before as, shrill and distant, the cocks of Adana crowed in answer. I remembered another cock-crow in the Straits of Mitylene; and the atmosphere of that other dawn came back to colour this one with its feeling of suspense. Soon the houses dwindled into huts, and the cobbles gave place to mud. Then the huts themselves grew meaner and wider spaced. Above them the stars shone weakly through a layer of thin cloud that would turn grey at daybreak.

Suddenly there was a shuddering cough in the darkness. It seemed to come from the mouth of an alley leading off to the left. There was another cough from the shadows of a house just ahead of me, then a low peevish grumbling began on my right. I seemed all at once to have become surrounded by the shadowy hosts of corruption and disease. There rose to my mind a picture of hideous lepers and outcasts, miserable exiles from daytime life, forced to forage pitifully by night among the refuse bins, or starve. Such people, in their extremity, could be dangerous as beasts. I clutched my stick firmly at the point of balance, and increased my pace. But I had hardly gone ten yards when I began to hear a slow, heavy tread almost beside me. Then I shied away to the left as a huge black mass detached itself from the house I was passing. I was about to break into a run, when another massive shape loomed up ahead, and glancing back in terror, I saw that a third had closed in behind me. I was in the middle of a herd of camels.

The camels were plodding deliberately westwards, out of the town. They were forming up into a rough caravan as they went. I passed them and found, at their head, a small donkey, picking its dainty way upon twinkling legs. The donkey, like the camels, carried a large bundle upon its back, but there was no sign of any human being. Then, twenty yards farther on, I came up with a second donkey, carrying a solitary Kurd or *Yuruk*, who sat hunched and huddled, in a mass of heavy coats and shawls, as though asleep.

I drew level, and was about to pass him, when I was astounded to hear a bright, "Good morning, Englishman."

I decided at once that this was no time to be mysterious and thereby to arouse suspicion. "Good morning to you," I replied. "D'you think it'll keep fine?"

"Sure it will. Where are you headin' for?"

"I'm going to Tarsus and Mersin."

"Best stick around with us then," offered the other, good-naturedly. "Police around here get tough with foreigners sometimes. Specially when they're moseyin' about on their own."

We talked on. I was surprised to learn that he was a genuine Kurd, who had lived all his life in a Cilician village. For many years, however, he had worked at the American Mission in Adana, until that institution had become reduced in size and scope by the rise to power of Kemal Ataturk. He seemed in no way surprised to find me walking alone to Mersin. I told him that I was joining a ship in three days' time and was filling in the interval with a tour of the ruins near Tarsus.

As the last few hovels of Adana fell away, the night began to congeal upon the meadows and thicken into dusty dawn. Then the sky receded and the stars went out.

Behind us the camels trudged ungainly, grunting to each other and coughing, or exchanging short worrying bursts of peevish argument. Looking back I saw a dozen or more of the great ill-humoured beasts and, behind them, half that number of donkeys. All were carrying burdens wrapped in ragged cloth or canvas. Behind the donkeys came a group of seven people—two Kurdish women with babies upon their backs, a man, a young girl and three ragged children who ran and capered with a pair of rough-haired mongrels.

I stayed with the Kurds until nightfall. They were friendly, and anxious to share with me their sour, white, goat-milk cheese and knobs of black bread. Their leader was irrepressibly cheerful. He was also eager to show off his English—or rather his American, though it seemed at times almost to out-yank the Yanks.

At dusk the party halted and lit a fire for the night. I shook hands with them all, including the children, and bade farewell to the boss.

"Say, wait a minute, Buddy," he objected. "You gaht to take a slug of gin with us first."

The gin, of course, was *raki*, and we downed it neat, in two great gulps.

"Hidy, Hidy!"

"Good health!" I replied, coughing as the frightful stuff filled my lungs with fire and aniseed. Then, with a final salute, I strode away towards the junction, whose lights I could see in the distance.

The moon rolled over the hills and shone full-brilliance upon the roofs and spires of a small town set in the wilderness.

Since parting with the Kurds, I had journeyed for several days, sojourning casually in Konya and Afyon. I had spent two nights as the guest of some Royal Engineers who were building an airfield for the Turks. Round Konya (St. Paul's Iconium) and the ruins of Antioch in Pisidia, I had watched the icy uplands crawling bleakly past the windows of a third-class railway carriage. For the rest I had kept myself apart, as far as possible, from my fellow-men, and the impressions remaining to me of my journey were few: the petulant soliloquies of a live chicken, flung trussed into a rack by a Turkish peasant; many flocks of sheep; gaunt, yellow dogs snarling at the train; dark shepherds standing in the snow in cloaks; *raki* and the smell of hot bodies in the night; wheels for ever "churring" and screeching and "churring"; more sheep and dogs and mountains, and yet more sheep.

At the end of it all I had collected my suitcase from the station-master's office at Ayasuluk, and now the town lay behind me as I trudged along, while before me was spread the Gulf of Scala Nuova, broadening towards the Aegean.

The Old Man had said he would pick me up soon after I had left the town; a recognition signal had been agreed upon. But I had passed the last houses at about five minutes to seven, and by now I must have been walking for nearly half an hour. I began to wonder whether a hitch had occurred; whether the car had broken down, or whether it might even have been waylaid by the Huns. Better not get too far away from Ayasuluk, I thought; besides, my bag was beginning to drag horribly. I looked about for a convenient rock upon which to sit and wait.

I found one at the top of the next rise, and flopped down upon it thankfully. The moon was now well above the hills; striking down into the folds and hollows below me, it set agleam a slender fragment of river beneath its mane of lacy, leafless trees. Here and there among the dells hung eddies of mist, like drifts of white wood-ash scooped into the pockets of the hills. In which direction should I look for Ephesus? Below me, where I sat upon a hill-side, lay the marshes of the Cayster River, and over beyond them rose the black wilderness again towards Mount Solmissus. The night wind came fitfully up from the sea and, in wavering chorus, the whimper of wimbrel and curlew. Who dwelt now in the marshes? Where was Artemis . . . the moon goddess . . . Great Diana of the Ephesians? The marsh reeds only sighed in answer, and the curlew complained to the moon.

The raucus call of a klaxon sounded from the direction of Ayasuluk. I stood up, and searched the road between myself and the town, watching for the prearranged signal. There it was—a long blast on the klaxon followed by headlights flashed twice and then turned out. I stepped into the middle of the road and waited. The car disappeared in a hollow; then suddenly shot over the crest of a nearby hill. I was struck by something unfamiliar about the vehicle; surely this was not the car old Mathews normally used! I hesitated for a moment in the middle of the road, as all sorts of wild notions chased themselves through my head. Had the plan failed then, and had the Germans found out about our rendezvous. Or they might have followed old Mathews out of Izmir and somehow . . . I leapt back from the road and threw myself down behind the rock upon which I had been sitting. Next moment the car roared past me, lifting a cloud of dust behind it. As it flashed by, the moon shone through it and silhouetted a well-remembered profile. I sprang back into the road, yelling at the top of my voice and waving my arms frantically. The car swerved under violent brakes and skidded broadside. Before it finally came to rest, the Old Man was out upon the road and bawling furiously.

"What the devil do you think you're playing at? Red Indians?" he roared. "Can't you see we're late enough as it is, without you trying to put me in the ditch for the third time in one evening."

I picked up my bag and hurried up to him, feeling more than usually foolish.

Old Mathews was once again not quite himself. It appeared that his own car had broken down, so he had been forced to borrow one from the consul at Izmir. He had arrived in that town at midnight the night before, having travelled by devious routes from Istanbul; and the whole of this past day been spent in violent telephonic battles with various authorities.

At 9.30 p.m. we reached the coast, somewhere west of Izmir. As it was a brilliant night—still, and reasonably warm—we took our sandwich supper on to the foreshore, where we were greeted by the familiar sight of a small boat lying close to the rocks, with a Turkish sentry on guard beside it.

While we were eating, the Old Man gave me my orders in great detail and, as he spoke, there crept into his voice a little of the old fire.

Briefly, the plan was as follows: *Orak* would reach Port Saip next evening, and would come on, after dark, to Gulbache Bay. *Olinda* was to weigh and steam up the eastern coast of the Kara Burnu peninsular, passing *Orak* off Ardic Burnu at eight o'clock on that evening. This the Turks had insisted upon . . . that both ships should be under way at the entrance to the prohibited area at the same specified time. As soon as the exchange had taken place, the ban on movement within the area would be re-enforced, and the batteries ordered to open fire on any craft approaching the anchorage. The Old Man went on to tell me about the patrols and observation posts in the Khios Strait. "The Germans seem to have a few small craft at sea each night," he said. "They patrol between Spalmatori Island, which lies across the northern end of the Strait, and Paspargos Island in the southern narrows; but they don't come east of Panayia Island, which is technically Turkish. Of course, if they knew that *Olinda* was at sea, there's no knowing what they would do. . . . However, we have every reason to hope that they won't know that until two or three days after you've left."

"What about observation posts? Have the Huns got any in the Straits?"

"Yes, there's supposed to be one on the eastern end of Spalmatori Island. And there used to be another in the lighthouse on Paspargos Island, but that one may have been removed; we don't know for certain. . . . Anyway, you'll need to keep as close to the Turkish coast as possible. Have you decided upon your exact route?"

"Yes, I had it all worked out last time, ready for making the passage the night after we reached Port Saip."

"Good. Well, we'd better be getting along then. I'll come out with you to the ship, but I won't come on board." He seemed a little more cheerful now that everything had been settled. "I'll hope to see you in a week or two's time then, in Beirut." His tone was almost jocular. "Oh, by the way," he added. "I nearly forgot. There's a note for you from Ankara. I've no idea who it's from; I think it came down by courier to Izmir yesterday."

He started fumbling in his pocket, and eventually fished out a rather crumpled envelope. I took it and read the address. Near the top was typed in block capitals the words: MOST SECRET. NOT TO BE OPENED BEFORE LEAVING HARBOUR. I put it in my inside pocket and followed the Old Man down to the beach.

The motor boat took about three hours to reach Gulbache. On the way we were unable to talk above the noise of the engine, so we huddled down into the most sheltered corners, making no attempt to converse.

It was nearly one o'clock in the morning when at last we nosed alongside *Olinda*'s familiar black hull. A heaving-line came hissing into the stern-sheets of the boat, which remained alongside just long enough for me to bend the line into the handle of my suitcase and leap for the end of the jumping ladder. Then the boat and the Old Man were gone, and I was scrambling awkwardly up the ladder in my heavy greatcoat and boots.

31

THE atmosphere on board *Olinda* had changed. Throughout next day I noticed this, even though my conversation
with the ship's company was confined to a few simple remarks
on the purely practical details of life on board. The Arabs
went about their work more cheerfully; Feodor was unusually
talkative, and the Master, as we discussed the route and laid
off all the courses on the chart, seemed almost enthusiastic
about the next stage of the voyage.

At first I was surprised as well as a little distrustful of this
new state of mind; I even began to wonder vaguely whether
they might not have put their heads together to decide upon
some plan for taking charge of the ship once she got to sea.
All the officers and the Bosun, I reflected, had been in the ship
under her previous owner and might reasonably have retained
some loyalty to him personally, whereas the Arabs could not
possibly care who ultimately obtained *Olinda*; they were, by
tradition, mercenaries, without much love for any Europeans;
so long as they were paid their wages and not subjected to any
undue hardship or danger, they were content to play their part
in the normal working of the ship down the coast; if not, not.
It was even possible that, during the past few days, someone
acting for the previous owner might have bribed his way on
board past the customs guards. I decided to sound Zamit
who, I felt sure, would be the last man on board to listen to
any proposal of treachery.

I found him sitting by himself on one of the hatches on the
foredeck. As I approached him, he gave me a friendly grin
and his eyes (or rather one of them) twinkled merrily.

"You've had a pretty dull time this last week," I began.

Zamit shrugged his shoulders and gave a little giggle. "No,
not dull. Plenty sunshine, plenty to eat. I bin catching fish
every day."

"Any visitors while you've been here?"

"No. Only Commander Mathews one or two times."

"What did he have to say?" I asked, more or less casually.

"One time giving us all long talk," said Zamit. "Him
telling us of *Orak* coming, saying the Turks very angry now

because the Germans bombing us in Suna Bay. Him telling that Turkish patrol boats keeping look-out in Khios Strait every night so we cannot be attacked there. We got to keep very close to Turkish shore all the time, he say, so the Germans not seeing us; but Turkish patrol boats looking out that no Germans coming in by the Turkish coast is catching us."

So that was why *Olinda*'s people were all so cheerful! Why, I wondered, had the Old Man omitted to warn me about the tales he had told them all? And what would the ship's company's reaction be if these supposedly Turkish patrol craft suddenly attacked the ship with machine-guns and torpedoes? Would not the shock of discovering that they were after all enemy craft throw them into a greater panic than before? It was difficult to say, but I hoped for the best. The main thing, in any case, was still to avoid being seen.

About eleven o'clock in the forenoon the murmur of an aircraft engine came to us from far off beyond the mountains to the westward, and a little while later we saw the white streak of vapour eating its way across the sky overhead. The reconnaissance plane passed over us at about 15,000 feet and turned north. No one on board took much notice; they had seen the same aircraft every morning for the past week.

The day wore on into afternoon and evening. The sun began to press down upon the mountains of Khios, and the air around us grew cooler quickly. I found Feodor Pavlovitch and Ivan Oreshkin on the poop, leaning over the side and gazing absently in the direction of Izmir, whose buildings and mosques were turning from white to creamy yellow in the ageing light.

"*Plus jolie qu'Istanbul*," I suggested to Feodor, whereupon he surprised me by saying that they were unable to judge which city was the fairest, since none of the Russians on board had ever set foot in either of them.

"But surely," I protested, still in French, "you have been trading between Istanbul and Rumania in this ship for the past two years."

"We are not permitted to land in Turkey," Feodor replied. "Turkey does not recognise the Nansen passports we hold.

17

As far as the Turkish authorities are concerned, we are people without a country."

Ivan Oreshkin, who apparently did not understand French, continued to gaze dispassionately over the side during most of this speech; but at the word Nansen he looked round and a faint smile hovered round his eyes for a moment. "Russian," he said firmly. And that was the first word he had ever addressed to me. Whether he was referring to modern Russia or the Russia of the days before the Revolution I could not tell.

Soon afterwards the sun set. For a moment bright orange streamers thrust upwards from behind the island of Khios. Then they became diffused and melted in the paler yellow of the evening sky. Within the bowl of the nearer hills it was quiet; not a ripple moved upon the water. A sea-bird alighted with a loud splash near by, and at once another made off upon hasty, pattering feet, struggling with difficulty into the heavy air. The dusk fell quickly then, and the mist rose to meet it, softening the outlines of the distant cliffs and beaches. We all went down to supper: when we came back on deck a little later, it was dark.

At 7 p.m. *Olinda* left Gulbache Bay and steered north towards the entrance. Off Ardic Burnu, at the mouth of the bay, she slowed down. The mist had risen by now all over the Gulf. It hung mast-high around us, but very thin; through it we could just see where the mountains came down to the water on either hand—black and steep to the water. Just before eight o'clock we picked up, from somewhere ahead, the measured commotion of a steamer's approach. Then *Orak* came, without lights, looming suddenly; first her mast-heads, then the dark mass of her hull plunging out of the mist before us, then swinging away to port to avoid colliding with *Olinda*. A hail from her bridge rang out thinly upon the darkness; we in *Olinda* answered it. Then she passed inwards and disappeared into the dark background of the hills astern. *Olinda* increased speed, heading north-westwards and hugging the dark fringes of the mountains towards the open sea.

At 9 p.m. we were abreast of Port Saip. The moon had not yet risen, but the sky was clear and full of stars which set the mist agleam. As we rounded the Island of Buyuk Saip, the mist thinned and then vanished before the first vague puffs of

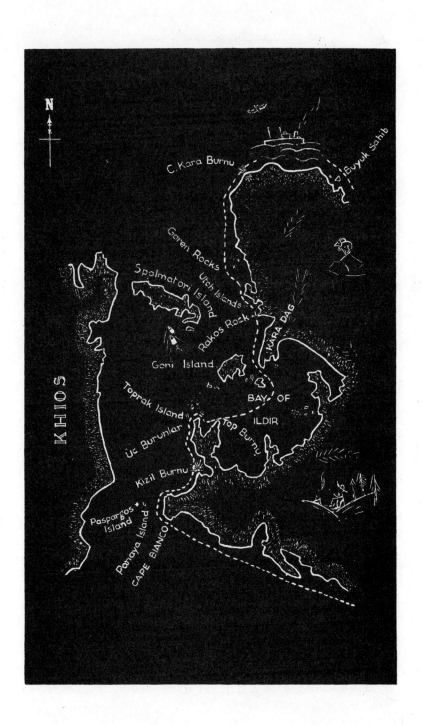

wind, coming from round the headland. *Olinda* turned west-ward, and crept in closer to the rocks.

To-night the shore defences had all been warned, so there was no firing. But we had, nevertheless, an eerie feeling of being watched all the time . . . the occasional glow of a cigarette in the hills; once or twice a thin cry or a laugh coming down to us upon the wind—a light north-westerly wind. As we rounded the headland of Kanli Kaya Burnu, the breeze freshened in our faces, dry and keen like the wine of Stromi. At ten o'clock we reached the north-western point of Kara Burnu, its lighthouse flashing out four times above us. We turned south into Khios Strait just as the first glow from the rising moon was beginning to edge the eastern hills with silver.

The night was very still, and the steady thump of *Olinda*'s engine rang and echoed among the rocks; but what little breeze there was still came from the westward, blowing against the sound of our passing, so that it would not carry across the Straits to the enemy shores; and the rising moon cast deep shadows about us, to hide us.

Throughout the ship there was an atmosphere of restrained excitement. The Master, who was standing beside me on the compass platform, was humming away to himself and scanning the pale moon-painted waters, bending away to the south-west and closing in gradually towards the narrows between Spal-matori and Goni Island.

"By and by coming Turkish patrol boats," he observed complacently.

"Yes, down in the narrows, I expect." That was the obvious place for the Germans to patrol, and I was banking on their doing the obvious thing again.

There was the usual crowd of sailors congregated on the tank-tops forward; but they were not lining the rail as they had during those anxious hours in Suna Bay; they were strolling up and down, or sitting about idly. After a while someone began to sing. A little later there rose the muted twanging of a balalaika, so I knew that the Bosun must be down there with the rest of them.

Just before 11 p.m. we picked up the glint of surf upon the Garen rocks ahead, and *Olinda* edged out a little to avoid them. Soon we were nearly a mile off shore, and next moment, as we slid out from the shadows, a bulbous moon, little more than half full, lifted above the hill-tops and shone directly upon us. We were still a good five miles from the enemy look-out post on Spalmatori Island, so as there was no sign yet of any patrol craft, we stood boldly on down the coast without any feelings of undue anxiety. Ten minutes later we were nearly abreast of Garen rocks; in less than five minutes more, we would be past them and able to creep back again into the shadow of the mountains.

Ah Fong's cheerful dish of a face appeared over the edge of the coaming as he scrambled up on to the monkey island with two large mugs of cocoa. He set them down beside the standard compass and remained for a few moments in the background, his bright eyes watching us shrewdly or gazing over the sea ahead. For the time being I was too occupied with conning the ship to pay any attention to Ah Fong and his cocoa. The surf was right alongside us now—only a hundred yards off. I felt very conspicuous out there in the moonlight, and an urgent longing for the deep shadows ahead of us began to possess me; I had to fight hard against the instinct to cut in closer past the shoals. Beside me the Master, sucking noisily at his cocoa, was also watching the compass and the rocks.

Ah Fong exclaimed suddenly in a soft guttural. The Master and I both turned to see him pointing out into the straits. We looked where he was pointing; then I raised my binoculars. Two small, dark shapes, which had just emerged from behind the bulk of Kara Ada, were moving slowly north-west across the narrows.

"Turkish boats," said Ah Fong confidently.

"Good job," pronounced the Master.

"O.K.," I agreed, and forced myself to turn away again without showing too much interest. But these were undoubtedly German E-boats or possibly Italian M.A.S. We were still some distance short of the direct line between them and the moon, however, so it was unlikely that they would have spotted us at once. All the same it was a great relief, when Garen rocks came abeam a few moments later, and we could alter course to port, and dive once more into the welcoming shadows of the cliffs.

Two miles ahead a huddle of flat-topped rocks, the Utch

Islands, lay upon the calm water like a cluster of water-lily pads. We steered to pass inside them. The gap between the islands and the shore was only about two hundred yards; but the water just there was deep, and *Olinda* went swishing through at full speed, trailing a glitter of bow wave that curled over and broke against the nearest island with a roar. It put up a roosting colony of sea-birds, like a cloud of spray, screaming and complaining into the night around us. We swept on past the Rakos Islands, where we sent another flock of birds scrambling noisily into the air. The hands on the foredeck laughed and jeered at the birds, and pointed out the distant patrol boats to each other in obvious high spirits. Then they settled down once more to their singing, and the gay blatter of the balalaika traced a lively counterpoint to the deeper rythm of *Olinda*'s screws.

For the rest of the night I laboured under an added distraction. Whenever I found it necessary to hug the rocks unusually close, the Master (and once even the Mate at the wheel) felt disposed to question the wisdom of hazarding the ship among the shoals, pointing out that "Turkish boats over there keeping Germans away." And the crew, almost as though they wished to advertise our presence and convey their gratitude to our supposed guardians, the "Turkish" patrol boats, played and laughed and sang away at the tops of their voices, until I began to fear, that even against the wind, they would be heard. Fortunately, however, the E-boats were still moving away across the channel, and soon they had faded into the hazy distances beyond the southern end of Spalmatori Island.

Olinda strode on down the coast, with the high central ridge of Kara Dag standing up before her. When she reached this headland she turned to skirt it, keeping less than a cable from the shore; then round the end of it and out into the moonlight of Ildir Bay. But now we had a whole group of islands between ourselves and the Khios Strait; for the moment, therefore, we were reasonably safe from observation and attack. The first stage of the passage had been accomplished without any trouble.

It was just midnight as we turned again to cross the bay. The moon was well up; but, below it, a heavy coating of black

cloud was spreading upwards and out towards us from the
mountains of Turkey. As we reached the middle of the Bay of
Ildir, a flurry of cold air came sighing over the hills and chasing
after us across the flat surface of the sea, ruffling it, and then
passing on into the night ahead. A few moments later there
came another puff that made us shiver. The Master wound
a scarf round his neck and I buttoned up my coat under my
chin. Ah Fong slid down the ladder and disappeared below.
Soon the music on the forecastle ceased, and I saw the hands
drifting away towards the shelter of the forecastle. *Olinda* was
steering a little south of west, towards the headland of Top
Burnu. Just as she reached it, the wind freshened to a steady
breeze from the eastward and, almost at the same time, the
leading edge of cloud shadow came racing down the hills
astern and out on to the water, like an angel's wing spread
swiftly to cover us with its friendly shadow. As we closed
the low, dark promontory of Üc Burunlar, the shadow over-
took us as the hem of the cloud itself rose up to cover the
moon.

Olinda plodded on towards the side of Üc Burunlar, close in
to it, and turning slowly north until her course was once more
parallel with the land. Beyond the end of this headland,
between us now and the open waters of the Khios Strait, was
a patch of shoals and rocks, about two miles square, through
which, close round the end of the point, was a narrow, un-
marked passage of deep water. The engines were rung down
to "slow ahead together" and *Olinda*'s speed dropped to no
more than three knots. But we held her in as close as possible
to the land, for less than seven hundred yards from the end of
the point, there lay a line of rocks and very shallow water,
waiting to trap the faint-hearted mariner, who might be
tempted to flinch away from the hard black menace of the
cliffs to port.

Just before we reached the end of the promontory, I picked
up my binoculars once more and swept the straits. A good
five miles away to the northward were the narrows in which
we had first seen the German craft. Yes, there they still were,
steering south-east now across the gap, and apparently quite
oblivious of our presence to the south'ard of them—of *Olinda*
having already passed them. I wondered whether they were the

same craft who had waited for us three weeks before in the Mitylene Channel. They must be having an arduous winter, these fellows, patrolling up and down, night after night, glaring into the darkness, into wind and weather, shielding their eyes as best they could against rain and sleet, only to find in the end that *Olinda* had managed somehow to slip by them once again.

I swung my glasses round to the tip of the headland which, by now, was close aboard to port. The low, black streak of Toprak Island was just swimming out clear of the point. This was our only guide to the inner channel round the headland. "Port fifteen. Steer 312." *Olinda*'s head began to swing slowly round to port until her stem was pointing directly at the island. A few minutes later the small cluster of rocks off the end of Üc Burunlar was right abreast of us. "Hard a-port," and the ship started a bold sweeping turn that carried her right round the headland, just clear of all the rocks. At last she was round and steering due south once more, towards the small, bright flash from the Kizil Burnu lighthouse, pricking the darkness every three seconds. South and away. And above us the cloud wrack spread no farther—seemed to be pierced and anchored by the mountain peaks climbing up through it in the east, as though indeed those mountains were the massy shoulders of some brooding Divinity whose pinions, spread to hide us from the moon, were now being folded once again.

About 1.30 a.m. the wind freshened from the south-east. When we rounded the next headland and passed through the southern narrows, between Paspargo islet and the shore, it was already strong in our faces, and the sea was curling in round the corner of C. Bianco. *Olinda* began to lift and wallow in the swell. We scanned the three miles of tumbling water between ourselves and Khios, but there was no sign of any more craft. The seas were breaking heavily against Paspargo and Panayia islands, the spray exploding over them like smoke. At 2 a.m. *Olinda* emerged from the straits into the open sea and turned south-east along the Turkish coast. For the rest of the night we went slogging and plunging into the weather down towards the cliffs of Teke Burnu.

Far out on the southern horizon, the dim ghost of Samos squatted in the moonlight . . . like some prehistoric monster lying in wait for us, waiting for our attempt to slip through between his rugged jaws and the coast of Turkey opposite.

32

JUST before dawn on February 8th, the wind flew into the south-west and freshened. But the sky remained clear, and at 5 a.m. *Olinda* rounded the headland of Teke Burnu to enter Sighajik Bay. Just as the sun was rising, we anchored at the mouth of a narrow inlet in the extreme north-west corner of the bay, where high mountains screened us from the north and west. We went below to our breakfast feeling confident that no aircraft, unless actually searching for us, would be likely to pick us up.

We had only just started eating, however, when the frenzied barking of Malu and the familiar fusillade of rifle shots, with the occasional clang of bullets coming inboard, brought us all out again on deck. Upon the hill-side nearby we saw a group of figures in khaki. From among them spurted an occasional puff of blue smoke, followed in half a second by the sound of a shot and then either a splash in the water alongside or the whine of a ricochet. What mistake could we possibly have made this time? After a while we decided to send a boat inshore to find out. Old Zamit immediately stepped forward and volunteered to act as peace envoy.

Feodor Pavlovitch went below, returning a few minutes later with a large piece of white linen torn from the back of an old shirt and tacked on to a broom handle to act as a flag of truce. At first Zamit refused to carry this ignoble emblem of surrender; but while we were all crowded round the boat, making ready to lower it, a stray bullet suddenly "whanged" into *Olinda*'s funnel and, rebounding at right-angles, came whining amongst us. It caught poor old Zamit on the shin, and made him dance with pain and anger. He snatched Feodor's flag and leapt up into the boat, shouting furious obscenities at the soldiers ashore. The Arab sailors began at once to lower away on the falls. From where I stood, a little way off, I saw the raging Zamit sink precipitately out of sight down the ship's side, waving his flag madly, more like a standard than a signal of truce. He looked like a fat and ferocious old pirate going down with his ship, but still bellowing defiance at his conquerors as she sank.

Johnny Caruana and the Bosun pulled the boat inshore, and we saw the soldiers come down to the beach as it approached; but at the last moment it disappeared behind a jutting rock,

so we were unable to observe the actual landing. About ten minutes later the boat reappeared from behind the rock, and came pulling back towards the ship. As it drew near we noticed that Zamit was no longer on board. We searched the shore with binoculars. At last we saw him, or rather his white flag, bobbing up and down violently over the heads of a group of khaki-clad figures, who seemed to be hunched very close together as they swayed and struggled up a goat track over the hills.

When the boat reached the ship's side, the Bosun looked very grim and Johnny Caruana somewhat mournful. Zamit, it appeared, had been arrested again and frog-marched away to the Turkish company headquarters. Apparently *Olinda* had once more chosen a prohibited anchorage; she was now ordered to shift at once to a small cove about two miles farther east, where there was a Turkish Customs post. This we accordingly did, and at 9.30 a.m. we entered Demircli Bay, to be met there by a boat full of soldiers who still held Zamit firmly clutched between them. He sat in the stern-sheets, between two of the soldiers, his broomstick between his legs, and the white flag hanging dejectedly from one surviving tin-tack at the middle of it. He was very dishevelled and muttering away to himself what appeared to be an endless stream of semi-defiant asides, directed at the floor-boards of the boat, but obviously intended for the ears of his captors. The soldiers did not look as if they were taking much notice of what Zamit said, though one could see their little black eyes snapping fiercely, and when the boat came alongside, Zamit was given a hearty clout on the bottom with the butt of a rifle, to help him on his way up the ladder.

Zamit, when he finally reached *Olinda*'s deck, was beside himself and chattering with rage. He was also streaked with perspiration from his arduous march over the hill. After we had managed to calm him somewhat, he informed us that *Olinda* might spend the day at anchor in her present berth; but on no account was she ever again to anchor anywhere on the Turkish coast *except at a place whose name was prefixed by the word Port*; such places, he explained, all contained Turkish Customs posts, and foreign vessels must enter no others.

"What about Port Saip?" I asked him. "That was a prohibited anchorage, wasn't it?"

Zamit went to the ship's side and shouted down to the N.C.O. in charge of the Turkish boat, which was just shoving off; but the Turk merely shrugged his shoulders and turned to give an order to the oarsmen. Immediately they began to pull away from the ship, followed by the maledictions of the furious Malu.

At 11 a.m. we once more heard the drone of an aircraft coming from over the mountains; but these mountains towered almost directly above us to 3,000-foot crags and ridges, so the aircraft itself never came in sight and we could only imagine him circling above Gulbache Bay, taking his daily photograph of the little ship he saw lying there. We hoped that *Orak* would have anchored accurately in the berth mentioned in the Old Man's letter to Vice-Consul Ensor, so that no slight change in position of the ship lying in Gulbache Bay could possibly arouse the suspicion of the Luftwaffe photographic interpreters.

Just before lunch I noticed Zamit, the Master and Feodor Pavlovitch standing together on the poop, discussing something which made the Russians glance at each other with doubtful expressions on their faces. As I strolled up to them, the Master turned to me: "Zamit saying patrol boats last night not Turkish boats," he announced. "Turkish officer telling him German E-boats."

I tried to look surprised and also not to show my annoyance at the indiscretion of Zamit, who was clearly both proud at being the bearer of important tidings and also rather triumphant over the ease with which we had once more slipped past the Huns. "Bloody sausage-eatin' square heads," he proclaimed with contempt.

"Anyway we're past them now," I said confidently. "Provided they go on believing we're still in Gulbache Bay, they'll go on waiting for us in Khios Strait; so all we've got to do is to push on through Samos and Kos Straits as quickly as possible."

The Master seemed satisfied with this, but Feodor smiled. In a faintly ironical tone he asked whether we had not already done enough pushing and pulling in Suna Bay.

By the evening the wind, still south-westerly, had freshened to a strong breeze, while the sky was becoming rapidly overcast. A little before dark we shortened in cable and made ready to sail, then waited for the light to fade. The air was cold and, out beyond the cliffs of Teke Burnu, we could see the white caps racing across the mouth of the bay. The barometer was falling slowly, which suggested that the weather was about to break in earnest. As I stood upon the compass platform, waiting for the night to close in upon the coast, I suddenly remembered the most secret letter which was still tucked away in the breast pocket of my greatcoat. I pulled it out now and glanced at the typewritten address upon it, trying to guess what might be inside, and also feeling a little guilty about my negligence in not having opened the letter as soon as we left harbour.

When I did open it, I found that it was not from Ankara at all, but from X . . . , the little foreigner in Izmir with suffering behind his eyes, the man who had pressed upon me those embarrassing tablets of dope for dealing with Fritz Scheibel. He must have slipped the letter in with the official mail from Ankara as the simplest method of ensuring that it would be delivered to me. The note ran as follows:

> It is your turn this time to help *us*. An agent for whom we are responsible has got into trouble with the Turks and must be removed from the country secretly and at once. There is no time to arrange things through the correct channels, nor can I be certain that such arrangements would be secure. *Enfin*, I cannot risk it, so will you please take my word that what I am asking you to do will greatly assist the Allied cause; and will you therefore help us if you can.
>
> I know that on your passage down the Turkish coast, you are likely to have to spend the day in the Gulf of Doris. Please, therefore, go to the landlocked Bay of Kiervasili. Our people will make themselves known to you there, and you will then be able to satisfy yourself further about details which I dare not write down even in a secret communication.
>
> Please do not let us down. Although this is irregular, you have my word for it that it is O.K.
>
> Yours,
X . . .

I put the note away. It was an odd and, as he had admitted, a highly irregular communication; and yet its very frankness seemed to give it a genuine ring. There had been no attempt in it to give a spurious authority to a perfectly straightforward request. In any case it seemed to me that very little harm could result from taking one of X . . . 's men back to allied territory, where he could be properly interrogated and looked after by the Army Security authorities. There would be time enough, in any case, to decide upon what action to take if and when *Olinda* reached the Gulf of Doris. Meanwhile the sun had gone down and dusk was already crowding in upon the anchorage. I shouted to the Bosun, who was standing upon the forecastle head, waiting for the order to weigh; and next moment the windlass came groaning and chattering to life.

It was 7.30 p.m., and quite dark, by the time *Olinda* reached the Island of Hypsili, off the eastern point of Sighsjik Bay. With a strong south-westerly wind piling the seas into the Gulf of Scala Nuova, she was beginning to roll ponderously and to swing wildly, yawing from side to side of her course like a drunken old trollop. The Master himself was steering and we passed, without incident, inside the black pyramid of Hypsili, then skirted the ten-fathom line round Lebedos Bay.

Just before we reached C. Bugali, I remember there were a couple of shots from a lonely watcher ashore, probably fired more out of boredom than in order to frighten us off. In any case the sea was still getting up and the wind seemed stronger, so we were all of us too occupied with handling the ship to pay much attention to stray explosions. All through the evening the wind continued to rise and, at midnight, the rain began, lightly at first, so that the visibility remained moderately good, but persistent enough, none the less, to hide us from any patrol craft who might chance to be at sea. The marsh reeds of Ephesus, just ahead of us, would be sighing more loudly, I thought, to-night; and the curlews would have cause for complaining.

Just after midnight, off Yarajik Point, a heavy, black squall came trailing its skirts up the gulf from behind the mountains of Samos; soon we could see the angry streaks of white water, lashed by hail and scurrying out before the fiercer gusts. At twelve-thirty, the squall burst upon us with a rush of wind and driving sleet that flailed the sea till it seemed to boil, and blotted out the land beside us. Just before the outline of the next headland disappeared, I managed to take a quick compass bearing of it. I shouted down the voice-pipe to the Bosun, who was now steering, to alter course a little, so as to carry us well clear. Then I scrambled down to the chart-room for oilskins. When I returned to the monkey island, I found both the Master and the old Mate standing there, already huddled in heavy coats and sou'westers.

For ten minutes we stood on into the smother ahead. It was pitch dark now, and the wind had risen to a screaming fury around us, with poor old *Olinda* careering wildly before

the seas. The Bosun had the greatest difficulty in keeping the
ship's head off before the wind. With only a few hundred tons
of ballast to steady her, she towered out of the sea, as awkward
as a houseboat and almost as difficult to manage. Time and
again she brought the wind well out on her beam, and all
the bridge superstructure and the funnel, acting like sails,
tried to force her round farther into the gale. In the end we
allowed her to have her way. In such weather there was no
longer any need to hug the coast, so we let her head come round
to south, and steered straight across the Gulf towards the
Turkish mountains of Samsun Dag, which stood guard over
the straits of Samos. We could no longer see them, of course,
but we knew that it would take *Olinda* at least two hours to
cross the head of the Gulf, so we had reason to hope that by
then the visibility would have improved.

The wind and sea were now upon the starboard bow, and
Olinda was pounding and plunging into the teeth of the weather.
We all crouched, to steady ourselves, against the rail on the
fore side of the monkey island, but continued to peer ahead,
shielding our faces as best we could with our hands and arms,
against the sleet. As the ship struggled ahead, she dug up
great lumps of sea and hurled them in sheet upon sheet of
hissing spray over her sturdy old shoulder. The tank-tops on
the foredeck were swept again and again; we could hear the
packing-cases, which still formed our dummy hatches, thumping
and straining against their lashings. There was no longer any
need for the dummy hatches; they must be shifted in the
morning. I turned to the figure crouching next to me in the
darkness—the Mate, I thought it was, but there was no way of
telling from the shapeless mass of his oilskins and the double-
pointed sou'wester crammed down over his face, which gave
him the appearance of a despondent and bedraggled old eagle,
perched precariously upon the top of the rail.

"To-morrow we must shift those dummy hatches," I yelled.

Olinda lurched into a heavy comber, and a cloud of spray
rattled over the bridge. The wind tore at the edges of my
mouth when it opened; half my words were lost in the sudden
pandemonium. "Yes, they are," said the figure beside me, but
he had not heard what I said. It was the Master; the Mate
was behind me, bracing himself against the binnacle. Another

large sea curled up to windward and hurled itself sprawling across the tank-tops. Next moment there was a tearing and thundering of sodden canvas, and the foremost tarpaulin was thrashing wildly, like a great black bird floundering about the deck. Then a furious gust of wind got under the packing-cases and tossed them into the air like leaves, like a handful of nursery bricks. In less than a minute the dummy fore-hatch had disappeared over the side, except for one black strip of tarpaulin which had fouled the shrouds and hung there a moment, cracking like a gigantic whip with a noise like a volley of rifle shots. Then it disintegrated in a final explosion, and followed the rest into the sea.

Just before 2 a.m. the sea grew less violent; *Olinda* steadied a little, but still listed heavily to port beneath the press of wind alone. Later the wind itself began to ease, so we knew that we must be approaching the high land to the south of us. The rain continued, if anything heavier than before, and impenetrable. We glared into it and waited. Whatever happened we must let *Olinda* run her full distance, otherwise, when the squall passed, we should find ourselves sitting out in the middle of the gulf, somewhere near the enemy harbour of Vathi, on the north coast of Samos.

At 2.30 a.m. the wind fell to nothing as though cut off by a screen. The sudden quiet was menacing; the hissing of rain all round us upon still water intensified the silence. *Olinda* could not be more than a mile from the cliffs. We rang down "slow ahead" on both engines and waited again. A few moments later the rain increased to a deluge, and the sea seemed to smoke and shiver beneath it; then quickly it passed, and there before us, almost on top of us, rose a hard, black wall of mountain, flat and forbidding, climbing into a clearing night sky three thousand feet or more above us.

"Starboard twenty." *Olinda*'s head swung away slowly from south to west. About five miles away to the westward stood the dark mass of Samos, garrisoned by the Italians, and we could just see the narrow gap of clear water between the island and the Turkish shore. We knew that somewhere near the tip of Samsun Dag was a Turkish look-out post. Presumably, also, there was an Italian one on the coast of Samos, less than a mile away across the Strait.

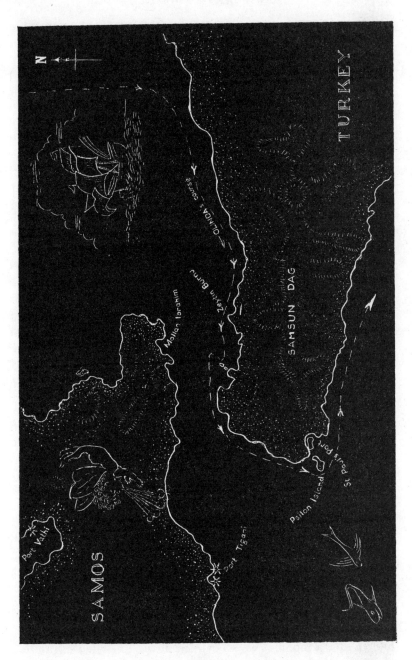

SAMOS

Port Vathi

Port Tigani

Mollar Ibrahim

Zeitun Burnu

OLINDA's course

Psilon Island

St Paul's Port

SAMSUN DAG

TURKEY

N

18

The sky cleared. First the stars and then the moon came out. We edged in closer to Samsun Dag, till the moon dipped behind the tops of the mountains, and their shadow swept over us; till the occasional streaks of pebbly beach gleamed palely beside us; till the cliffs and crags seemed almost to curve in overhead. All around us now was deathly quiet, and just across the water the hills of Samos were crowned in moonlight. The houses of Port Tigani, on the south coast of the island, stood out white and clear and very close. The olive groves, covering the mountain-sides in a thick unbroken mat, like chocolate icing, fell darkly to the shore in tongues, fanning out where the valleys broadened to the sea. The jagged course of a mountain stream zigzagged through them like a streak of silver lightning.

No one spoke on the bridge. Zamit heaved himself up the ladder and settled against the after rail, where he remained almost unnoticed; Feodor came out on to the wing of the lower bridge to watch.

In the unnatural stillness under the lee of the mountains, *Olinda*'s engine sounded loud, and the pounding of her screws echoed back to us from among the cliffs. We felt that the noise of our approach must easily carry across the water to the Samos shore. We rang down "slow" on both engines and edged in a little closer still to the Turkish side, till the rocks and the occasional trees growing among them seemed to be flying past us. Silently, from here and there, the hands came out upon the foredeck. The Master went below for a moment to make sure that Malu was safely locked in his cabin. We rounded a point of land and swept on past a long straight beach. We could hear the hiss and rattle of our bow wave stirring up the pebbles as it raced along after us. We all held our breath. Instinctively I lowered my voice when giving orders down the voice-pipe; I could hear Zamit behind me murmuring in urgent undertones to the Mate.

Suddenly, from the shore, there rose a furious barking of dogs, disturbed by the "churring" of our bow wave along the shingle. They were racing after it down the beach, yapping and snarling their defiance. In an agony we turned with one accord and "hushed" at them madly; but of course they could not hear us, and would certainly have taken no notice if they had. After a moment we all calmed down, and then began to laugh at ourselves and at each other, which made us feel a good deal better, causing the tension to relax.

Just ahead of us now stood the point of Zeytin Burnu, with the ruin of a watch-tower upon it. A mile away to the northward we could see the Samian village of Mollah Ibrahim, tucked into all the dark corners of a cove. Then we swept out round the point, and a sharp exclamation from the Master, on his way back to the bridge, made me turn to look at where he was pointing. . . . Directly ahead of us, less than a mile away, two E-boats lay close together, just clear of the Turkish coast, waiting for us!

It was too late to stop; we were almost upon them. " Full ahead together ! " *Olinda*'s engines burst into life again, and she turned a little more to port, so as to bring herself stem on to the E-boats, thereby presenting for them the smallest possible target. For a full sixty seconds we bore down upon the enemy, expecting at any moment to see the first torpedo come streaking towards us. Then suddenly I was struck by something odd in the appearance and behaviour of the E-boats—they remained dead still, broadside on to us and directly in our path. Were they anchored then, and their crews all asleep below? Would we be able to ram and sink them? No! "Hard a-starboard." There was a terrible, shivering moment as *Olinda* hung agonisingly, under full helm, before she began to turn. Then slowly she swung away . . . out into the moonlit straits, with only yards to spare between herself and the two squat lumps of rock at which we had been charging in the extremity of our desperation!

"Hard a-port." *Olinda* steadied up; then she began to swing back again towards the shore, just in time to avoid plunging out of the mountain shadow and into the glaring whiteness the straits. "Slow ahead together," and she crept back once more into the pitchy shelter of the Turkish cliffs. Five minutes later we rounded another point, and before us were the nar-rows, with a flat, green-topped island about four hundred yards out towards the middle of them. We slid in between the island and the shore, then turned due south . . . away from Samos.

The moon shot out from behind the mountains; the wind swept in against us fresh and cold. In twenty minutes we had reached the ancient island of Psilon, sheltering the entrance to St. Paul's Port, and had turned the corner once again, placing the mountains of Samsun Dag between us and the island of Samos. Then, with the wind behind us and a brilliant moon-light setting the wavelets a-glitter, we worked up once more to *Olinda*'s best speed and went galloping away to the eastward; towards the plains and marshes of Miletus and the mouth of the Meander River.

33

BY dawn on February 9th we reached Mandelyah Gulf. Into early morning sunlight we plodded eastwards towards the head of it, and so into the Bay of Asen, which we reached at about 8 a.m. We all felt very tired after the physical and nervous strain of the past two nights, so there was considerable relief when *Olinda* sauntered into the roads abreast of the small country town of Küllük; there to anchor for the remainder of the day.

We were now snugly hidden in the depths of Turkish territory, with the nearest enemy island more than twenty-five miles distant, and the enemy base of Leros at least fifty miles away to the westward. Not a sound of any aircraft, nor the evidence of any other warlike activities came to disturb us. We thought of *Orak*, sitting peacefully upon the sheltered waters of Gulbache Bay, with the old Hun buzzing round close above her, assiduously taking photographs. We wished them both well, commending them to a continuance of such laudably peaceful pursuits; and, in a benevolent frame of mind, we clattered down the companion into the saloon for breakfast. This meal, since leaving Izmir, had taken on a strangely convivial character for the time of day at which it was eaten. Breakfast had become, in fact, our main meal, and consisted always of large quantities of raw salt herring, scrambled eggs and *vodka*. After such a feast we found that we could all roll into our bunks and sleep like the dead until late in the afternoon.

But to-day, after breakfast, I wandered up on to the poop to bask for a moment in the sunshine, and to gaze at the friendly little township of Küllük, lying so snugly against the side of a pine-covered hill. There were no high mountains hereabouts, and most of the hills were thickly wooded. The landlocked harbour was calm and blue, with one or two small sailing craft ghosting across its surface in the light airs that came slithering over the tree-tops to brush the water. Away up at the head of the bay, upon a small hill jutting out into the sea, stood the ruins of the ancient walled town of Iassus, looking, at that distance, in the slanting yellow sunshine, quite fresh and scarcely tumbled.

The coastline of Asia Minor, we had already noticed, is thickly sprinkled with these ancient Greek, Byzantine, Roman and Saracen ruins. They seemed also to have held a fascination for the worthy hydrographers who had so studiously compiled and drawn the Admiralty charts. I fetched a chart from the bridge and began to study it in the sunshine. Wherever one looked upon it there were intriguing little notations such as: "Probably the ancient Mount Cragus" or "scattered sarcophagi, colonnades and a ruined theatre, surrounded by luxuriant gardens," all lovingly penned in the neatest copperplate; or again, with a hint of disdain for such tawdry modernity, the laconic comment: "Middle Age Fortress." And at one point on the chart, many miles inland among the peaks of the Latimus mountains, was the surprising assertion: "Temple of Hecate (by Lieutenant Smith, Royal Engineers)," as though it might have been "*Décor* by Oliver Messel" at the beginning of a theatre programme, and the good Smith the architect of this ancient edifice.

I was still smiling at my last discovery when a movement nearby caused me to turn my head; I was surprised to find Ivan

Oreshkin leaning over the rail beside me. For a moment or two we smiled at each other, but rather shyly, seeking and hoping for some means of contact—a contact so far denied to us by the lack of any common tongue. After a while I saw him screwing himself up for some carefully practised observation— possibly the only words of English that Ivan knew. I grinned encouragement.

"Lord Byron," said Ivan, and added, almost desperately, "Roas' Beef."

But with these words he had clearly shot his linguistic bolt; he turned away blushing, to glare across the harbour with a deeper, fiercer scowl than ever before upon his sharp features. The effort, however, had been made; and, for ever afterwards, there was an added feeling of goodwill between Ivan and myself, as though from a secret shared. It was frequently reaffirmed, when we met alone, by one of us hailing the other with "Lord Byron," to which the other automatically replied "Roas' Beef"—unlikely partners perhaps; but so, in fact, were Ivan and myself.

It still wanted two hours to sunset when *Olinda* sailed again. Since there was no risk of our being seen by enemy craft until we once more reached the open sea, we had decided to take advantage of a couple of hours' daylight to help us upon our way. Wind and rain had come in again from south-west, but on the southern shore we were sheltered from the full strength of it. As we steamed through the narrow pass between the first small island and the mainland, the rain began to fall more heavily and the ruined monastery, near the crown of the island, stood out dimly through a film of low cloud, like the carcass of a long-dead monster. At dusk the rain eased off, and the cloud wrack seemed to lift a little. By the time we had rounded the Sandama Peninsular, leaving the ominous-sounding pinnacle of Wreck Rock well away to the northward, the night had closed in dark and over-burdened, conceiving more rain.

We slipped in behind Kiremit Adasi, then on past the mouth of Gümüslük harbour. The two small islands of Kiremit and Kato were both nominally Greek; but no one lived on them, so although we passed within half a mile of them, we did not expect any trouble.

Next the loom of the lighthouse on Hussein Point, in Kos Strait, glowed in a pale half-halo over the end of the land; a moment later the light itself flashed out above it. We watched the bearing of the lighthouse closely; when this reached 162 degrees we turned again to port and steered towards it, keeping it all the time upon the same bearing, so as to pass to seaward of the spit of shoal water off Karabackla point. Then in again, as close in as we dared to the rocks, and on down the coast towards the straits.

Ten miles away to seaward lay the enemy-occupied island of Kalimno, its higher mountains dipped in cloud; and, beyond it to the north-west, the island of Leros, which contained the main Italian base. Ahead of us, on the other side of Kos Strait, which was two miles wide, stood the large island of Kos, with its main harbour facing north across the straits. Between us and these three larger islands were several clusters of smaller ones, some inhabited by Greeks or Italians and some deserted. The nearest of them was only a mile or so from the Turkish shore. Kos Strait itself was the main thoroughfare between Rhodes and Leros for coastal shipping.

The middle of Kos Strait is clear and free from shoals or other dangers; but on the Turkish side there are two off-lying rocks—Pasha Rock, which lies no more than two feet above the surface, and Magpie Rock, which is never less than four feet under water. Between Magpie Rock and the Turkish shore there is room for a ship to pass, but no buoy or other sea-marks to assist her in doing so. Consequently the channel is never used, and all craft keep well out in the middle of the strait.

At 8.30 p.m. we were nearly abreast of Hussein point and had just picked up the small, black streak upon the water, which was all that was showing of the top of Pasha Rock, when the look-out in the wing of the bridge sang out and also pointed. . . . Away in the middle of the channel we could make out the familiar dark shapes of small craft.

I examined them through my glasses. The leading one looked like a *caique* without any canvas set; I could see a tall mast forward. She seemed to be towing another smaller boat, and beyond her were two more vessels, apparently steaming north in company with her. There were no E-boats among

them, but vessels under way at this time of night would
scarcely be Turkish, so whatever they were, we must avoid
being seen by them for fear of their reporting us.

At first I thought of stopping and waiting until the other
craft had passed northward, for the sweeping shaft of light from
Hussein Point lighthouse would be sure to silhouette us for the
caiques, even if we passed by at a fair distance from them.

But there was no telling which way they would turn after they
had passed through the straits. If they were bound for Samos,
they must pass quite close to where *Olinda* now lay. There was,
therefore, only one thing to do: to risk the inside channel past
Pasha and Magpie, and to try to get so close to the lighthouse
that we should be past it in a flash and into the darkness beyond.
In this way, we and the *caiques*, going in opposite directions at
a combined speed of perhaps fourteen knots, would only be
in line with the lighthouse together for two or three seconds
at the most, so the risk of our being seen would be slight.

I settled myself behind the standard compass bowl, and
glanced over the dim face of it at Pasha Rock ahead. "Port
easy." I heard the Master suck in his breath sharply; then he
lumbered over and stood beside me. "I'm going close round
Pasha and inside the Magpie," I told him. We had discussed

the possibility of this before, and though he had been violently and fairly reasonably opposed to such a manœuvre, he had reluctantly agreed that a situation might arise in which it would be necessary to take the risk.

It was fortunate that we had already discussed this plan, for I was now able to give him the first course, and leave him at the compass, while I turned away to train my binoculars on two of the southernmost lumps of black rock which lay upon our seaward side. I knew that when these two islets came in line with each other, *Olinda* must be upon a course that would take her *directly away* from them. She must keep them in line until she was past a certain bearing of the lighthouse; then she must turn at once on to a fresh course. If she deviated more than fifty yards or a handful of seconds from this procedure, she would take the ground either on the rocky spit stretching from Hussein Point itself, or upon the dreaded Magpie, which would tear the bottom right out of her and sink her at once.

Luckily the rain was still holding off and the visibility was good; but, just as the gap between the two islets was beginning to close up perceptibly, I heard a muttered curse from the Master.

"Rain coming," he growled.

I glanced round and saw the dark curtain of a squall gathering off the eastern point of Kos Island. The wind was fairly fresh, but even so, it would take the squall fifteen or twenty minutes to reach us. With luck there was still time to get through the most difficult part of the channel before it arrived.

Pasha rock swept by, looking cruel and close to port. We could see the jagged, saw-like ridge of it, low upon the water beside us. For a moment we heard the sigh and gurgle of the surf welling over it and pouring down again in frothy cascades into the sea. A mile away on the other side, the four boats were still plodding north-westwards out of the straits. We were as close as we would ever be to the lighthouse. Its beams flashed over us in groups of three every twenty seconds, like three flashing swords—slashing the darkness to pieces, whistling over our heads and lighting the ship from end to end. Soon the two edges of the islets were very close to each other. "Hard a-port." *Olinda* began to swing steadily away, and the tips of the islets came together more slowly.

"Mid-ships." The islets were nearly in one, and almost dead astern of the ship. "Meet her and steady." *Olinda* stopped turning and steadied upon her course. Then I felt a surge of sudden fear bursting upwards through my body as I saw the islets just kiss and then draw apart again at once. There must be a current setting us towards the coast. "Steer fifteen degrees to starboard." The gap between the islets was opening slowly; but as soon as *Olinda* began to turn, and the islets drew out a little way upon her starboard quarter, the gap no longer widened . . . then at last it began to close again very slowly. I kept facing aft, however, with my eyes glued to those two small rocks astern of us, while the Master at the standard compass looked out ahead and watched the bearing of Hussein Point to port.

"What is the course now?" I called over my shoulder.

"131 degrees," replied the Master gruffly.

"Steer 126 degrees." At last the islets were nearly in one again and seemed to be holding together. Unless the current changed we would be safe upon this course for the next few minutes.

I glanced once more at the *caiques* out in the middle of the channel. They were well past us now and fast disappearing in the direction of Leros. They had ceased to be of the slightest importance; our two immediate and most deadly enemies were lurking beneath the surface of the sea nearby and not upon it. I looked round at the rain squall, and noticed that it was already half-way across the straits towards us; it had spread out east and west in a solid wall of inky black. It seemed to be moving faster than I had expected; no doubt it was bringing a strong gust of wind along with it. Yes, I could see a fringe of whitecaps chasing across the water ahead of it, and tall pillars of rain striding after them. Then I noticed that Feodor Pavlovitch was standing at the top of the ladder. When the next flash from the lighthouse lit up his face, I caught a glimpse of a sardonic smile upon it. I raised my glasses and trained them once more upon the islets astern.

"Ah! now we have the fancy tricks," suggested Feodor, with a not unfriendly touch of sarcasm, "you have grown tired of the ordinary methods, I see, and prefer now to steer the ship backwards. Can you also do this standing upon your head?"

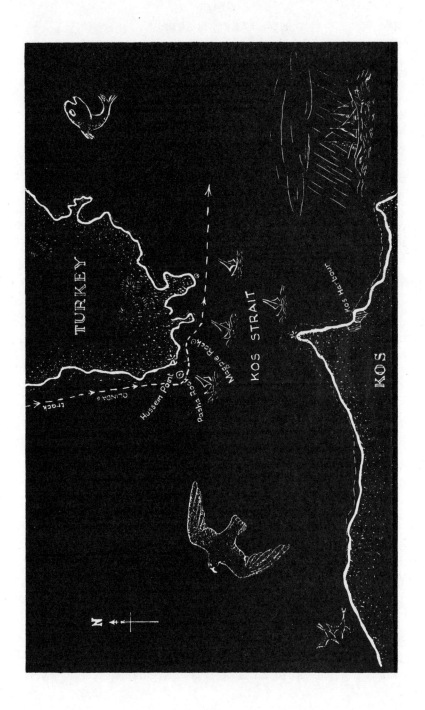

TURKEY

KOS STRAIT

KOS

Kos Harbour

Hussein Point

Pasha Rock

Mappa Rock

OLINDA'S

Track

N

But I was too busy just then to bandy words with Feodor; nevertheless, I somehow found his slightly supercilious remark encouraging. It bred a mild atmosphere of competition, the everlasting rivalry between deck and engine-room, between ourselves and the pig-iron polishers, the grease-wallopers.

The Master stood crouched over the compass bowl, carefully noting the rapid change in bearing of the lighthouse as we slid past it. "Bearing 047 degrees," he said, then a little later "040 degrees . . . 035 degrees . . . 030 degrees."

When the bearing had passed through north (or 000 degrees) to 355 degrees, we would be right off the end of the shoal spit stretching out from the point; Magpie Rock would be a few hundred yards to seaward of us, off the starboard bow. We must then turn at once, under full helm, round the end of the spit, and steer east until the bearing of Hussein light was exactly 320 degrees. After that we would at last be clear of the Magpie Rock as well. I began to feel excited; so far everything was working according to plan. If only the rain would hold off for another few minutes, we would be clear of the worst danger.

Feodor called to me and pointed. I followed the direction of his arm, and saw a paler streak of grey running out towards our bows through the black water ahead. Yes, that would be the spit; it looked alarmingly near, but at all costs we must not lose our nerve. If we turned away now, *Olinda* would be just about in the right position to charge straight over the sharp pinnacle of Magpie Rock. I could imagine the huge lurch she would give, rearing up forward and heeling over; then sliding into deep water beyond, to settle quickly and finally to the bottom.

"005 degrees," called the Master.

"Port fifteen," I sang out down the voice-pipe.

"000 degrees" . . . *Olinda* was already turning slowly. But the spit looked very near; glancing over the side, I could see the mottled outline of rocks and sand in the water directly beneath the ship. We seemed to be racing over the ground; it was difficult to believe that there was at least four fathoms of water under us. . . . But the chart said so; so there must be. There'd got to be, or else. . . . Feodor remained leaning over

the rail and gazing calmly down into the water. I marvelled
at the coolness of the man; at his mild and seemingly academic
interest in matters outside the sphere of his own department;
at his air of detached superiority during a time when we were
all holding our breath and controlling with difficulty a craven
impulse to ring down "full astern" on both engines.

"355 degrees," called the Master.

"Hard a-port. Steer east."

I kept my eyes on the darkness ahead now . . . away
from the shoal water into which Feodor was still gazing dis-
dainfully. The Master kept on watching the bearing of the
lighthouse.

"345 degrees . . . 335 degrees . . . 325 degrees. . . ."

If we were too far off shore; if we were going to strike the
Magpie, it would come now . . . the shock, the tearing and
grinding, the heavy stagger . . . involuntarily we stiffened, the
Master and I, as though bracing ourselves to meet it; our arms
straightened out against the binnacle and gripped it hard; but
we said not a word. And Feodor continued to loll over the
port rail, gazing placidly down into the water.

"320 degrees." We were there; on a direct line between
the lighthouse and Magpie Rock; it would be now or not at
all. "315 degrees!" We were past . . . we were through. . . .
Olinda was through the channel and safe.

"Starboard fifteen—steer 125 degrees." The Master
straightened up and, drawing out his watch, held it with
exaggerated deliberation over the compass bowl, to take the
time for the next course. Feodor raised himself slowly,
whistling between his teeth. Then he jerked his head round
and gave us a quick, ironical glance as he wandered across
to the ladder and disappeared without a word below.

I turned and squinted across the compass at the lighthouse,
now astern, to watch for any sign of drift due to current.
Suddenly I felt an icy draught round the back of my neck;
then, with a moaning and hissing, the squall swept in upon
us, and the rain poured down in a solid torrent, blotting out
everything. Once or twice more we picked up the dull gleam
of the lighthouse, looming through the deluge weakly; then it
was finally obscured, leaving *Olinda* to stand away clear and
free into the middle of the straits.

A little later we turned east up the Gulf of Kos, feeling confident that we would be safe enough from observation in the weather which had fallen upon us. After forty minutes the squall passed over as suddenly as it had come; but by this time we were abreast of Budrum (the Halicarnassus of ancient fables) with a fresh southerly breeze upon our starboard beam. A little later, the low scud lifted farther and the light on Cape Krio, fifteen miles to the south'ard, on the end of the Dorian Isthmus, shone out and winked us a cheerful greeting. *Olinda* turned into the wind and headed for the southern side of the Gulf. Thankfully we shed our oilskins, and settled down for two hours of steady plodding into a sea which was already too rough for E-boats, but not yet high enough to cause us any great discomfort.

From 10.30 p.m. onwards a watery half-moon peeped occasionally through the gaps in the scud flying north above us. Kos, grim and mountainous, crouched upon the western horizon, with infrequent lights twinkling from near its town and harbour. Once, for a few minutes, we followed the headlamps of a car, creeping tortuously along the coast road of the island, flashing and winking as they turned the corners. And all the time the look-out kept his glasses sweeping ahead for any other ships that might "pass in the night."

At midnight we reached the Dorian coast and skirted it close, passing inside the islands of Mordala and Kuchi, till we came to the cliffs of Cape Krio itself. By now the clouds had blown away, and the moon shone down brilliantly upon the ruins of Cnidus, where St. Paul had put in on his famous voyage, as a captive, from Palestine to Rome. There was no village at Cnidus now, only the gaunt skeleton of the ancient city, crowded upon a narrow neck of land between the end of the mountains and the crag upon which stood Cape Krio lighthouse.

Cape Krio was another turning-point on the *caique* route from Rhodes to Leros, so we swept in close under the cliffs as we rounded it, and saw the beam of the lighthouse whirling high above our heads, leaving *Olinda* in dark shadow beneath it.

We encountered no more ships that night as we trundled

peacefully down the southern coast of the Dorian Isthmus. We passed by the Island of Piscopi without further alarms; the coast of Rhodes made a dim border to the southern horizon. Before dawn the wind fell away to nothing, and Symi grew out of a hazy sea.

As the first light was making, we crept between the friendly arms of the ancient Gulf of Doris. I remembered the note I had received from the Consul at Chanak, who came every summer to collect the Dorian honey. Then I remembered also the letter from X . . . and wondered what strange excitements the day would bring.

The sun rose, and with it a faint breeze from off the land, whispering to us, full of the wild enticement of pine. Then came the smell of the heather from high in the hills and of wood smoke from a village, waking among trees by the water's edge. *Olinda* drove majestically on towards the head of the gulf; past a row of bright islands, where patches of brilliant green came out of the forest and down to the sea; where the sunshine was already warming the grey sides of boulders streaked with orange, and lizards were beginning to stir. The sun was well up; the sea had turned blue beneath it as we rounded a jutting point on the southern side of the gulf, and swung in among the mountains of Kiervasili Bay.

This deserted haven surpassed, in beauty, anything that we had yet encountered. It lay smooth and blue and placid as a lake before us, surrounded by lofty peaks and rich, dark forests. In the middle of the bay stood a steep, green island with the ruin of a small chapel upon its summit. Beyond the island, at the head of the bay, the mountains fell back to enclose a sheltered plain, only a square mile or two in area, and covered with olive groves and fruit trees. At the water's edge stood a cluster of huts; in front of them a sand bar stretched a sheltering arm to form a lagoon, upon which lay a solitary *caique* at anchor.

The surface of the lagoon was glassy, reflecting the mountains and the *caique* and a man upon her deck in a bright blue shirt, with a red scarf round his neck. *Olinda* slowed and stopped, drifting in gently behind the island. Then, with a mighty splash, her starboard bow anchor plunged into the sea, and a shackle or two of cable went clattering merrily after it. We stretched ourselves and yawned; we felt at peace with each other and all the world. Even Feodor nodded contently and smiled about him before turning to lead the way down to *vodka* and caviare and raw salt herring.

VII

HONEY FROM DORIAN HEATHER

34

FOR mid-February the sun was very hot, beating down upon the hill-sides so that the moisture rose steaming between the pines from last night's rain. The smell of it—the smell of pine needles and hot, wet earth—went eddying lazily round the sides of this amphitheatre of mountains, and out to us across the water.

After breakfast, when we came up again on to the poop, there was a small boat alongside, with a solitary customs guard sitting patiently upon the thwart. He did not come on board, possibly because of Malu's noisy objections; in any case he seemed only to have visited us for the purpose of bartering a large comb of black honey and a dozen eggs in exchange for some cigarettes. He poked his basket of "trade" up to the level of the deck on the muzzle of an ancient rifle.

It was easier than I had expected to get ashore.

I told Zamit to explain to the soldier that I wanted a hot bath; the latter immediately offered to take us ashore in his boat. We scrambled down the jacob's ladder without further bargaining, and just in case there really was a bath somewhere amongst that odd little group of huts on shore (I could not for the life of me imagine where; anyway not a hot one), I took with me into the boat a cake of soap and a towel.

On the way across the harbour I fell to wondering just how X . . . 's people were going to make themselves known to us; how they would manage to establish their identity beyond all reasonable doubt. Zamit sat quietly beside me in the stern-sheets, whistling (or rather hissing) a quiet little tune through a gap in the side of his lower front teeth. He looked very pleased with himself, perched there on the edge of the transom seat, like a battered old Humpty-Dumpty. The edge of the seat made a deep furrow across the tightness of his old and dilapidated black cashmere pants; his tummy, barely covered by the lower half of a grey-looking vest, parted the two halves of a blue tweed jacket in front, so that the bottom button would not do up. In spite of the fact that he sat so far forward upon the seat, the toes of his worn (though at one time fashionable) brown shoes, only just reached the floor-boards of the boat. He wore nothing upon his head, whose scattered tufts of occasional hair clung damply, in many different directions, to his scalp. Round his neck a black-and-crimson scarf was wound once only, the ends left loose to hang.

Yes, Zamit was happy. He had begun to regard himself as the mainspring of the operation, and with some justice, since he was perhaps the only man on board who could have boasted a wholly disinterested determination to make it succeed. This voyage was at one and the same time his blow for freedom, endorsement of his British nationality and his only vacation from business for the past six years. One gathered that he had a wife in Istanbul: "she was immense business woman . . . sitting on my business now in Istanbul," he had said at some time or other . . . a strange description, which conjured up all sorts of pictures; a bulging blonde maybe, with a shrill, hectoring voice, or a placid, deep-bosomed, motherly creature with shrewd eyes and a bun. One could have imagined Zamit's wife as anything from the erstwhile principal of a women's college to a blowsy old madame in perennial furs. Anyway, she was a sitter on businesses, whatever that meant; no doubt she sat upon Zamit somewhat when he was at home. I glanced across at him now. He had stopped whistling and was snuffing happily at the scented atmosphere, and jogging backwards and forwards with each sturdy stroke of the soldier's sculling.

Soon we were rounding the end of the sand spit and turning into the lagoon. It was well on in the forenoon; the sun poured down upon us burning hot. The soldier was sweating prodigiously in his heavy rough-spun tunic; but this seemed to cause him no unusual discomfort. He kept up a steady "chunking" stroke, and smiled at us occasionally in a friendly way.

Ahead of us lay the *caique* at anchor. I gazed at her idly as we drew nearer. Subconsciously, in the way one often does, I noticed something strange about her appearance. There was a queer-looking object hoisted up in her rigging, on the end of the jib halliards, to dry; not that this was unusual in itself, odds and ends of sails and gear always need drying whenever the opportunity of a fine day presents itself. But what *was* odd was that this particular object should happen to be a mattress—quite a new, clean mattress. The *caique* men never use mattresses; there is no room for them in the tiny cubby hole forward, where they curl themselves to sleep, among the ropes and spare gear.

We passed within a few yards of the *caique*, whose deck was at first deserted. But just before we reached her, I saw a head pop up out of the cuddy aft; then pop back again at once. Immediately the silence around us became intensified, and I realised that someone on board the *caique*, who had been singing, had suddenly stopped. I had not noticed this before, because the tune was the same one that Zamit had been hissing to himself most of the way across the bay, and I suppose it had been running round in my head all the time as well. Nor had I noticed until now what tune it was. It was one that had already become so popular in the night-clubs of Istanbul, that you lived with it all day long as well as most of the night. . . . It was *Lili Marlene.* In the cosmopolitan bustle of Istanbul I should have thought nothing of hearing it, but it was still new enough to harmonise ill with the remoter creeks of the Turkish south coast and the cuddy of a diminutive *caique.*

Next moment we were abreast of the *caique*, and the unnatural quiet on board her, as well as the absence of anyone on deck to pass the time of day with us as we went by, gave me a strong sensation of being spied upon. I kept my eye on the black square of the hatch leading down to the cuddy. Just before our movement forward closed it from sight, I thought I caught a glimpse of a young face—a boy's, I decided—watching us from the shadows within. Shortly afterwards, the *caique* and her crew went out of mind, for our boat had reached the shore, and we were clambering out to help the soldier haul her up on to the shingle.

As soon as the boat was safely beached, the soldier slung his gun over one shoulder and, leaving the oars with their blades poking up over the gunwales, he led the way up the beach. We halted at the foot of a great limestone cliff, which climbed sheer into the mountains a thousand feet above us, sheltering the hovels of the village from the north. He pointed at the base of the cliff and said something to Zamit in Turkish, then turned to me with a triumphant grin all over his face. "Hot bath," translated Zamit, also grinning. I looked again at the rocks round the foot of the cliff and saw that he spoke the truth. A small spring was welling out of a deep crack in the limestone a few feet up, and from it a waterfall came tinkling down over the boulders into a deep, green pool about six feet in diameter. Above the surface of the pool lay a mist of steam, eddying away

round the corner of the cliff and renewing itself continually. I dabbed my hand into the water; it was warm, almost hot. And when I put my finger into my mouth there was a bitter sulphurous taste upon it, but no trace of salt.

Zamit and I dragged off our clothes and waded into the pool, then threw ourselves down, wallowing about luxuriously. I was pleased to find, a moment later, that the soap I had brought with me lathered magnificently. Soon both Zamit and I were standing knee-deep near the edge of the pool with the rest of our bodies, faces and hair smothered in soapsuds. Then we plunged in again and splashed about like schoolchildren, shouting out to each other and laughing. Our soldier stood watching us for a few moments with a friendly tolerance.

He had removed his cap and was giving his closely cropped black head an airing. His face was daubed with sweat. After a while, still carrying his cap in his hand and his rifle slung over his shoulder, he sauntered off towards the village.

The pathway leading up to the village forked before it reached the houses, one branch leading away into the hills that crowned the limestone cliff on the northern side of the clearing. Zamit and I turned away up this branch, intending to climb to the top of the cliff, where it would be cooler. The customs guard seemed to have vanished completely, so there appeared to be no reason why we should not wander about the countryside at will. The path we followed was no more than a goat track, faltering this way and that among the boulders and trees, till it came out at last upon the barren scree. As we trudged along, we could see it zigzagging away above us over the heather to the top of the cliff. Once we were clear of the trees, and out upon the open hill-side, there was a breath of air drifting in lazily from the north-westward against our faces. This air tasted fresher, and the perspiration soon dried upon us.

All at once a succession of familiar sounds, the hollow ring of wood upon wood that tells of a man dropping into a boat and getting out the oars and thole pins, made us pause and look down into the harbour below. The *caique's* dinghy was bearing off from alongside her. There were two figures in the boat; one pulling, and one sitting in the stern-sheets. The boat was coming inshore now; we could hear the steady thud as the looms of the oars brought up against the pins at each stroke, like the beat of a distant tom-tom echoing across the harbour and re-echoing among the crags above us. Soon we could also hear the swishing of a bow wave, then the harsh grating of the boat's keel on the pebbles of the beach. Both figures leapt out, and together they hauled the boat high and dry on to the shingle. From where we stood, five hundred feet directly above them, at the edge of the cliff face, we could recognise one of them as the man who had been standing on the *caique's* deck when *Olinda* had arrived in the bay; the other looked like a young boy—doubtless the one who had peered at us out of the *caique's* cuddy half an hour before. They left their boat and set off along the path towards the village, disappearing at once beneath the forest trees below us.

Zamit and I turned and clambered on up the slope. Ten minutes later we reached the top of the cliff and sat down beside a large boulder, which hid us from the village and also gave us a little shade. For some time neither of us spoke; it was pleasant just to sit and look out across the mountains to the open sea. Rhodes was hidden from us by the hills, but we could just glimpse a narrow strip of the Gulf of Symi and all the water to the north of the island—between Nimos Island and the Dorian Isthmus.

A shrill whistle rang out from high above us, near the top of the mountain behind the cliff; then there was a clatter of stones upon rocks; then the musical clang of a goat bell. We looked up, searching the peaks above us until a sudden move-ment against the heather showed a flock of goats feeding indolently across the higher slopes. Their patchy browns and yellows and blacks toned in with the boulders, making the animals almost impossible to see. But now the small boy minding them, perched upon a rock above them, was hurling stones down into the flock which began to move on in short, skittering rushes and swirls, like a cluster of autumn leaves disturbed by quick eddies of wind. We were still lying upon our sides, staring up the slope, watching the goats, when a young voice close beside us said . . . "What a terrible long way you've come to find somewhere to sleep." And there stood Nadia with X . . . . beside her.

Nadia was gazing down at me in that serious way she had, with just the hint of a smile around her eyes. She wore her beret at an angle upon her head; but her hair was short, like a boy's, and she was dressed in blue dungaree trousers rolled up at the bottom, also a red high-necked sweater and a ragged old jacket of some dark material whose sleeves, being far too long, were turned back at the cuffs. The jacket hung loosely from her shoulders, hiding her breasts; the skirt of it fell down low upon her thighs, so that she looked the picture of a *caiqui* "boy" of fifteen or so, forced to make do with the men's dis-carded clothing.

She flopped down, her feet tucked up beside her, her hands clasped together in her lap. For a moment no one spoke;

I myself was too startled by her sudden appearance and all that it implied; I was trying to work out at lightning speed just what it did imply. Zamit was completely at a loss: to him Nadia was just a girl, and rather a pretty one at that, but otherwise she was nothing; he could not possibly have connected her with *Olinda* or the voyage. X . . . . leaned his back against the nearest boulder and, folding his arms, stared down over the harbour in silence, waiting for me to say something—to make the next move.

"It goes without saying that Nadia is the 'agent' who is to be removed from Turkey?" I ventured at last. But X . . . . continued to stare moodily down over the harbour without saying a word.

"You realise, of course, that one of the strictest rules in the Navy is that no women are on any account to be taken to sea without Admiralty approval?" But my tone was now half-hearted, because I knew what X . . . . would say.

He said it at once. "*Olinda* is not a naval vessel."

"Well, anyway," I burst out, in desperation, "who *is* Nadia? And why couldn't you apply for her evacuation through the usual channels at Ankara?"

"Nadia is an Allied agent," replied X . . . . , without turning his head. He paused for a moment, then turned to stare at me almost truculently, as though defying me to question his statement. He heaved himself away from the boulder against which he had been leaning, and slumped down beside us on the turf. He looked straight at me, but his eyes were more friendly as he went on talking. "You must, I'm sure, be well aware," he went on, "that the fact that Nadia is the agent of another Power, even though that Power happens to be one of our most gallant allies, makes a great deal of difference to our people at Ankara. Although we and Nadia's people are fighting on the same side in this war, that does not mean that either we or they are prepared to pool our Intelligence Services."

I nodded, but not very encouragingly.

"You can easily imagine," X . . . . continued, "the difficulties that would be encountered in trying to establish Nadia's *bona fides* with the regular British Naval authorities in Ankara, or in persuading them to risk putting the Turks' noses out of joint

by smuggling a non-Britisher out of the country illegally—
especially one who is *wanted by the Turkish police.*"

"Well, if that is the case, how on earth do you expect a com-
paratively junior and totally uninformed naval officer to take
a responsibility that even his staff would jib at?"

X . . . . came back at me at once: "And on whose authority
or instructions then," he wanted to know, "did you employ a
young cabaret artiste, whom you had frequently been warned
to avoid"—(I wondered how much of our background X . . . .
knew; most of it, I decided gloomily)—"to assist you in ad-
ministering drugs to a German national in Ayvalik? And whose
fault is it that Nadia is being hunted by the Turkish Police for
complicity in a flagrant violation of Turkish neutrality? Can
you tell me that?"

X . . . . glared at me angrily for a moment. Then his face
cleared suddenly, and he gave a little chuckle of triumph as he
scrambled to his feet. He said something in Turkish to Zamit,
who also got up; then he turned to me again.

"I am being rather unfair to you, my friend. Don't take it
too seriously. Situations like this are always cropping up in our
game, and when they do, one just has to make one's own
decisions; and to hell with precedent."

X . . . . continued to look at me for a few seconds longer; then
he transferred his gaze to the hill-side above us. . . . "It must
be nearly noon," he remarked, in a more matter-of-fact tone.
"This chap and I"—(indicating Zamit) "will go on down into
the village and see if we can find a meal for all of us. You simply
can't leave Kiervasili without tasting the honey; it's been
famous throughout the Eastern Mediterranean for over a
thousand years. Nadia had better stay and tell you about all
that's happened to her since you left her in Ayvalik a fortnight
ago. Then you can follow us. Nadia knows the house where
we usually eat . . ." and, motioning to Zamit to follow him,
he set off back down the hill-side towards the trees.

After X . . . . had left us, Nadia and I sat in silence for
several minutes; I gazing moodily down at *Olinda* and the
caique where they swung quietly at their anchors upon the flat
sheet of the harbour, dark green and brown, with tree shadows;
Nadia sitting beside me, plucking at the little tufts of spring

grass and pale blue scillas that grew near her, and glancing
up at me occasionally as though waiting for me to speak.
The wind had freshened from the north, ruffling the heather
and stirring the dust on the pathway. "It's getting cold
here," I said at last. We got up and strolled away down
the path, round on to the southern slopes of the mountain,
overlooking the village and the trees. Here we were sheltered
from the wind and, when we came once more to a small patch
of grass beside an outcrop of rock, Nadia threw herself down
upon it and looked up at me smiling.

"Don't you want to hear the thrilling story of my life?" she
asked, mocking me and my surly looks. I sat down beside her,
clasping my hands round my knees.

"I don't awfully want to be *convinced* about you," I admitted,
smiling back at her faintly.

"I know you don't," she said. "You're afraid of having to
make a decision about me."

"Yes, I suppose I am."

But this was not all. I was also ashamed of myself. I knew
that I had been responsible for getting Nadia into trouble (with
her own people as well as with the Turks), and I also felt
instinctively that Nadia did not particularly resent it; she just
thought me rather a fool, which was worse.

"Tell me," I said. "Is it really the Turks who are after you
or your own people? Or are you in disgrace with your folk
because you've got yourself into trouble with the Turks; or . . .?"

"Never mind about that," she interrupted, but I sensed none
the less that Nadia's plight was a good deal more serious than
it appeared at first sight.

"Anyway," she went on, with a trace of irritation in her voice,
"I don't know exactly what you mean by talking about *me*
getting *myself* into trouble with the Turks. I can understand
that an ingenuous, clean-living, open-air young British officer
(bless him) would not realise or even believe that I was an
Allied agent, ordered by my headquarters to keep an eye on
all of you and to see that you didn't get too friendly with agents
from the other side who would have had all the facts about your
activities out of you in five minutes without asking you a single
question. . . ." She paused for breath and looked at me very
gravely, so that I felt uncomfortable beside this intensely

self-possessed young woman, with the face and appearance of a schoolboy. "I can even forgive you," she went on, more bitterly, "for not appreciating that it was not very thrilling to spend night after night playing up to that conceited, half-baked young imitation Casanova, Jesse Matheson, only because he was the most likely one of you to get caught by someone else, and having to keep him interested, and having to spend all my evenings capering round the night-clubs, and getting all my stockings torn to bits, and then, at the end of it all, getting into a disgusting public brawl, which made all the other girls giggle behind my back for days. . . ."

Nadia paused again for breath, her eyes flashing dangerously; looking adorable as she always did when she was angry. It occurred to me, none the less, that she had more to say about Jesse than was entirely relevant. I began to smile, glancing away hurriedly to hide my amusement as she went on talking. "I can forgive you for all that," she said, "and I can understand it, but what I could not have anticipated—and will never understand—was that this fine, straightforward, upright, down-right and totally idiotic Englishman should suddenly walk into a restaurant with a pocket full of dangerous drugs and start handing them round, about as obviously and indiscriminately as a missionary handing round tracts in a public-house," and as an afterthought: ". . . didn't you even notice that there was a mirror on the wall opposite to the bar?"

Getting this tirade off her chest seemed to have done Nadia good. She was smiling again when I looked round at her.

"What, in the name of goodness, made you do it?" she asked. "And since when have they begun to include doping in the British school curriculum?"

I said nothing but waited for her to go on.

"You English are the most unpredictable people." There was a note almost of admiration in her voice. "No wonder nobody can understand you and most people distrust you."

"I had to do something, didn't I?"

"Why? I would have looked after Fritz all right."

"Don't be silly, Nadia." It was my turn to be impatient. "You've just said yourself that I couldn't possibly know you were on our side . . . anyway X . . . . gave me the dope."

"Peter should have stopped you," she asserted, rather

unreasonably. "Anyway I'm not on *your* side; my people are the . . ." Nadia checked herself before saying the name.

"Who *are* they? And anyway, why don't you go to them for protection?"

"Oh! you won't understand. . . ." Nadia's voice was scornful, but I could see that she was worried all the same. "Besides that's nothing to do with it. What *is* important is that I'm in a jam, and you got me into the jam, and you happen to be the only one, at this moment, who can get me out of it."

I hedged. "You were smart enough in preventing yourself from getting doped. Why on earth couldn't you stop Fritz from drinking his *vodka* too?"

"Oh, Fritz!" and she made a contemptuous little gesture. "That good-natured old half-wit wouldn't have cared if he'd known his drink *was* doped. All the poor boy wanted to do was to get his job over and go back to Istanbul . . . just then he wanted more than anything else to be friends with everyone and to get drunk as quickly as possible. He had most of that *vodka* inside him before I could even turn round."

"Isn't he a Hun secret agent then?"

Nadia snorted impatiently. "Of course he isn't. He's a fat nincompoop with a much too wealthy father, who has interests and relatives in Germany. The German Intelligence use him occasionally for a few small jobs; he does as he's told." Her expression softened a little, became almost wistful. "He'll be doing what he's told now all right. They got him over the border into Bulgaria last Thursday. . . . Poor Fritz."

I did not ask Nadia how she knew just when Fritz had been smuggled out of the country. I had come to the conclusion that all these people knew more about other folks' affairs than I could ever know, or wanted to know for that matter. Instead I asked her how she herself had managed to get away.

"Peter bundled me out of the restaurant and into his car just as the police came up . . . two of those Turks standing by the bar were secret police, you know; they'd been watching us all along . . . then we drove straight down to Manjik, where X . . . . keeps this *caique*."

"Couldn't the *caique* take you down to Cyprus?"

"Don't be silly, darling, it would take her a month or more to get there and back. . . . And she'd probably be arrested by some idiot of a Port Security officer when she got there; it would take us another month to get her free again. Anyway she's needed for more important work here."

"What about you, when you get to Syria?"

"Oh, I shall be interned," she announced calmly, even gaily.

I looked away over the sun-struck valley, with its acres of olive groves and fruit trees in blossom. The air around us was baking hot and dry, full of the scent of heather and the incessant whisper of cicadas, like the clashing of a million cymbals in a fairy symphony, based upon the low, lilting music of the bees. High above, round the tops of the mountains, a steady north wind had fashioned a turban of cloud, white and woolly and motionless round every peak, for ever piling up upon the northern side and tearing off to leeward in soft streamers that melted and vanished again in the hot air rising out of the valley to meet them.

"You *will* take me, won't you?" The note of timid appeal in Nadia's voice made me turn quickly to look at her. All her self-assurance of a moment before, all her impatience at my bungling ignorance had vanished. She looked exceedingly young again and her eyes, serious and childlike as always, were frightened now.

I felt myself wavering, and it made me angry at first, made me resent the womanly appeal in her voice, in her eyes, in every-thing that went to make up Nadia. The world these days was full of people who were frightened, and with far better cause; thousands of women and children were being butchered daily. Why should Nadia claim special privileges? If she was indeed such a competent agent as she made out; so cynically unmoved, for instance, by the courtship of chaps like Jesse, could she not extricate herself with ease from her present position . . . without complicating a naval operation that I had already found quite complicated enough? Women in ships! There was always trouble with them.

And then I knew that I was wrong; that Nadia had been far from unmoved by Jesse; that she would never have got into trouble at Ayvalik if it had not been for a sudden genuine impulse to be with us there for a day or two, to have fun and to be made much of. I thought also of what her present position really was. . . . Sooner or later, if she did not leave the country, the Turks would catch up with her. X . . . . was only able to help her temporarily. If the Turks found her (and their secret police were among the best in the world) he would be forced to give her up; his organisation would never agree to flout the Turks for the sake of a foreign agent, discredited, even with her own side. That would mean prison for Nadia— prison with bugs and lice and filth for several years.

Of maybe she would be handed back to her own people; there was no telling these days. And to be handed back to them would mean . . . I didn't really know, but one had heard terrible tales, and once I had seen a man sitting in an office at Istanbul, palsied with fright, pleading, almost on his knees, for protection; merely because he had received some message which ran ". . . you have made an error in judgment over the interpretation of our wishes. You have been very foolish. Return to P—— before June 6th and report to your head-quarters. . . ."

But still I hesitated. "You don't realise how difficult it is for me. I'm not just hiding behind the regulations. It's really that *Olinda* is by no means out of the wood yet. By noon to-morrow, at latest, the Huns will know that she has excaped from Izmir, and the following morning they'll be on the look-out for her. Whatever happens she *must* be past Castelorizzo by then. I've enough 'problems' among the crew as it is— especially if we run into any trouble—without adding a woman to them."

"Even in these?" said Nadia ruefully, flapping the great tails of her ragged old coat round her, and lifting one leg off the ground to display the horrors of her ill-fitting trousers.

I couldn't help smiling at the gesture. "If anything, my dear, they add, by suggestion, to the intoxicating delights which they obviously conceal."

"Do they really?" said Nadia, brightening visibly in a womanly way and forgetting everything, for the moment, in her pleasure at knowing that her frightful rags did not entirely hide her charm.

It was this remark, and the way in which she made it, that decided me. It made her suddenly seem very human and brave, with that inner bravery that only women seem able to retain in the face of utter adversity and hardship.

"I suppose I am most of all to blame for getting you into this mess," I said doubtfully.

"Then you *will* take me?" Nadia took me up eagerly and a little breathlessly. I nodded, and she scrambled into a sitting position, catching hold of my hand and squeezing it in an unaffected passion of relief and gratitude.

The afternoon wore on, breathless and drowsy with the noise of insects and the heavy smell of spring flowing up warm out of the valley. The breeze died away at last, and the rocky mountain peaks stood out brazen and hard-edged against a brassy sky. The hill-sides over against us caught the afternoon light; the green and grey of them was washed with orange, and stood out towards us, near and clear and stereoscopic with the promise of rain to come. Over in the south-west, beyond the ragged outline of Symi, a grey bank of cloud was already lifting above the edge of the distant skyline. High on the mountain-side a goat bell clanged twice, very clear, then fell silent.

All at once we both felt hungry; scrambling to our feet, we set off again, down the pathway, to the valley.

35

IT was dark in the anchorage. A solid, leaden sheet of cloud obscured the stars. The mountains, in their inky coats of forest, stood up all round us, shutting off the last glimpse of light that might have filtered into the bay to help us. As the Master manœuvred his ship gingerly to turn her short round and head her out of the fjord, it was impossible to tell, except from the compass, which way she was moving and how fast she was turning. "Slow ahead port . . . slow astern starboard," he sung out now, then settled himself behind the standard compass to watch the "lubber line" as it began to creep slowly round the card.

Not a breath of wind had yet found its way down into the fjord; but the barometer had begun to fall, and the sky above us was already spitting with rain; so we knew that, by the time we reached open water, the wind would be rising from south-west and that conditions would be ideal for slipping down the Gulf of Symi, round on to the open south coast and away to the eastward.

It was now about 8 p.m. Soon after dark X . . . . had pulled us quietly off to *Olinda* in his boat, and Nadia had gone straight to the spare cabin, previously occupied by myself, where she had promised to remain till we anchored next morning in the Gulf of Fethieh. The only other memento which I had brought away with me from our "run ashore" in Kiervasili was three combs of magnificent dark-brown wild honey, crammed into an old biscuit tin, which in turn was wrapped in a scarlet cloth. There was about ten pounds of it in all, tasting of heather and the scent of orange blossom. It came from a peasant's hut in which we had all eaten numberless eggs and cheese and black bread and bowls of soup, with several eggs floating in each, and

also as much of this same honey as we could cram into our mouths.

X . . . . had many and mysterious friends along the coast. This peasant had been one of them—an aged woodsman, by the look of him, who lived in a tiny and very broken-down old shack among the trees a little way from the village. Here he dwelt pleasantly and peacefully, surrounded by his goats and chickens, a plump little dormouse of a wife and innumerable children of various ages, all incredibly ragged, cheerful, impulsive and very healthy. We had spent an hour or more with these people, eating the food they gave us and basking in the sunshine of the small clearing in which their dwelling stood. I looked back now towards the valley, already lost in the surrounding darkness, and could not help reflecting upon the illogical idiocy of our daily life, compared with that of the old peasant or, in fact, with that of any of the villagers of

20

Kiervasili, whose only link with the outside world was the visit of an occasional *caique*, come to pick up a cargo of olives or oranges.

My meditations were cut short by a loud hail from the Mate forward, followed by a grinding, shuddering crash which made *Olinda* whip and shiver like a branch in an autumn gale. Then there was a muffled clatter of violently agitated dentures close beside me and, "Ah!" said the Master philosophically, "now we know where we are."

In fact, instead of swinging short round under the impulse of her two screws turning in opposite directions, *Olinda* had all the time been creeping very slowly ahead, without any such movement becoming visible in the darkness. She had butted her stem straight into the cliff on the western side. No real damage was done however (the stem had merely been crumpled back upon the plating for a few feet above the water-line) and, as the Master had pointed out, we were no longer in doubt as to our exact position in the bay! So, after allowing the ship to bounce back a few yards into clear water, the Master completed his turn and headed *Olinda* for the harbour entrance.

As we were passing the island in the middle of the anchorage, I suddenly noticed the dim outline of Nadia standing beside me in the gloom and looking ahead, as I was, towards the Gulf of Doris, opening out before us.

"You promised to stay in your cabin," I said, feeling rather cross.

"I thought we must have arrived somewhere," she answered sweetly, in a suspiciously naïve tone of voice, and then, "this is what you call pushing on through the narrows, isn't it?"

"Feodor Pavlovitch has been preaching to you, I suppose," I said accusingly.

"He did come in for a moment or two. I think he's a wonderful old man. He reminds me of an old goat I used to ride on when I was a little girl . . . that was on a farm in Hungary. We used to dress him up in a cap and an old blue shirt. He looked just like Feodor Pavlovitch, and he was just as patient.

"You'd better get back to your cabin and turn in."

Nadia turned her head quickly to look at me, and I felt sure that she was making a rude face. But next moment she had whisked round without a word and disappeared below.

By now, having reached the harbour entrance, we were turning west down the Gulf of Doris. It was time for me to take over again from the Master. The mountains fell away behind us, no longer casting their shadows upon the water, which began to gleam a dull grey in the darkness, returning the sky. *Olinda* plodded on past the mouth of Losta Bay, and in among the islands that line the southern side of the Gulf. The narrow gaps of sea and sky, between the islands and the shore, shone pale and definite, like bright chisels of steel plunging down from the clouds and slicing dark chunks out of the land. *Olinda* pointed her stem at each chisel blade in turn, till it broadened before her, and the sea about her turned black once more with the shadows of the island to starboard and the cliffs of the mainland to port; for a minute or two there was a swishing and a sighing of her bow wave as it curled upon the beaches on both sides of her together; then she was through the pass and turning slowly to stem the next.

Karamea, Kaloyeri, Mikale, Ikinji . . . one by one the islets went sweeping past, were done with and forgotten . . . Ikinji, Omeah; then the broad sweep of the open Aegean before us; and, as we swung round the headland of Cape Apostoli, the wind came whistling in our faces up the Gulf of Symi, clammy and cold and full of salt and the threat of heavier weather.

Olinda steered due south for Capes Volpe and Alupo. Soon she began to lift jerkily to the short seas hurrying against her. The Gulf of Symi was nearly four miles wide at its narrowest point, and there was no sign of any other craft upon its surface. It was with easy minds, therefore, that we plugged along from headland to headland and round the corner at Cape Alupo. More by force of habit than of necessity, we passed inside Ipsera and Elesa Islands; or it may have been in order that a long and gloomy night should be pleasantly punctuated with sudden, surging rushes of apparent speed as we swept through narrow places; or because we liked to listen to the sound of our engines echoing from the cliffs, unsynchronised and for ever catching each other up; then beating together once or twice, then separating again in a homely little competition to see which side of the ship should reach the harbour first.

Abreast of Cape Aspro-mitas we left the shadows of Turkey and stood due east across the bay. By now it had begun to rain steadily; the dim outline of Rhodes Island, nearly fifteen miles away to the south'ard, had disappeared. Soon a rising sea told us that the sheltering bulk of that island was already well astern. Then the wind died away, and at the same time the rain became a blinding downpour, teeming upon us out of the fat, dark belly of the night, obscuring the two red lights on Cape Marmarice, sweeping over us and rattling upon the surface of the sea in a wavering cadence of showers and lulls, like a succession of steam trains hissing and thundering past a wayside station.

Olinda chuffered stolidly eastwards through the deluge, a simple but stout-hearted little pilgrim. After a while the rain eased off, but overhead still the clouds, bulging and loath-some, like pregnant black spiders, hovered and crawled upon each other, moving in many different directions before uncertain slants of wind. The barometer was falling more rapidly than before; and long, ominous swells, running in from the south-west, told us that a heavy gale could not be far away.

At 5 a.m. on February 11th a wall of inky cloud was building rapidly in the west, and the first harsh puff of wind came moaning over us. Hastily we scuttled round the cliffs of Cape Suvela into the Gulf of Fethieh, and anchored, just before dawn, in the landlocked Bay of Skopea.

Skopea Bay, though a much larger sheet of water than Kiervasili, is also completely hemmed in by hills. But most of it is very deep, eighty fathoms or more; too deep for anchoring. *Olinda* found a berth at last in about twenty fathoms of water, in a small cove, in the crook of an arm of those mountains which shelter the bay from the south. Here she rode uneasily, though fairly securely, while we all went down to breakfast.

Nadia was already at table with Feodor Pavlovitch beside her. The Master took his place at the head, and I sat down opposite Nadia. A moment later the Mate shuffled in and sat down on the Master's right hand. Coffee was brought, and cakes; then Ah Fong set the bottle of *vodka* before the Master, who immediately passed it to Feodor Pavlovitch, who poured

some out for Nadia, and so on, until the bottle had come round
to each of us in turn, and so had reached the Master once again.
By now Ah Fong was busily piling plates of raw salt herring,
caviare, peeled hard-boiled eggs and anchovies upon the table.
The Master splashed a generous helping of *vodka* into his glass
and raised it before him.

"For Hell with National Socialism and all the other ''isms',"
he proclaimed; then drained his glass in one sonorous gulp.
Feodor and the Mate raised their glasses to drink sedately,
though more moderately, to the Master's toast. Nadia, who
had frequently declared herself to be an ardent Malinist,
glowered at the Master but said nothing, then glanced round
and caught me smiling to myself.

A strong gust came funnelling down between the shoulders
of the hills; we heard the rising whine of it approaching,
surrounding us and passing on. As *Olinda* began to swing in
the urgent embrace of the wind, we all paused in the business
of draining or refilling our glasses, preoccupied for a moment
with the familiar sequence of sounds and movements that
played the pantomime of a passing flaw. We felt *Olinda*
shudder as her cable came suddenly taut; heard the crumbling
grate of a rusty link, riding up restlessly upon the lip of her
hawse pipe. Then the air fell calm again and very quiet.
Olinda swung on round the compass slowly, aimlessly; the shaft
of weak sunshine, dropping through the skylight of the saloon,
swung round in the opposite direction, lighting Nadia's rather
petulant expression, then falling upon calm Feodor, then upon
the Master with the *vodka* bottle poised over his glass, then the
Mate, and finally settled in a corner of the saloon near the door.

"To Hell with the Germans," said Nadia pointedly.

"And the Grovoniks," retorted Feodor at once, making a
face at Nadia.

"Lord Byron," announced Ivan Oreshkin as he bustled in
at the door. "Roas' beef," I replied quickly, thankful for the
interruption. Ivan turned to the others with some jovial
obscenity, but checked it at the sight of Nadia; then completed
the phrase slowly and rather absentmindedly, gazing at Nadia
with a puzzled puckering of his forehead. Nadia looked back
at him calmly, but a tiny flash of sudden interest seemed to
pass uncertainly between them. Then Ivan shuffled his way

round the end of the table, and since Nadia was occupying his usual seat, he planked himself down in the one beside her.

"Nadia feels very strongly about politics," I observed to the table in general. "You'd better be careful what you say."

"And you too," retorted Nadia. At which we were all able to laugh, and I hoped that the conversation would take a lighter turn. But a few moments later Feodor made some remark in Russian which earned an immediate and rather heated response from Nadia; within a short while they were hard at it, worse than the Greeks, bandying Facists, Partisans, bandits and Communists, all of which words were easy to recognise in the language they spoke. Ivan Oreshkin egged Nadia on and grinned rather wickedly from the background. I finished my breakfast and rose from the table. It looked as though Nadia's femininity, well swaddled in the ragged garments in which she had joined the ship, would prove a less formidable catalyst for commotion than her violent taste in politics.

I left them to it, and went up on deck for a final look round before turning in. On my way up I glanced at the aneroid in the chart-room. It had fallen sharply since I had last looked at it an hour before. I gave it a tap; the needle trembled down another hundredth. Then I climbed to the monkey island and looked round.

The sky was completely overcast. To the westward, stretching from the tops of the hills half-way to the zenith, it was black as ink. As I watched, a hieroglyphic of lightning was scrawled abruptly, by an invisible stylograph, upon the stormy black tablet of cloud; then another, and every few seconds they were repeated, as though God were writing upon the wall a message of hasty warning. The silence continued menacing, but for the time being the storm approached no closer; it seemed to be passing north-westwards parallel with the shore.

I turned to look inland at the mountains south-east of us, standing on guard above the small town of Fethieh. These mountains were taller than any we had seen so far, they rose straight up from the harbour to five and six thousand feet, and their higher slopes were painted white with snow against a leaden sky. Even as I watched, the sky behind them darkened, and above the hard ridge of advancing cloud the first filmy

tentacles of storm wrack came writhing through the passes,
clutching the peaks and smothering them. A moment later
a posse of cold air, like a sudden sortie of tribesmen, tumbled
pell-mell over the nearer hills into the anchorage, and came
frisking and skirmishing across the bay towards us. *Olinda*,
like a rheumaticky old lady taking a nap, was caught broadside on to the hooligan assault of the wind, which buffeted her
and whisked her round with a creaking and groaning of cable.
It plucked at her clothes and hair; the jury mast shivered, and
the shrouds twanged humming taut; the skylight windows
rattled; the tarpaulin on her one remaining dummy hatch
lifted and slatted back convulsively. Then the wind swiped
up a plume of salt spray in *Olinda*'s face, and screamed and
whistled in aggressive derision as her anchor cable lifted out
of the sea bar taut, and the old lady began to shudder and
heave against it. Next there was a trembling "chunk" as the
anchor dragged once, then held again, then dragged, then held.

The Master poked his head out of the chart-room door; but at
the same moment the wind passed on, leaving *Olinda* to swing
indecisively, shaking her old head as she settled herself down
again to doze.

I did not in the least like the look of things, nor did the
Master. If it came on to blow, we agreed, *Olinda* would be
worse off here among the mountains than anywhere else.
Squalls would come whistling down the hill-sides without
warning, and from all sorts of directions; nor was there anywhere, except dangerously near the shore, where the water was
sufficiently shallow to offer good holding ground in a really
heavy blow.

"Why not move into Fethieh harbour?" suggested the Master;
but I had had enough, with Ayvalik and Port Saip, of regular
ports; it seemed futile to risk being arrested again or being
spied on by enemy agents. In the end, as the storm seemed to
be holding off for the time being, and might, we thought, even
be diverted entirely by the mountain range to the south of us,
we decided to wait and see.

A tremendous rumbling and jarring started me out of a deep
sleep as though a cannon had gone off in my ear. *Olinda* seemed
to be lying over with a heavy list to port; as I shot out of my

bunk and began to scramble into my clothes, I was sent staggering across the cabin, with one leg half into my trousers and the other one fumbling after it. I brought up heavily against the opposite bulkhead, with my face against a little colony of Nadia's "smalls," which hung incongruous and shameless, drying, upon a strand of hastily rigged sail twine. Subconsciously I registered the fact that women, however hard they try, are by nature unable to prevent their femininity from impinging, in a thousand little ways and at all sorts of odd times, upon the lives of men with whom they live or consort. Nadia had only spent a few hours of the night in this cabin, and would not return to it until *Olinda* was at sea again; but already it had ceased to be a cabin; it had taken on a new personality, the personality of Nadia; it had become a boudoir. There was even a trace of scent in the air and the inevitable sprinkle of powder at one corner of the table. These thoughts and others continued to saunter through the background of my consciousness as I struggled into oilskins and sea boots with desperate haste.

The racket outside increased, and into it merged the more persistent clatter of the windlass. I heard a shout or two; *Olinda* was clearly trying to get her anchor. The windlass paused and laboured, then hurried on again and, overlaying the sound of it now, came the deep tumult of wind rising around us. Then both main engines exploded into life, one after the other. The ship struggled slowly on to a more even keel; the windlass fell into a steadier beat as the engines, going "slow ahead," took a little weight off the cable.

When I reached the bridge I saw that a veritable tornado had come tearing down upon us out of the southern mountains, which were now obscured by a phalanx of rain or sleet. The sea was being lashed and tortured, white and seething, by the wind; a couple of small whirligigs of spray came dancing over the water. From the opposite direction another one was also advancing towards the centre of our cove. The first gust took us and bludgeoned us back; then the other swept in on our defenceless port quarter, clouting us unmercifully; poor old *Olinda* staggered and swung round again towards the land. Fortunately, by now, our single anchor was well clear of the bottom and the cable was coming in steadily over the windlass.

The Master shouted at the top of his voice to make an order heard above the din of the wind and the smashing of spray against the wheelhouse windows. I felt one engine stop and then go "full astern." *Olinda* recovered herself and began to struggle stern foremost into the wind, which was now dashing in upon us from the north.

I put my mouth close to the Master's ear and yelled, "It's hopeless to try and anchor anywhere in this bay. It's too deep except right inshore." He seemed to have heard enough of what I said to nod his head violently in agreement. Next moment the wind was ahead again (that is from the south) and with it, this time, came the hail and the sleet in such a raging fury, tearing and thrashing at us, that we were forced to cower down beside the sandbags for protection. It was the sort of hail that might have killed cattle, and for a moment we were fearful of being knocked out by it ourselves.

The worst of the hail passed quickly and turned to sleet, then rain, then the shower was over; but the wind remained, leaping out at us through each gap in the hills in turn; blasting the ship round and baffling every fresh attempt to manœuvre her clear of that lunatic vortex. The cliffs and crags formed the sides of a monstrous "puff ball" table, with *Olinda* as the luckless little ball of pith, caught in a pocket in its southern corner.

At last a chancy gust twirled us round, so that *Olinda*'s head was pointing nearly north—towards clearer water and the entrance to Skopea Bay. With our hearts in our mouths we slammed both engines "full ahead." There came a quick lull in the wind, *Olinda* gathered way, began to answer her helm. Before the next gust struck her, she was sufficiently under control to hold fairly steady upon her course, gathering momentum as she went.

Twenty minutes later *Olinda* was heading south out of the Gulf of Fethieh. The nearest harbours which might offer adequate holding ground in this sort of weather (except for Fethieh harbour itself) were Marmarice or Karagatch. To reach these would involve retracing our steps to the westward, but I think we had all had enough of delays and doublings back upon our tracks. One tiny enemy fortress only, the island of Castelorizzo, remained between ourselves and freedom, so in a fit of weary impatience with both our enemies —the weather and the Axis—we determined, on the spot, to barge our way at all costs past Castelorizzo, nor anchor again until we had cleared it.

We expected to meet steadier winds as soon as we reached the open water—a gale, no doubt, and mountainous seas, but conditions, none the less, which a well-found ship can be expected to survive fairly comfortably—provided her engines keep turning.

There was no air base on Castelorizzo, and Rhodes Island was already forty miles to the westward of us (seventy miles west of Castelorizzo), besides which we felt that this violent wind, with incessant rain squalls, would keep aircraft grounded at least for to-day. It was therefore almost with a sense of relief that we altered course to round the rocky point of Cape Angistro. The time was about 3 p.m., and the visibility, in between the frequent rain squalls, was fairly good; so we continued to hug the Turkish shore as far as the Seven Capes.

It looked as though the true wind must be from the south-eastward for, although a few stinging gusts fell upon us from the high mountains alongside, the sea remained fairly calm, and *Olinda* made her full eight knots down the coast.

Once, in between two squalls, the sun teetered uncertainly through a ragged gap in the clouds. I saw Nadia and Ivan Oreshkin come out on to the poop, still talking earnestly together—about politics I imagined. A little later the bosun joined them. After a while Nadia fell out of the conversation and wandered over to the ship's side to gaze at the mountainous coastline. She snatched off her beret just in time to prevent it from being blown into the sea; next moment the wind had ripped open her ragged old coat and set it flapping wildly about her shoulders. She struggled with it for a moment and, once or twice, she glanced up at the monkey island with an expression of mocking despair upon her face; then she slipped into the lee of one of the boats to re-arrange herself.

Ten minutes later Nadia appeared on the monkey island itself bringing, as a passport or peace offering, a cup of tea each for the Master and myself. She remained for a few moments looking about her with interest. "How far is it," she asked, "to the place where John was attacked in *Kirilovka*?"

"About another thirty miles," I told her; "but it's too rough for E-boats to-day. Anyway, in this sort of weather, we ought to be able to get past Castelorizzo without being seen."

"How dull," she pronounced, then brightening: "but Feodor says we're bound to get into some sort of mess. He says you always have, every night so far."

This remark was presumably intended to provoke a discussion sufficiently acrimonious to keep Nadia on the bridge for some time; so I only smiled at her and, in the end, she wandered off in search of a more sensitive antagonist.

By 5 p.m. we were approaching the first of the Seven Capes; it was here that a decision had to be made: whether (a) to continue to hug the coast and try to sneak through between Castelorizzo and the Turkish shore, or (b) to stand well out to the southward of the island throughout the night, and endeavour to return to the Turkish cost *beyond* Castelorizzo before the following dawn.

In favour of hugging the coast was:

1. The fact that a current of 1 to 1½ knots was known to set westwards (against us) past Castelorizzo; it would be likely to affect us more if we were offshore than if we were close in to the coast.
2. That on the inshore route we would be able to keep an exact check upon our progress throughout the night.
3. That close to the land we might continue to receive some shelter from the wind and sea.

Against it was:

1. The fact that we had no proper chart of the channel inside Castelorizzo island.
2. That if the wind came southerly, we would be on a dead lee shore, without a decent offing from an ironbound coast in case of engine failure.

As we approached the Seven Capes, we could see a heavy sea rushing past the end of the first one, carrying a great white streak of broken water well out to sea. It was clear from this that the wind was coming in from well south of east and that no further shelter could be expected along that coast. One of the main conditions in favour of keeping close to the shore had in fact been removed so, without further deliberation, it was decided that *Olinda* should take her chance that night in the open sea.

We rounded the first cape, and immediately a powerful blast of wind came howling at us along the cliffs. At the same time the sea, piling up against the land into miniature Alps and glaciers, came thudding and smashing upon *Olinda*'s port bow. In the first few minutes after passing the cape, our remaining dummy hatch (which we had ultimately decided to retain in case we were still forced to make some part of the voyage in daylight) evaporated into the air like a waking dream. The jury mast, being a more logically designed structure, still held; and both the false derricks remained like a couple of disconsolate mantises, praying and nodding shamefacedly to each other across the naked tank-tops.

Half a mile clear of the coast, the seas fell into a longer, steadier stride, and the wind settled down strong and even from the south-east. Seeking southward, away from the land, *Olinda* blundered doggedly into the eye of a making gale. The scud ran low above her, and the squalls gave place to a continuous drizzle, which soon joined forces with approaching night.

36

IT was a night of turmoil and doubt and sudden hope, then gnawing doubt again. The wind increased steadily until nearly midnight, and the sea with it. *Olinda*'s speed fell off from eight knots to six and then down to five knots or lower. Soon it was no longer possible to tell her actual speed of advance because, in such a sea, no faith could be placed in the ordinary taffrail log, streaming out astern of her. But, hour after hour, we forced her into the weather with all the horse-power she could stand. She slogged and butted and wallowed. The steering became wilder than ever before. Green water swept the foredeck at every plunge and burrow of her bluff old bows into the rollers.

After a while it began to feel as though she were becoming unusually sluggish in lifting to the seas; she seemed tired, almost dazed, and we began to suspect that she must be making water forward. The bosun and I watched our chance for a dash across the tank-tops and succeeded, after two abortive attempts, in reaching the forecastle—half-drowned when a big sea caught us and rolled us in the scuppers, but with our limbs providentially intact. As we lifted the hatch leading to the forepeak an ominous hissing and gurgling greeted us. We lowered ourselves into the darkness below, then shone a torch upon the stem. As we had feared, *Olinda was* making water. Where her stem had been buckled against the cliff in Kiervasili, a thin crack about eight inches long had appeared near the butt of one of the plates. It was well above the water-line; but at every plunge of the ship's bows into the head sea, a silvery fan of water came spurting through. Gallon by gallon the forepeak was flooding. It was not a serious matter—a wisp of oakum, a batten and a shore of stout timber reduced the leak to a harmless trickle—but it worried us none the less, and made us ease down a little on the engine speed, for fear of driving the ship too hard and thereby placing an unfair strain on her weakened stem.

At midnight the wind suddenly died away, leaving an oily, black swell running sleepily by. It was an uneasy lull, for the glass was still falling, while the sky was as lowering as before. Then the rain stopped. All at once the mastheads and the funnel-top and odd pieces of *Olinda*'s rigging glowed out green and ghostly with St. Elmo's fire. Looking round, I noticed that even the peak of the Master's cap shone faintly green in the darkness. For a few moments the glimmer grew and spread about the ship, until one imagined that anyone seeing her must take her for a phantom, stealing across the sea to some long-forgotten doom. Then, softly, the green light faded as it had come, till only the mastheads, green-tipped, like spears with emerald points, lunged and feinted at the clouds. A moment more and these also had vanished. Now there was no light anywhere except the orange loom above the compass bowl, like a brazier upon an altar set in a high place, or as though the good *Olinda* were bearing the fires of Marathon, through storm and tempest, to a new Olympiad.

By 1 a.m. the swell was moderating; but it seemed, from the uneven motion of the ship, as though another line of swell from the south-west were slowly overlaying it. Judging that

Olinda was already well south of the latitude of Castelorizzo Island, we altered course to the eastward; the new swell, thereafter, was running in upon the starboard quarter and *Olinda*, though still steering somewhat wildly, went plunging along again at her full eight knots. Allowing for 1½ knots of current against us, we hoped to pass six miles south of the island at about 4 a.m. on February 12th. Then we would turn north-east to regain the Turkish coast a short distance west of the black headland of Phineka promontory. This bold cliff, with the mountain of Beimelik Dag climbing to 4,700 feet above it, would provide us with an unmistakable landfall. Meanwhile there was nothing for us to do but to stand on into the darkness and wait. The Master went down to take the wheel; the Mate relieved him on the monkey island. I clambered down the ladder and went below to look for cigarettes and maybe a cup of cocoa.

I knocked on the door of the spare cabin; then heaved my way in against the roll of the ship. As the door began to open, the ship rolled back, making me lurch and stagger in the square of the door. My oilskins and seaboots were awkward and none too clean. Water ran from them on to the deck of the cabin.

Nadia was sitting up in the bunk, with a pillow and an old coat behind her back. She was still fully clothed, except for her beret, and she held a book of some sort before her. The main light in the cabin was turned off. She was reading by a small oil bracket lamp, which was loosely secured to the bulkhead above her; it moved and its glass chimney rattled with every roll of the ship. For a moment I stood in the doorway, recovering my balance and getting accustomed also to the light. "I came for some cigarettes," I excused myself, sounding rather gruff in my effort to appear casual. Nadia put down her book and looked at me. "It's very rough to-night, isn't it?" she asked. She seemed anxious to make conversation; to keep me there if possible. I realised that she was afraid, and also rather lonely.

The wind by now had died, and the sea had abated somewhat but there was still the continuous clanging slap of the wave-tops against *Olinda*'s hull, the violence of her rolling and the tearing hiss of white water turned back from her bows as she went. Nadia knew that we were well out in the midst of enemy-controlled water. I felt a certain admiration and gratitude for the self-control which had kept her to her cabin.

"It's not rough any more," I reassured her, "and when it does come on to blow again, it will probably be from astern of of us, so we shan't feel it so much."

"Where are we?" Nadia then asked.

"About twenty miles south-west of Castelorizzo, I hope. But there's no way of telling how strong the current is here. We may be farther west."

"When will you be able to find out?"

"When we reach the coast again at dawn," I told her cheerfully; and she smiled at me and looked more cheerful herself on account of my obvious optimism. This optimism was quite genuine. After all these weeks of cowering and calculating and contriving, it was fine to be out at sea again and going somewhere; it was exhilarating; one felt almost like laughing at everything that had gone before. *Olinda* was striding along again at eight good sea miles per hour over clear, black water. Already she had nearly reached the outer fringes of the islands, the last tenuous barrier between herself and freedom.

I collected my cigarettes and wandered along to the saloon. As I passed the galley I saw Ah Fong lounging against the bench, blandly contemplating a kettle upon the stove. Zamit came out of his storeroom to see who it was; then went back again. In the saloon the bosun stood talking quietly to Feodor. Everyone, on various pretexts, seemed to be about; there was an atmosphere of studied calm throughout the ship; but no one had thought of turning in. While I stood talking to Feodor and the bosun, we heard and felt the wind come back to us. It swooped suddenly upon *Olinda* from the south-west; we felt her lean to it for a moment, then surge ahead before the swell. And the rain came also, driving in flat sheets over her.

Up on the monkey island conditions were a good deal easier, with the wind upon our starboard quarter instead of in our faces, battering us. At 4.15 a.m. *Olinda* altered course to north-east. Now, with the wind and sea dead astern of her, she became more difficult to steer, while the exhaust gases from the funnel, driving over the monkey island, made us blink our eyes and cough. The fumes piled away ahead in a filmy, brown cloud that grew denser with distance, till it looked like an island upon the horizon. Huge rollers came galloping after the ship, lifting her up, as though with giant hands, out of the sea; then letting her fall, to lie for a moment wallowing, as they hurried on past her and away towards distant Turkey.

Soon after 5 a.m. the darkness assumed that powdery texture which tells of approaching day. The rain had stopped, but the sky was still heavily clouded. As it grew slowly lighter, we began to imagine the dark shadow of the Turkish hills spreading east and west upon the northern horizon. A few moments later we could see them, no more than five miles distant and extending unbroken except where the blurr of *Olinda*'s own dim smoke lay ahead of her upon the water. Very dark, opaque smoke it seemed, when looked at from end on, down the whole length of it. Very low it lay upon the sea, as though weighed down by the heavy damp air—very low and squat and thick and . . . *it was an island.*

It was the island of Castelorizzo itself! Not away in the western gloom astern of us, as we had hoped; but right in our path, no more than three miles ahead—and daylight was growing fast across the sea.

"Steer east." *Olinda* swung off a point or two, bringing the island upon her bow. It stood out plainly now, dark and rugged, with a tiny white chapel or look-out post at its highest point. It was a sickening sight; but there was little use in crying now over the luck that seemed to have destroyed, in a moment, the value of all our previous efforts at concealment, all our tricky ruses and subterfuges. The fact remained that the current and the weather had been too much for us during the dark hours of the night before; *Olinda*, instead of having at last escaped from the Aegean net and being safely upon her way across the relatively neutral waters between there and Cyprus, had, at the very last moment, blundered straight into one of the outer meshes.

We stood on eastwards; but with a dull foreboding as we gazed in despair at that infuriating little block of land, imagining its inhabitants glaring back at us and chuckling to themselves triumphantly. The weather, of course, was impossible for E-boats; but, unless the rain closed in again, there was every chance of aircraft from Rhodes. Castelorizzo would report our passing by W/T at once; after that it would merely be a question of time.

Then something occurred which changed the whole situation in a matter of moments. A fresh squall of rain blew up, sandwiched between water and dull sky, and in a short while the land had disappeared again from view. With the squall came more wind and a sea that grew quickly precipitous. Soon we had nearly forgotten all other worries in our efforts to keep poor old *Olinda* away before the weather. She was still heavy forward and this, coupled with her high superstructure aft, caused her to struggle again and again towards the wind. If she once flew round, it would be difficult—might even be impossible—to get her back upon her course. In our minds was the embarrassing picture of a defenceless lump of a tanker, driven round into the wind, out of control and pinned down upon a westerly course . . . unable to do otherwise than to waddle, very laboriously, stern first, past the enemy base or, alternatively, *to steam westwards straight into Rhodes harbour.* Very tricky indeed it would appear to the puzzled Spaghetti boys, watching us from the top of Castelorizzo island; excessively ingenious—"Ah, magnifico," we could hear them exclaim. "But what cunning, what craftiness, what deep hypocrisy; ze English son-of-a-beach."

Meanwhile, however, behind a blanket of cloud and rain, Castelorizzo was invisible to us, and we to it. This squall might last for an hour; but we must hurry on at all costs, and endeavour to be out of sight of the island before the rain had passed. The wind increased in violence till it had become a whole gale. *Olinda* fled and squattered before it like a terrified duck with a broken wing, and every bit as ungainly. By what seemed, at times, a miracle of helmsmanship, the bosun managed to keep the old ship away before the wind. One by one, the men off watch began to drift towards the bridge and boat-deck, as though unwilling to remain below in case one of those huge cliffs of sea should suddenly smash aboard, and the ship founder miserably, without warning. Nadia and Feodor were in the port wing of the bridge, gazing calmly enough towards the north, where the land lay behind the rain; but I noticed that

Feodor had fitted a cork life-jacket over the girl's chest. She looked up and smiled at him occasionally; otherwise they made no movement. Ivan Oreshkin and Chinese Mickey were still below at their posts in the engine-room, and I thanked God for their courage as one always thanks God, in times of stress, for the cold courage of stokers and engineers.

At 8 a.m. the wind flew round to the north-west and the sea went down. I slipped below to the chart-room to look at the glass; *it had already risen five hundredths since dawn.* Ten minutes later the clouds lifted and, at last, we could see the round, black lump of Phineka promontory, lying broad on *Olinda*'s port bow. Then the sky cleared, and the sun shone out brightly. Looking astern, we discovered that we were now well hidden from the enemy—a long and mountainous head-land had interposed itself neatly between ourselves and Castelorizzo Island. In the wave of optimism which this realisation and the sudden return of the sunlight brought bursting over us, we began to feel that we had probably never even been sighted from Castelorizzo.

"Italians!" we scoffed, "a lazy, sloppy bunch. They'd never keep a proper look-out anyway." After all, we had only been in sight of the island for about ten minutes, and just before dawn at that—with the light growing upon us from the opposite direction, not silhouetting us. One could not imagine an Italian look-out being particularly bright at 5.45 a.m.— more likely to be asleep, or making coffee, or love to one of the local Greek girls. We realised, however, that it was now nearly twenty-four hours since the enemy reconnais-sance aircraft over Gulbache Bay would have noticed that *Olinda* was gone. We wondered whether they would start looking for us; but decided, in our new spirit of optimism, that they would hardly know where to begin; they might even have finally given us up as a dead loss.

At noon that day, February 12th, we passed between the Khelidoniah Islands and the Cape of the same name. The crew of the lighthouse came out on to the mountain-side and waved to us cheerily; Malu barked energetically in reply. The wind was still from the north-west; so, in a fit of high-spirited temerity, we gave the lighthouse people a jaunty salute on *Olinda*'s syren—a hail to Khelidoniah and a farewell, at last, to the Aegean disappearing astern of us. Then we whipped round the corner into the sudden calm and sun-baked shelter of the mountains marching northwards into the Bay of Adalia.

All day the barometer rose, and joyously we trundled upon our way; following closely the configuration of every bay and headland; gazing with something near to rapture at rivers coming down to the sea, dressed in expensive gowns of birch forest and native oak; at regiments of pines upon the higher bluffs; at a very occasional hamlet or a woodsman's hovel, nestling in some cleft of the rocks, a hundred miles from nowhere, across trackless mountains; at the ruins of ancient cities, far more numerous than the modern villages. These ruins were in every cove and at the mouth of every small river; their names were still the names of the Acts—Myra, Patara, Olbia, Attalia and Side. As we passed them, the walls and colonnades and even a Roman theatre or two stood out white and magnificent against the darker forests. It was almost as though these cities still lived, and were watching us pass as they had watched the triremes of old . . . before malaria brought silence to the whole of this coast and an end to its civilisation.

We became so absorbed in the passing scene and in its ancient enchantment, that we hardly noticed the hours as they flew by. Above us stood the snow-capped giants—Mount Taktalu, 7,800 feet high, and Mount Climax; and, behind these, the first of the Lysian and the Pamphylian Taurus, striding round the horizon like an army of benevolent Titans, guarding us and going with us into Cilicia.

THE END OF THE STORY . . .

IT was on a wintry afternoon, just one year after *Olinda* had escaped from the Aegean, that I came again to the village of Erekli, on the northern shores of the Sea of Marmara. My business was not the same, and the craft in which I had made the voyage from Mersin was minute . . . a tiny coastal *caique*, no more.

I had had my corvette for a while—on the Western Desert run; and now the Eighth Army, starting from Alamein, had passed Benghazi, and was well on the way to Mareth; and my corvette—she was at the bottom of the sea, poor thing; somewhere between Tobruk and Derna. So I was back on the Turkish coast; back at Erekli.

There seemed to have been heavy snow in Thrace during the past twenty-four hours, and the cold, leaden appearance of the sky spoke of more snow to come; but my instructions had been to reach Istanbul as quickly as possible—doubtless for some conference or to receive special orders. As usual, my arrival must, if possible, be unnoticed by the enemy; but I had no idea how to set about achieving this, since landing was prohibited in Thrace and I had noted, on our approach to the port, the familiar little group of Turkish cavalry rattling down the hillside to congregate upon the beach ready to enforce the law. I called to Zamit.

Yes, Zamit was with me once again. In fact this was his home-coming from the year of service with the British forces, which he had so passionately longed for and which his wife had at last grudgingly permitted. He had spent the past eleven months in an orgy of boyish and warlike self-fulfilment. He had adventured as far as Tripoli in a merchant ship, which had been sunk in Tripoli harbour by one of the first of the circling torpedoes used by the enemy. He had been a member of a naval advance-base party in the desert, acting as interpreter and, I have no doubt, as self-appointed chief of police or assistant town major into the bargain. He had even managed to wangle a short visit to Malta, where I pictured him cocking a magnificent chest before the elders of his native village. But now he was returning from this spectacular truancy, at the stern demand of his wife, to relieve her of business worries and responsibilities, which had apparently begun to bore her beyond endurance. "She is very great," Zamit had explained, "business was too easy for her—after a while she spit on it for pastime for a beautiful woman." I was a little doubtful about the exact meaning of this declaration, and wondered whether I would ever be lucky enough to meet this fiery, this all-conquering amazon, who appeared to be the only creature on earth whom Zamit held in any awe.

We were allowed to land; but one of the sentries kept us covered with his carbine while Zamit engaged in a long argument with the other. At last we were taken to the police station in the centre of the village, where we settled down to about an hour of argument and round after round of black coffee in tiny brass cups. Zamit argued with a great variety of people from police officers to peasants. The discussion was sometimes bitter to the point of violence, sometimes a long and apparently indolent exchange of courtesies. It flared up and died down like a dog fight. I felt that we were getting nowhere until, right in the middle of a lively duel between Zamit and the sergeant of police, there was a clatter on the cobbles outside, and a small cart, drawn by two shaggy ponies, came to an uneasy halt. It appeared that the argument proper had been over and won nearly twenty minutes back; the rest had been just a "friendly," to fill in time.

.   .   .   .   .

Zamit arranged himself cross-legged upon the seat of the railway compartment (of which we were the sole occupants) and lit a cigarette. He muttered to himself occasionally. I felt he was still a little upset at the indignities he had suffered earlier in the afternoon. All at once he fell into a rumble of deep laughter, saying something in Maltese which ended with the familiar "Zamit, he fix." Then he settled his feet more firmly under his great buttocks and sat there, plump and upright, gravely smoking; silent except for, now and then, a deep chuckle or a muttered word or two in his native tongue.

.   .   .   .   .

It was a long, bleak, all-night journey to Istanbul. The countryside was featureless and white with snow; the train seemed to be wandering all over it in long, lazy and rather pointless curves. There may even have been frozen marshes; one could not tell in the vague fluorescence from snow and sky. Zamit and I sat in opposite corners by the windows—he Turkish, cross-legged and dozing; me British, slouched and thinking. As I knew little about the future except that I was to report at the Embassy in Istanbul, I was thinking mainly about the past—about Nadia and about Ivan Oreshkin; Jesse and John; old Mathews and the rest; and about all that I knew of what had happened to them. . . .

Nadia's character had seemed to change from the moment *Olinda* rounded Cape Khelidoniah and entered the calm, sunny waters of the Bay of Adalia. We had trundled happily round the coastline of that great bight of water all through one hot and peaceful day; past the ancient Roman town of Adalia itself; past the ruins of Eski-Stambul in the evening. On through a soft, warm night—still and hazy at sea-level, round the feet of the mountains; clear overhead and rich with stars— till we came at dawn to Cape Anamur on the eastern side of the bay.

It had seemed as though all Nadia's fierce partisanship, all her youthful imperiousness (contrasting so remarkably with a childish appearance, accentuating the latter), all her impatience and all her cynicism had fallen from her during this sunny day. Before nightfall she had slipped easily—one felt thankfully—into the part of an amiable and beautiful young woman surrounded by a crowd of pompous, ardent, worshipful or enchanted males. She no longer seemed so childish, but a good deal more appealing, she was frankly enjoying, at last, a state of comfortable womanhood.

Just beyond Anamur the morning sun had played upon the yellow magnificence of an old Saracen castle, standing in a plain of quiet, green parkland beside the water. And so we had come, at last, to Cyprus; and thence to Beirut throughout another breathless day.

The Syrian sun was almost touching the horizon astern of

Olinda as the first dark stencilling of pine trees and veins of rocky gorges began to appear, join together and grow real out of the heat haze to the eastward. All round us, upon the blue-white sea, the mist was turning from brown to purple; and now the green-ribbed countenance of the Lebanon mountains was beginning to add new colours to the picture.

The western sky turned red; the mist in the east reflected it till, in a little while, a rose-coloured cloud, high up ahead of us, well up in the sky, became a castle, a ship in full sail; then, growing brighter and firmer in outline, it formed at last into the snow-covered crest of a great mountain. . . . Rose-coloured and gleaming out of the sky, like a heavenly promise, stood Sanine of the Lebanon peaks.

The hour was full of the relief and the joy of home-coming. Though none of us had ever been to this land before, it was nevertheless our journey's end and our haven. Sanine brooded above us like a great white bird, settled calm and unassailable upon a nest of green forest and mountain pastures, ready for *Olinda* to creep in beneath her feathers for comfort. Thankfully I handed over the ship to the Master, and clambered down on to the lower bridge.

Nadia was there and Ivan, leaning with their elbows on the wooden rail. Nadia had her head in her hands and was gazing at the mountains before us, half-smiling a thoughtful sort of smile; Ivan was watching her and occasionally glancing ahead also. When I joined them, Nadia turned to me:

"So we have arrived," she said, "and I have caused no mutinies. Are you pleased with me?"

"Yes. Have you enjoyed it?"

"I love it more every minute. I only wish it could go on for ever. It seems so many years since I have had real friends—people for whom I was not for ever acting a part. Can you understand that?"

"I think so. But what will happen now?"

"I told you before. I shall be interned. There will be no one to speak for me here; I shall be treated like any other alien. I have a Rumanian passport—you didn't know that, did you?"

"But won't you claim to be pro-Ally?" I suggested.

"You mean pro-British, don't you?" she said, with a little

mocking laugh, and when I looked away uncertainly she added . . . "No, I won't do that. Besides I want rest, real rest, complete isolation from the war and the world. I am looking forward to that more than anything."

"You realise that I shall have to report your presence on board to the security people as soon as we arrive? Would you like me to ask them if I can give you a good dinner somewhere before you go?"

"My dear, it is sweet of you to think of it; but you need not concern yourself. They will know already that I am on board; they will be waiting for me."

And so it turned out. The last we saw of Nadia was the flash of a white hand at the window of an army staff car as she drove away, with a corporal from the Port Security Office beside her.

I was thinking of Nadia now as the train tantivied along over the plains of Thrace, with an endless, repetitive nagging of wheels. The dim, blue glow from the tiny police light in the roof of the compartment lighted the bald patch at the back of Zamit's head, which was already sunk upon his chest so that he snored and gruffled stentoriously. I sat on, hunched in my corner and glaring out across the snow, thinking of Nadia and of the others as well.

Olinda had been ordered away to Port Said, where her crew had been dispersed in various directions and she herself remanned by the Greeks. I never saw any of the original crowd again. John Hilton also disappeared—home to England, to a fresh appointment. It was not until many years later, when I had already begun the writing of this story, that I ran across him one day by chance.

Jesse I met only once more. My corvette happened, one day in the summer of 1942, to be berthing alongside a destroyer in Haifa and, on hearing a loud voice with a Canadian accent exchanging brisk and provocative backchat with someone else on the "iron deck" of the destroyer, I looked over the side of my bridge and saw Jesse.

At noon that day he came across for a drink, and we sat in my cabin talking for a while. He was navigating officer of the destroyer, he told me, and hoped to be returning to Canada shortly to become first lieutenant of a frigate.

"You made quite a public commotion out of that little trip in *Olinda*," he said, grinning. "Why didn't you do like I did— go straight down outside of everything at full speed. No trouble at all. Saw nothing; heard nothing."

"No. I suppose you didn't." The conversation turned to other things. But after a while he said:

"And Nadia. She was kind of cute, wasn't she? I tried all I knew to make her, but I guess she was out for something better. Wonder what became of her?"

"She's interned over at Mie-Mie; just outside Sidon."

"You don't say!" Jesse was astonished; then triumphant. "Glad I got clear of her before that happened. But how in hell did she get down here, and how and why did she leave Turkey?"

"She got into some sort of trouble; had to get out."

"I suppose she got found out by our people and they thought she'd be safer inside the wire down here than loose in Turkey, is that it?"

"No, not quite." But I didn't want to get into a long argument with Jesse over Nadia. I felt sure he would only scoff and, in the end, start even wilder theories about Nadia's sympathies than before.

"I always knew she wasn't on the level, that kid," said Jesse provocatively, and added: "you were a bit soft over her yourself, I'd say." But I refused to be drawn—to attempt to champion Nadia when I myself still knew so little about her.

Quite recently, when I met Nadia again (and John Hilton, too!)—near Leeds, of all improbable places—I was pleased that I had kept my counsel. For her true story, which I then heard for the first time, was one which might have made poor Jesse wince.

At dawn on February 24th, 1943, the train carrying Zamit and me reached Constantinople main station—on the European side of the Bosphorus. It was just getting light as we slipped out of the station with the crowd.

We were both well wrapped against the intense cold; but I had taken the added precaution of winding my scarf round the lower part of my face, and of keeping my head bent down into the collar of my coat, in the hope of escaping the eye of any German agent, told off to make a routine check of passengers arriving. I dropped Zamit near his home in Pera and took our taxi on to the Embassy, where I settled myself in the Old Man's office to wait for him to arrive.

About 9.30 a.m. he came tramping in: "Good God Almighty! What are you doing here?" he shouted, then added more amiably. . . . "Still I'm pleased to see you. Where are you staying? The Park?"

"I just arrived this morning, sir . . . most secret . . . by *caique* from Mersin."

"God stuff me with artichokes! What the hell for?" He looked genuinely puzzled as he stood there scratching his head. "I wonder if there's anything in to-day's mail about you. Someone down in Alexandria must have come over queer and thought up some fantastic new scheme." He moved across to his desk and started opening letters. I picked up the daily paper.

All at once the Old Man began to bubble and puff to himself. I looked up to see him glaring at a letter and a signal in his hand. "H'm," he snorted, and then, "never heard such nonsense. . . ." He read on, and a little later. . . . "Oh! . . . ah! . . ." followed by, "yes, I suppose so." He reached the end of the letter, glanced at the signal, and then threw both of them down. Next moment he was marching across the room towards the well-remembered chart locker. On the way over, he suddenly whipped round upon his heel, and fixed me with a baleful stare. . . .

"Now look here . . ." he began. I registered deep attention. "This time there'll be no women. None whatever. Get me?" I nodded. "Never mind who they are," he continued. "Americans, Swiss, Greek, French . . . pro-British, pro-Russian or just *pro bono publico* . . . they're all offside; every bloody one of 'em. Is that quite clear?"

I nodded again, whereupon he opened the chart locker and waved me across to the table, upon which he was soon laying out all the old familiar charts (a good deal grubbier and more ragged, I noticed, than they had been a year before; but still quite serviceable). Then out came the dividers, and we were soon both immersed in the age-old routine of measuring, laying off courses, remeasuring and glaring at rocks and islands. After a while the Old Man straightened up:

"Now this is the general picture," he began . . . which brings me to the end of this story and also, of course, to the beginning of another. . . .